THE INVISIBLE JUSTICE SYSTEM
DISCRETION AND THE LAW
Second Edition

THE INVISIBLE JUSTICE SYSTEM
DISCRETION AND THE LAW
Second Edition

Edited by **Burton Atkins**, *Florida State University and*
Mark Pogrebin, *University of Colorado at Denver*

Criminal Justice Studies
Anderson Publishing Co.
Cincinnati, Ohio

THE INVISIBLE JUSTICE SYSTEM: DISCRETION AND THE LAW

Second Edition

Copyright © 1978, 1982 by Anderson Publishing Co.

Library of Congress Cataloging in Publication Data

The Invisible justice system.

  (Criminal justice studies)
  Includes index.
  1. Prosecution — United States — Decision making.
2. Police discretion — United States. 3. Corrections —
United States — Decision making. I. Atkins, Burton.
II. Pogrebin, Marc. III. Series.

KF9640.I58 1982	345.73'05	82-4024
ISBN 0-87084-058-4	347.3055	AACR2

The editorial supervisor for this book was Candice Piaget, Anderson Publishing Co.

To our children — Amy and Stephen

CONTENTS

ACKNOWLEDGMENTS

We are grateful to the following persons who helped us with the planning, criticisms, and production of this book: Dr. John Stratton, Sociology Department of the University of Iowa and Dr. Justin Green, Political Science Department, Virginia Polytechnical Institute, who greatly aided us in the initial planning and ideas for the anthology.

We would further like to thank Fred Friedberg and John Memory of the School of Criminology at Florida State University for their help with the collection of articles and other tasks which made the producing of this book less difficult.

I. Discretion and the Criminal Justice System

1. DISCRETIONARY DECISION-MAKING IN THE ADMINISTRATION OF JUSTICE

BURTON ATKINS and MARK POGREBIN

ONE OF THE most demanding intellectual tasks that observers of any institution or process must undertake — be it public or private, political or nonpolitical — is that of analytically and empirically distinguishing symbol and myth from reality. As Max Lerner so aptly expressed it several decades ago, we react, in many ways, like children to our surroundings — imbued with myths that provide us comfort as we contend with the realities of our environment.[1]

Our legal system is shaped by innumerable myths and symbols. Perhaps the most significant one within our constitutional framework is that of due process. As it has evolved in a constitutional context, due process generally refers to rules of fundamental fairness that dictate the broad assumptions and values guiding our criminal justice system. Due process also denotes a belief in governmental limitation, of barriers to whimsical authority by political officials. It suggests an adherence to the old adage that ours "is a government of laws, not of men"; that our system of justice is premised upon rules and upon structure, not upon the personal idiosyncracies of public officials. We take great comfort in the symbol of due process, we virtually pay it homage and we seem to feel more secure in the knowledge that our criminal justice system is operating by norms of regularity and restraint.

Against this symbolic frame of reference, the issue of discretionary decision-making in the criminal justice system poses substantial tensions. Discretion refers to a situation in which an official has latitude to make authoritative choices not necessarily specified within the source of authority which governs his decision-making. Kenneth Culp Davis, a recognized commentator on discretion, argues that a public officer exercises discretion ". . . whenever the effective limits of his power leave him free to make a choice among possible courses of action or in ac-

tion."[2] Discretionary justice thus suggests latitude of decision-making rather than formality or certainty. It suggests that, unlike the symbolic idea of due process, idiosyncracy rather than rules may guide decision-making within the administration of criminal justice.

Discretion is exercised in the police officer's decision to apprehend a suspect, the prosecutor's decision to file, dismiss or reduce formal charges, the judge's decision to admit a defendant to bail, release on recognizance, grant or deny trial motions, suspend sentence, release on probation, impose severe or minimal sentence in prison, and the parole board's decision whether or not to release a prisoner from incarceration. It is a critical element at almost every point in our criminal justice system. Yet, our legal system's reliance on discretionary decisions is not unique. As Davis has observed, all legal systems in history have utilized such power.[3] But it is not simply its existence which draws our attention to discretionary decision-making. Rather, discretion is important because it maintains a flexible, individualized system of justice. Nevertheless, it is a system vulnerable to abuse. Roscoe Pound wrote: "A balance between rules of law and discretion which will give effect both to the general security and general life with the least impairment of either is perhaps the most difficult problem in the science of law."[4] The question, then, is not how to avoid all discretion, since discretion and justice are not incompatible concepts, but, in the words of Justice Charles Brietel of the New York Court of Appeals, ". . . how to control it so as to avoid the unequal, the arbitrary, the discriminatory, and the oppressive."[5]

If discretionary decisions are inevitable, then the issue is not whether or not they *should* occur but rather determining the degree of impact the exercise of discretion has upon the administration of justice. The invisible system of justice that lies beyond the formal scriptures of the law derives its energy from the failure of statutory law or any administrative code of regulation to specify all contingencies of decision-making. The essential problem becomes that of discovering the elusive balance between structuring decisions and providing for individualized justice.

Davis has suggested three concepts that can be applied to the task of limiting or regulating discretion. The first is confining discretion. This refers to keeping ". . . discretionary power within designated boundaries."[6] This may be accomplished through statutory or administrative rule-making. Confining, in other words, refers to setting the limits beyond which decisions may not reach. Discretion may also be structured by controlling boundaries established by the confining process.[7] Finally, discretion may be checked by imposing the supervisory controls of one decision-maker upon another.[8] These concepts are useful because they provide a starting point for conceptualizing the issue of discretion. Yet their intrinsic limitation is that they presume the problem of discretion to be similar, if not identical, in a variety of institutions. The use of discretionary judgments by all those involved in the various components of our legal system is not a clear case of right or wrong, lawful or unlawful.

Each part of the criminal justice system utilizes discretion in different ways for a variety of reasons. Because each part of the legal structure is primarily concerned with its own particular needs and functions, it becomes difficult to resolve conflicts that involve the actual utilization of discretionary judgments or the authority to exercise it. The variety of contexts in which discretion may be employed, and the details concerning its actual exercise, are endemic to our justice system because each component of the system is organized more for its own purposes and concerns than formulated for the common good of the criminal justice system.

This anthology examines the exercise of discretion in the administration of justice. Obviously, the particular circumstances and the broad parameters of discretion exercised by those in the criminal justice system differ. Also, the conditions permitting the exercise of discretionary judgments, the statutory authority defining the formal limits of power, the effective limits of authority, and the degree of control exercised by higher authority over decision-making vary considerably. The articles in this collection present a variety of perspectives on the existence and impact of discretion on the due process of law.

POLICE

Contrary to myth, most police work does not necessarily involve cornering bank robbers and muggers on the streets. A considerable amount of police activity is directed towards service functions, areas of activity which entail a particularly high degree of discretionary judgment. Police officers have considerable discretion to invoke or refrain from invoking arrest when they confront low visibility offenses or crimes which have little impact on anyone but those directly involved. Much discretionary behavior stems from the ambiguity of criminal statutes. It remains, in most instances, a matter of judgment for patrolmen to determine whether or not particular activities fall within the legal sanction, and if so, whether or not the particular circumstances require arrest. As one observer has noted:

The law contains certain guidelines about the boundaries of legality. Within these boundaries, however, there is located a vast array of activities that are not important since determined by considerations of legality. . . . The effective reasons for the action are not located in the formulas of statutes but in considerations that are related to established practices of dealing informally with problems.[9]

Discretionary decisions by actors at one point in the system can have important effects on decisions made elsewhere. When law enforcement agents, for example, choose not to invoke their arrest powers for routine, low visibility and particular victimless crimes, their decisions define the outer limits of sanctions to be imposed by the political system regardless of what the statutory law may provide. In this context, the police become law interpreters since their discretionary judgments on the streets give concrete meaning to vagrancy, prostitution, gambling, and intoxication laws. As Joseph Goldstein has argued in a now classic article, a patrolman's discretionary judgments on the streets ultimately affect others in the system who make decisions — prosecutors, grand jury, judges, probation officers, correction authority and parole and pardon boards.[10]

Discretionary policy judgments not to arrest a suspect who has committed a low visibility offense, moreover, are rarely subject to review by other decision-makers in the system. There are some situations, however, in which police discretion is scrutinized by other participants in the criminal justice process. One circumstance is judicial assessment of the evidence, circumstances of arrest, and confessions. A court decision to accept or reject a police officer's discretionary judgments helps to establish the limit of the officer's legal behavior. Yet, the vast majority of criminal cases are plea bargained and never come before a judge and jury in an open trial. In reality, then, the discretionary judgments that law enforcement officers make in deciding whether or not to arrest are rarely scrutinized by other decision-makers in the legal process. This is particularly troublesome when illegal discretionary decisions are made. Rosset and Cressey have observed that:

When there is no announced norm to govern decisions, it is hard to know what evidence is relevant and what procedure is appropriate. Where there is no defined process for making decisions, it is difficult to discern what standards are being used. Rules and norms become little more than suggestions to the decision-maker. When a policeman decides not to make an arrest, or a prosecutor declines to file a charge against a person accused of a crime, the official is on his own, because there is not likely to be a formal hearing or other procedure. In these situations there are few determinative legal criteria to effectively bind the official because his decision is not subject to review.[11]

The President's Task Force on Police proposed that police departments develop clearly stated policies that would enable police to have specific guidance for those situations which often require the exercise of discretion. The report stated that:

Policy should cover such matters, among others, as the issuance of orders to citizens regarding their movements or activities, the handling of minor disputes, the safeguarding of the rights of free speech and free assembly, the selection and use of investigative methods, and the decision whether or not to arrest in specific situations involving specific crimes.[12]

More than a decade after this recommendation was made, there are still very few police departments that issue formal guidelines on the use of discretionary policy to the rank and file patrolman. The same problems still exist because of the unwillingness of police administrators to state departmental discretionary policies as clearly as possible in order to avoid ambiguity in the line officer's use of discretion. The absence of clear guidelines which would aid the patrolman in his everyday encounters with suspects and complainants perpetuates the ambiguity of his responsibilities. Instead of attempting to make decisions based on familiar departmental policy, he continues to depend on his personal judgments which often have little or no legal basis. It is to the policeman's disadvantage that he is forced to make factual judgments rather than legal judgements due to the lack of stated normative administrative guidelines in the exercise of discretionary judgments.

On what basis are discretionary judgments made? What cognitive processes, in other words, affect the latitude of decision-making by the police officer? Surprisingly little research has been conducted on this issue. Many studies are now available which describe the policeman's working environment and how discretion is exercised, but few scholars have directed their attention to the variables that affect discretionary judgments. One exception is a study of police discretion by James O. Finckenhauer. In his study, Finckenhauer examined the effect of education upon the discretionary judgments of police recruits. His procedure was to offer the subjects ten hypothetical scenarios representing a variety of problems a police officer might confront. The hypothetical situations involved legal violations relating to prostitution, gambling, obscenity, and pornography. That is, each situation posed a technical legal violation which allowed the police officer to arrest the violator, take some official action other than arrest, or do nothing. Finckenhauer found some differences in college and non-college educated recruits' reactions to these hypothetical situations, particularly that ". . . college educated police officers are less likely to advocate involving the criminal process in such situations."[13]

Finckenhauer's research is important because it suggests that education does have an effect upon how discretion operates in the adminstration of justice. These findings also are in conformity with, and lend support to, goals set by the Task Force on the Police, part of the President's Commission on Law Enforcement and Administration of Justice, which has suggested that the quality of police departments was ultimately tied to the educational level of recruits brought into the system.[14] Besides the obvious implication linking education to police professionalism, Finckenhauer's research clearly suggests that discretionary decision-making involves a behavioral component. In other words, how discretionary judgments are made and in what circumstances they are not likely to be maximized and minimized, relates to each decision-maker's cognitive processes. While the psychological dimension of decision-making is related to discretion within the legal system, little research has been done directly applying behavioral concepts to police and prosecutorial decision-making.[15]

PROSECUTION

A prosecutor's discretion is extensive. It encompasses the power to selectively prosecute suspected offenders, to give strength to, or emasculate, law enforcement policies by not prosecuting violations of certain laws, to drop charges once having initiated a prosecution, and, of course, to plea bargain with a defendant.

Probably the least publicly visible aspect of prosecutorial discretion is the charging decision. While most jurisdictions have statutes which require prosecution of all offenders, and frequently dictate that prosecutors shall "diligently enforce"[16] all law within their jurisdiction, the fact remains that total enforcement may be both impractical and undesirable as a matter of public policy. Un-

doubtedly, some discretion has to be exercised if only because limited resources of money, personnel, and time prevent a prosecutor from initiating a complaint against all offenders. Apart from resource limitations, prosecutors may be motivated by political ambition or even corruption. Thus, the decision to charge or not to charge may be tied to their own personal motivations.

The disparity between what statutes provide and what political realities dictate similarly affects the removal of prosecutors who have abused their discretionary powers. State statutes provide for removal of prosecutors by courts, voters, governors, and legislature. For the most part, however, these processes are ineffective checks to prosecutorial discretion.[17] In some instances, courts may suggest that prosecutorial action is mandatory in certain circumstances. Nevertheless, most jurisdictions have taken the position that a prosecutor's charging decision is beyond judicial scrutiny.[18] Some courts, in fact, have gone further, interpreting statutes conferring authority on prosecutors quite broadly so as to actually legitimize discretion not to prosecute.[19]

The decision to charge a defendant is frequently made with the ultimate aim of plea bargaining. The informal negotiation towards a plea stems from a promise by the prosecutor to reduce the original charge, often comprised of multiple charges, to a lesser criminal offense if the defendant agrees to enter a guilty plea. Excessive plea bargaining discretion has been the focus of reform policy that seeks to place restraints on the prosecutor's flexibility in dealing with criminal defendants. Some jurisdictions, for example, have experimented with a policy precluding plea bargaining for drug violations.[20] Need for controls, however, extends to other aspects of prosecutorial decision-making. Remington and Rosenblum, for example, argue that although the prosecutor's discretion is widely acknowledged, little attention has been devoted to developing a system of internal rationalization and accountability. Remington and Rosenblum advocate the formulation of institutionalized procedures making it possible for discretion to be utilized, but in a manner which is visible and subject to review in order to insure that it is not abused.[21]

Courts have, for the most part, remained curiously silent on plea bargaining. However, some courts have begun to confront the plea bargaining issue directly, but unfortunately, emerging judicial policy has provided little beyond a tacit recognition that plea bargaining is a catalyst for an efficient, or perhaps more accurately, expeditious administration of justice. A few courts have been candid in their approval of plea bargaining. For example, in *U.S. v. Wiley*, a federal district court noted that:

If, in one year, 248 judges are to deal with 35,517 defendants, the district courts must encourage pleas of guilty. One way to encourage pleas of guilty is to establish or announce a policy that, in the ordinary case, leniency will not be granted to a defendant who stands on trial.[22]

The Supreme Court has similarly condoned plea bargaining. In *Brady v. U.S.*, the Court ruled that a guilty plea conditional upon a prosecutor's leniency does not violate the Fifth Amendment protection against self-incrimination.[23] In *Santobello v. New York*, the United States Supreme Court implicitly recognized that plea negotiations were an essential component of the administration of justice.[24] The current position of the federal courts on the issue of plea bargaining was set forth in *North Carolina v. Alford* which held "the standard was and remains whether the plea represents a voluntary and intelligent choice among the alternative courses of actions open to the defendant."[25] Still, there is little policy primarily concerned with the procedural exercise of prosecutorial discretion to charge or not to charge a defendant, or policies designed to guide discretionary judgments affecting the process of plea negotiation. The Supreme Court had, however, taken some initial steps toward a policy in the *Santobello* decision when it ruled that prosecutors must adhere to promises made to defendants in plea bargaining. Yet as even Chief Justice Burger had recognized (while a member of the federal court of appeals), courts may only be capable of performing a limited role in curtailing prosecutorial discretion:

[F]ew subjects are less adapted to judicial review than the exercise by the Executive of his discretion in deciding when and whether to institute criminal proceedings or what precise charge

should be made, ... ing once brought.

Whereas co ... check abuses of ... play between jud ... cretion is more an ... that prosecutors ha ... in negotiating plea ... stered by the hesita ... ...o interfere with bargains struck between prosecutor and defendant. In some circumstances, however, the courts will intervene. The circumstances surrounding *United States v. Ammidown* represent one such instance.[27] In this case, the defendant, Ammidown, had pleaded guilty to second degree murder after having been initially charged in the first degree for planning his wife's rape and murder by a friend. Federal district Judge John Sirica, however, refused to accept the negotiated plea on the grounds that the crime was so heinous that the public interest would not accept a mere "tap on the wrist."[28] At Sirica's insistence, the defendant pleaded guilty to the charge in the original indictment and was found guilty of first degree murder. Ammidown then appealed his conviction to the court of appeals for the District of Columbia. In vacating the judgment and sentence, the court of appeals sought to formulate policy that would guide judicial discretion as it affects prosecutorial plea bargaining. The essentials of this policy are that a bargain may be rejected only if (1) it is inherently unfair to the defendant; (2) it represents an abuse of prosecutorial discretion, or (3) it interferes with a judge's sentencing prerogative without any overriding prosecutorial interest.

Ammidown is actually only one of a series of decisions in which federal courts have opted for a presumption in favor of prosecutorial discretion in plea bargaining. The emerging doctrine appears to be that prosecutors will be given a generally free rein in plea bargaining but the judiciary will nevertheless reserve the right to intervene when the prosecutor abuses his discretion. Courts have occasionally taken a more extreme view that the judiciary has no power whatsoever to oversee prosecutorial discretion because of the separation of powers doctrine. This argument, adopted by Chief

Newman v. U.S.[29] when ... ourt of appeals, was based on ... at prosecutors are executive offi- ... oject only to executive controls over ... internal decision-making process. Yet, ... *mmidown* seems to reflect the drift of opin- ion at least within the federal courts. It would be reasonable to conclude that the po- litical and organizational necessities of pros- ecutorial decision-making combined with a hesitancy by the courts to impose judicial supervision provide the conditions in which prosecutorial discretion can flourish.

THE JUDICIARY

Judicial discretion, like police and prose- cutorial discretion, is inevitable. The issue here is probably more complex since certain strains of jurisprudence are tied to interpre- tations of judicial behavior that view a judge as a legal automaton applying statutory and common law rules to particular cases in a rather mechanical fashion. Ultimately, this formalistic view of decision-making would have to reject the notion of judicial discre- tion since the concept implies ambiguity and flexibility, whereas mechanical jurispru- dence emphasizes certainty and even rigidity in judges' opinions.[30] The mechanical theory is also founded upon the assumption that ju- dicial decision-making is qualitatively dif- ferent from other kinds of political decision- making. However, discretion may best be interpreted as the inevitable result of a human decision-making process that applies with equal force to judicial and non-judicial institutions.

A trial judge has considerable discretion in setting bail, conducting a trial, and impos- ing sentence. The function of bail is to se- cure a defendant to the court's authority. At least in theory, the amount of security re- quired to bind a defendant should be depen- dent upon his financial status, opportunity for employment, and roots in the commu- nity. Unfortunately, the bail process rarely works as intended. The root of the problem is that judges and court-support personnel usually do not, and perhaps cannot, process the kinds of information relevant to fitting the amount of bail to the particular circum- stances of each defendant. This is not meant

to suggest that the imposing of bail, or for that matter, the determination of whether or not a defendant should be released on his own recognizance, is entirely haphazard. In some instances, it may be. But more often, judges develop their own *modus operandi* not only in relationship to how much the amount of bail should be and how it should be set, but also in relation to the function that pretrial release or detention should serve. Not surprisingly, then, judicial discre- tion has a considerable impact upon the bail decision since each judge has his own per- ception of the seriousness of a crime and of the defendant's moral character. It is not at all uncommon for judges to set their own bail rate schedules. In some instances, these schedules are idiosyncratic in that they re- flect the judges' perception of the serious- ness of offenses and not society's view of the severity of crime. One study conducted in New York, for example, found that judges generally imposed higher bail in robbery and burglary offenses than in sex-related of- fenses even though the latter are crimes against persons as opposed to crimes against property. In fact, the view of the New York judges that robbery and burglary offenses should be treated more severely than sex- related crimes, even though burglaries do not necessarily involve any contact with the victim, suggests a priority of legal values that might very well be questioned.[31]

It would be erroneous, however, to sug- gest that the judge proceeds entirely by whim. As Suffet has suggested in his study of bail setting interaction, the actual determi- nation of bail is the result of an exchange re- lationship between judge, prosecutor, and defense attorney.[32] In the end, like the po- liceman and prosecutor, a judge's discretion is frequently controlled by his role relation- ship with other actors in the system. Never- theless, how this bail decision is reached and the impact of discretionary powers within the process can have an enormous impact upon the defendant. In one respect, the bail system as it operates in most areas discrimi- nates against defendants because of eco- nomic statutes, particularly when judges im- pose bail based upon the type of offense with little or no consideration for the charac- teristics of the defendant, the amount of money necessary to bind him to the court's jurisdiction, or even whether or not the defendant should be released on personal recognizance. For defendants who must experience pretrial detention because of an inability to raise bond, the repercussion can be serious indeed. There is some evidence to suggest that these defendants receive more severe sentences because of their handicap in preparing defenses within the confines of a jail.[33] Equally as damaging is the fact that those who are ultimately released or found innocent by the court nevertheless have no recourse from the social stigma of jail or the economic inconvenience of having lost their jobs through the ordeal.

As much, if not more, discretion exists in the sentencing process. Numerous studies have documented the scope of this problem. For example, one study of sentencing discretion and disparity in federal district courts found that judges in North Carolina imposed an average sentence of 77.6 months upon narcotics violators, whereas those in South Carolina, working within the same statutory parameters and generally within the same geographic area within the United States, sentenced narcotics violators to an average of 56.3 months in jail. A similar tendency was found for forgery convictions. One federal district court in Texas sentenced forgers to an average of 43 months. Yet, another in the same state sentenced forgers to only 27.2 months.[34] This amount of sentencing discretion is not limited to felony offenses in federal courts. One study of the New York City Magistrate Court found considerable variation in intoxication, sanitary law, and speed ordinance violations over a 15 year period. For example, New York judges varied from 1.3% to 73.4% in the percent of intoxication cases discharged; from 18.8% to 87.6% in the rate for imposing fines for sanitary law violations; and from 1.0% to 79.0% for the frequency with which speed ordinance violators received suspended sentences.[35]

The causes of sentencing disparity and discretion lie in the combined effect of legislative policies that impose maximum and minimal thresholds for sentence, indeterminate sentences, and the judge's perceptions of the utility of certain legal policies. Few legislative policies exist that are designed to limit judicial discretion. Some states, however, have recently experimented with "flat-time" sentencing in which a judge must impose a legislatively fixed sentence for certain kinds of offenses. Appellate review of trial judge sentencing, considered by many commentators to be a more viable solution than flat-time laws, is virtually non-existent in our country. Appellate courts in Arizona, Connecticut, Hawaii, Iowa, Massachusetts, Nebraska, New York and Oregon do have power to review and modify sentences alleged to be too severe, but these are more the exception than the rule. In six other states, courts are empowered to "reverse, affirm, or modify" criminal court judgments, but the "suitability" of a particular sentence is normally unreviewable. Federal appellate courts generally face similar constraints.[36]

While appellate review might appear as an attractive solution to abuses in sentencing discretion, several limitations of the process must be recognized. One is that while many jurisdictions might favor the appellate review process, they commit themselves to an exponential increase in criminal appeals at a time when many courts are seeking ways of reducing the seemingly endless number of appeals. Organizational demands, in other words, may place some restraints on this approach. Another problem is that appellate review does not necessarily reduce discretion in sentencing. Instead, it creates another layer of discretionary decision-making intended to check decisions of trial judges. There is also evidence that few sentences would actually be changed. For example, the New York experience with appellate review of sentencing has shown that about 90% of appeals raised on grounds of legality, propriety, or excessiveness were affirmed. By contrast, slightly more than 5% were modified and slightly less than 5% were actually reversed.[37] Obviously, appellate judges are not prone to disturb a trial judge's sentence except in the most extreme situations.

If a certain amount of discretion is inevitable in judicial sentencing powers, there is still the problem of contending with the idiosyncratic role behavior of judges. Since judges are human beings, they will obviously be susceptible to human frailties such as bias and bigotry. In theory, a judge's sentencing decision is supposed to be premised upon legally relevant criteria such as the severity of the crime and whether or not the defendant has a prior criminal record. Supposedly irrelevant are such factors as the defendant's demeanor in court, his deference or lack thereof towards judicial authority, and even his attire in court. Nevertheless, it has been proven that sentencing decisions are related to legally irrelevant criteria. One study of Detroit Traffic Court, for example, found an inverse relationship between the defendants' mode of dress and whether or not they received a jail sentence as opposed to receiving a fine or suspended sentence. Those defendants whose attire was more dignified were less likely to be jailed. This relationship held even where the severity of offense was taken into account. Although the relationship was not statistically significant, the Detroit data also suggests that defendants' demeanor was also related to the magnitude of fines imposed; that to the extent defendants failed to use honorific titles, expressed disrespect for the court and the like, they were more likely to receive larger fines.[38]

While justice is supposedly blind to legally irrelevant criteria, it is clear that maintaining the tenuous balance between discretionary justice and discretionary abuse involves more than simply drafting model penal codes or model sentencing acts. It may entail some type of cue-taking and consensus-building among judges. On-the-job socialization to agreed upon sentencing norms may reduce some disparity. But more fundamental problems remain. Most proposals have not dealt with the process by which lawyers become judges and how ill-equipped many lawyers are to undertake the burdens of judicial decision-making. Few law school graduates are trained in legal aspects of sentencing, no less the psychological dimensions of the process. Few attorneys who become judges have had much, if any, criminal law practice. As federal judge Marvin Frankel has observed, too much attention has been paid in the sentencing debate to what the judge should do, and too little attention to the problem of who the judges are:

The most notable thing about this group . . . is that its members have mostly remained unencumbered by any exposure to, or learning about, the problems of sentencing. Characterized by their dominant attributes, our judges are men (mostly) of no longer tender years who have not associated much with criminal defendants, who have not seemed shrilly unorthodox, who have not lived recently in poverty, who have been modestly or more successful in their profession. They are likely to have had more than an average lawyer's amount of experience in the courtroom, though it is a little remarkable how large a percentage of those who go on the bench lack this credential. They are unlikely to have defended more than a couple of criminal cases, if that many. They are more likely to have done a stint as prosecutors, usually as a brief chapter in the years shortly after law school. However, much or little they have been exposed to the criminal trial process, most people ascending (as we say) to the bench have paid only the most fleeting and superficial attention to matters affecting the sentences of convicted defendants. In this respect, the pattern set in the law school is carried forward and reenforced.[39]

PRISON ADMINISTRATION

Considerable discretion exists in prison administration. It is at the last stages of the criminal justice process that we find the lowest public visibility in discretionary decision-making. Prisons, far removed from the public eye, have until recently been generally free to utilize their administrative authority in any manner they thought consistent with their control policies and goals. Perhaps the most flagrant examples of abuse in discretionary decision-making have occurred in the procedures adopted for disciplining inmates. For years now, prisoner behavior has been guarded by petty rules which are, for the most part, unwritten and vague. Quite often these rules are arbitrarily and discriminately enforced. Even with the numerous federal court cases that have recently begun to restrain some of the discretionary abuses of prisoner rights, corrections still has a major problem of finding ways to combine the need for flexibility and discretion in decision-making with the need to make fair and sensible decisions.

A major cause for extensive discretionary decision-making among correctional officials stems from the lack of restraint placed upon administrators by statutory law. Legislatures grant broad authority with hardly any restrictions on the exercise of administrative authority. The grant of authority given to prison officials by legislation is usually broad. The statutes normally stipulate that correction departments can make and enforce all rules regarding regulating and disciplining inmates. In other words, the content of the rules, as well as their interpretation, is left to the discretion of the prison administrators. Many states grant broad power to allow officials to freely alter such rules as it may become expedient. For the most part, the statutory language allows the officials to use their own judgment in deciding when such alterations should be imposed.[40] For example, under the old indeterminate sentencing law in California before the recent change to a more determinate sentencing system, the California Adult Authority was charged with overseeing the administration of the indeterminate sentencing procedure and parole system. It was given extensive authority to grant and revoke paroles, to fix length of sentences, to establish the conditions of parole, and to restore a prisoner's political and civil rights to the extent that the Authority saw fit. Through its statutes, the California legislature had imposed no restraints upon, and had created no standards for, the Adult Authority's decision-making.[41]

This statutory ambiguity providing prison officials with vast discretionary power has, at the same time, contributed to the erosion of the "hands-off" doctrine. This doctrine had been used extensively by courts to justify their reluctance to intervene in the administration of correctional institutions. Now courts have become more aware of prisoner demands, in part, because legislatures had virtually abrogated their responsibility in providing external controls over prison administrators.

Courts have also begun to accept the proposition that correctional abuses often deny prisoners their constitutional rights. This modified position is indicative of the recognition by courts that the imposition of arbitrary punishment in the form of disciplinary hearings often deprives prisoners of certain rights such as earned good time and other institutionally earned privileges. Proceeding from this assumption, courts have ruled, for example, that prison officials cannot unreasonably censor prisoners' mail in violation of the First Amendment;[42] that prisons must adopt minimum housing standards for inmates;[43] that restraints may be placed upon disciplinary procedures em-

ployed by prison officials;[44] and that the religious freedom of incarcerated offenders must be protected under certain conditions.[45] In fact, *Holt v. Sarver* went so far as to declare the entire Arkansas penitentiary system to be in violation of the Eighth Amendment protection against cruel and unusual punishment.[46].

Perhaps the most auspicious Supreme Court decision has been *Wolff v. McDonnell*.[47] In *Wolff*, the court ruled that certain constitutional rights should be afforded to prisoners prior to punishment by prison officials. While the inmates do not have the right to confront their accusers and are not entitled to counsel, a hearing is nevertheless required. While this is a limited protection at best, it does indicate that the Supreme Court is not going to allow the "hands off" doctrine to hamper all attempts at curtailing discretionary abuses in prisons. To the extent that *Wolff* and other precedents effectively limit disciplinary practices, an area usually considered to be entirely within the domain of the prison administrators, they establish the constitutional basis necessary for extending judicial supervision to other spheres of internal decision-making. This trend towards more judicial intervention should not be interpreted as suggesting that abuses will necessarily be curtailed at a pace commensurate with judicial supervision. Judicial policy evolves slowly and one cannot always predict just how vigorously future courts will defend the interest of prisoners. The exercise of discretionary power remains a real problem. At the very least, however, prisoners now may have access to grievance mechanisms when abusive discretionary decisions are alleged to occur.

Positive judicial intervention could have some unforeseen benefits beyond the curtailment of discretionary abuse. It may well be that the imposition of external control mechanisms will limit disciplinary situations that lead to inmate frustration and violence. The Attica prison revolt of 1971 is the most vivid example of problems that were smoldering long before the riot occurred — problems that still exist unabated in other prisons around the country.

Regardless of the preconceptions that the public may have concerning the effect of a prison sentence on modifying criminal behavior or the threat of jail as a deterrent to crime, two facts emerge from even a casual observation of the American penal system. First, a large proportion of prison inmates are recidivists, a fact that suggests that prison environments do little to alter an individual's penchant for violating societal norms. In this context, it would seem reasonable to hypothesize that discretionary abuse on the part of prison administrators undermines any attempt by authorities to instill within inmates' minds a sense of equity or justice regarding the legal system. In the final analysis, the purpose of rehabilitation must be to reshape prisoners' values towards society. Yet it would seem that abused discretionary power would very likely reinforce prisoners' attitudes that the system is corrupt, and that survival either in or outside the penitentiary depends as much upon illegal means as it does upon legal ones.

PAROLE

The parole decision represents another critical point in the system in which enormous discretionary powers occurs. Considerable variations in parole board decision-making existing across the United States are fueled, in part, by the belief among many officials that the granting of parole is a purely administrative task to be performed without judicial or legislative interference. The granting of parole has been alluded to in one study as decision-making by "an act of grace."[48] To the extent that such a perception permeates decision-making in parole boards, it certainly impedes any attempt to balance discretionary abuse with decision-making structure and rules. One of the few existing nationwide empirical surveys of parole board decision-making found that less than half of the parole boards studied adhered to standards suggested by the Presidential Task Force Report on Corrections as minimally necessary for limiting discretionary abuse. The study showed, for example, that as of 1972, 60% did not permit counsel at the parole hearing; 69% did not permit inmates to present witnesses at the hearing; 78% did not record the reasons for the parole decision; only 40% made verbatim transcripts of the proceedings; and only 43%

informed the inmate directly of the decision.[49] With such practices in effect, it is clearly difficult to impose restraints upon parole boards, particularly when the absence of complete records of the proceedings makes it virtually impossible for courts, or any institution for that matter, to review the boards' decisions. The fluidity of decision-making in parole boards is not limited to the state board. The United States Parole Board had been accused of exactly the same type of amorphous decision-making that allows discretionary abuse to flourish. As Kenneth Culp Davis has written:

In granting or denying parole, the board makes no attempt to structure its discretionary power through rules, policy statements, or guidelines; it does not structure through statements of findings and reasons; it has no system of precedents; the degree of openness of proceedings and records is about the least possible; and procedural safeguards are almost totally absent. Moreover, checking of discretion is minimal; board members do not check each other by deliberating together about decisions; administrative check of board decisions is almost non-existent; and judicial review is customarily unavailable.[50]

Although courts have imposed some restraints on prison discipline and administration, they have been more hesitant to extend judicial control over the process by which correction officials grant or deny a prisoner release on parole. Typical of their response is the one made in Scarpa v. United States Board of Parole, where the court of appeals ruled that due process rights do not attach at parole hearings and that ". . . in the absence of flagrant, unwarranted, or unauthorized action by the Board, it is not the function of the courts to review such proceedings."[51] Another court of appeals similarly augmented the Board of Parole's discretionary powers when it wrote that "the question of parole is . . . a matter entirely for the judgment and discretion of the Board of Parole."[52] As far back as 1935, the Supreme Court has held that parole is not a right but an "act of grace" and that due process standards do not apply.[53]

While courts cling to this "hands off" doctrine, it may appear that the seeds for change already exist. One important inference of Wolff v. McDonnell, for example, is that the arbitrary disciplining of an inmate may delay the timing of his ultimate release from prison. If the denial of a request for parole is the consequence of the inmate's failure to conform to prison regulations and if, in fact, disciplinary actions taken against a prisoner occurred in the absence of due process safeguards, or even if the decision to deny parole is interpreted as simply another form of disciplinary action, the necessary linkages are established to extend the due process cloak to the parole hearing. In this context, *Wolff* clearly emerges as a critical decision.

Another source for change is that the Supreme Court has been willing in recent years to extend constitutional guarantees to individuals seeking what has traditionally been referred to as privileges rather than rights. For instance, *Goldberg v. Kelley*[54] suggests that this legal dichotomy may no longer be a barrier. In that case, the court ruled that a welfare recipient had the right to a hearing, conforming to due process standards, before welfare benefits could be terminated. The decision is premised on the fact that due process standards need not be negated simply because a privilege was involved. When tied to the Court's decision in *Morrissey v. Brewer*[55] that parole revocation must be guided by due process, it would seem but a short step to extending the doctrine backwards to the initial parole decision.[56]

If and when parole is granted, the offender is placed under the supervision of a parole officer. At this stage of the system, the parolee has the obligation to abide by the rules agreed to as a condition of release from the correctional institution. Here too, the authorities have a wide latitude of discretionary authority in their supervision of the offender. A report on the New York parole system found that the parole officer can exercise a great deal of discretion in seeing that the parole agreement is satisfied.[57] In general, the parole officer prizes his right to use his discretion because it helps to maintain the current parole system. Because the parole agreement entered into by the offender contains so many technical rules, nearly all parolees violate parole at one time or another. If an officer were forced to recommend revocation for all violations of parole rules and regulations, he would be revoking a large majority of his caseload back to prison for only minor infractions. It must be understood that parole revocation cuts across both the discretionary release decision on the part of the parole board and the community supervision aspects of parole.

The Supreme Court decision of *Morrissey v. Brewer*[58] provides the revocated parolee with many rights. The due process requirements imposed upon a revocation hearing included (1) written notice to the parolee of alleged violations; (2) providing the parolee an opportunity to appear in person at the hearing and to bring witnesses and evidence; (3) the right of confronting and cross-examining hostile witnesses; (4) a neutral and detached hearing body; and (5) a written statement by the revocation board concerning reasons for its decision and providing the evidence to support the conclusions. The Court nevertheless left many issues unresolved in *Morrissey*. Whether or not evidence obtained by a parole agent in an unauthorized search is admissible at a revocation hearing was not considered by the Court. Nor did the Supreme Court decide the issue of whether an indigent parolee is entitled to appointed counsel. However, *Morrissey* represents an initial attempt, and thus a very important step, towards imposing some restraints upon parole decision-making.

The articles appearing in this anthology expand upon the themes identified in this essay; they have been chosen on the basis of their relation to the central theme of discretion. This book is not intended to provide a systematic review of criminal justice decision-making per se. Rather, its focus is upon the points in the system at which discretion appears to have its most visible and important impact. Moreover, the selections in each section do not purport to encompass all aspects of decision-making. Of course, editors of any volume are bound somewhat by the available literature. Not surprisingly, the balance of our selections must reflect the focus of scholars and practitioners in the field.

Equally important, the selections in this volume reflect an express desire to provide an interdisciplinary approach to the study of discretionary justice. It is the editors' belief that a proper understanding of how our legal system operates cannot be conveyed by a single tack, be it legal, political, sociological, or criminological. The legal scholar, for example, may see the problem of discretionary abuse as stemming from ambiguity in existing statutes. Solutions, accordingly, flow from a desire to correct existing legislative deficiencies or by proposing new legislation. The further development and refinement of judicial policies might appear of equal importance. The sociologist, on the other hand, may interpret the issue of discretionary decision-making from the perspective of interaction among actors within the criminal justice system. Social scientists, be they sociologists or political scientists, might view the issue from an empirical paradigm and thereby utilize empirical evidence tested with sophisticated statistical techniques to explore the complexities of discretion.

The fact that the quality of our system of justice depends, in large part, on the discretionary decisions of others is an uncomfortable reality. Our system of justice is not staid; the decisions that define its character are often the result of complicated, subtle, and sometimes irrational processes. They reflect a critical interplay between formal and informal legal norms, political events, organizational necessities, and psychological motives. In short, within the formal structure of criminal justice, they constitute the invisible system of *human* justice.

NOTES*

1. Max Lerner, "Constitution and Court as Symbols," *Yale L. Rev.*, 46 (June, 1937), pp. 1290–1294.

2. Kenneth Culp Davis, *Discretionary Justice: A Preliminary Inquiry* (Baton Rouge: LSU Press, 1969), p. 4.

3. Kenneth Culp Davis, "Discretionary Justice," *J. Legal Ed.*, 23 (1970), pp. 58–59.

4. Roscoe Pound, "Discretion, Dispensation and Mitigation: The Problem of the Individual Special Case," *N.Y.U. L. Rev.*, 35 (1960), p. 925.

5. Justice Charles Breitel, "Controls in Criminal Law Enforcement," *U. Chi. L. Rev.*, 27 (Spring 1960), p. 427.

6. K. Davis, p. 97.

7. *Ibid.*

8. *Ibid.*, p. 142.

9. E. Bittner, "Police Discretion in Emergency Apprehension of Mentally Ill Persons," *Soc. Prob.*, 14 (Spring, 1967), p. 278.

10. J. Goldstein, "Police Discretion not to Invoke the Criminal Process: Low Visibility Decisions in the Administration of Justice," *Yale L. Rev.*, 69 (1960).

11. A. Rosett and D. Cressey, *Justice by Consent* (Philadelphia: Lippincott, 1976), p. 190.

12. President's Commission on Law Enforcement and Administration of Justice, *Task Force Report: The Police* (Washington, D.C., Government Printing Office, 1967) pp. 19–20.

13. James Finckenauer, "Higher Education and Police Discretion," *J.P.S. and Ad.*, 3 (1975), pp. 450–457.

14. *Task Force Report: The Police*, 1967, p. 126.

15. Certainly an exception to this is considerable work done on the psychological and group dimensions of judicial choice. Useful summaries of this research can be found in Glendon Schubert, (ed.), *Judicial Behavior: A Reader in Theory and Research* (Chicago: Rand McNally, 1964).

16. Private Prosecution: A Remedy for District Attorney's Unwarranted Inaction," *Yale L. Rev.*, 65 (1955), p. 209.

17. *Ibid.*, p. 211.

18. *Ibid.*, p. 213.

19. *See* comment, "Prosecutorial Discretion in the Initiation of Criminal Complaints," *S. Calif. L. Rev.*, 42 (1969), p. 523.

20. Thomas Church, "Plea Bargaining and the Courts: Analysis of a Quasi-Experiment," *Law and Society Rev.*, (Spring, 1976), pp. 377–401.

21. F. Remington and Rosenblum, "The Criminal Law and the Legislative Process," *U. Ill. L. Forum*, 481 (1960), p. 497.

22. 184 F. Supp. 679, N.D. Ill., (1960).

23. 397 U.S. 742, 1970.

24. 404 U.S. 257, 260, 1971.

25. 400 U.S. 25, 1970.

26. *Newman v. U.S.*, 382 F.2d 479, 1967 D.C. cir.

27. 497 F.2d 615, D.C. cir 1973.

28. Cited at p. 618 of *Ammidown*.

29. Newman v. U.S., *loc. cit.*

30. For a discussion of the "No Discretion" thesis, see Ronald Dworkin, "Judicial Discretion," *Journal of Philosophy*, 60 (1963), p. 624; *see also* Rolf Sartorius, *Individual Conduct and Social Norms* (1975) and Sartorius "Social Policy and Judicial Legislation," *Am. Phil. Q.*, 8 (1971), p. 151. For a review of their work, and a contrary position, *see* Kent Greenwalt, "Discretion and Judicial Decision: The Elusive Quest for the Fetters that Bind Judges," *Columbia L. Rev.*, 75 (1975), pp. 359–399.

31. Charles E. Ares, Anne Rankin, and Herbert Sturz, "The Administration of Bail in New York," *N.Y.U. L. Rev.*, 38 (1963).

*Footnotes have been abridged, edited, and renumbered.

32. Frederick Suffet, "Bailsetting: A Study in Courtroom Interaction," *Crime and Delinquency*, (October, 1966), pp. 318–331.

33. Compelling Appearance in Court: Administration of Bail in Philadelphia," *U. P. L. Rev.*, 102 (1954) pp. 1031–1043; 1051–1054.

34. Julian C. D'Esposoto, Jr., "Sentencing Disparity: Causes and Cures," *J.C.L.C. and P.S.*, 60 (1969), p. 183.

35. *See* Albert Somit, Joseph Tanenhaus and Walter Wilke, "Aspects of Judicial Sentencing Behavior," *U. Pittsburgh L. Rev.*, 21 (1960), pp. 613–621.

36. Charles B. Burr, II, "Appellate Review as a Means of Controlling Criminal Sentencing Discretion — A Workable Alternative?" *U. Pittsburgh L. Rev.*, 33 (Fall 1971), pp. 5–6.

37. James D. Hopkins, "Reviewing Sentencing Discretion: A Method of Swift Appellate Action," *UCLA L. Rev.*, 23 (1976) p. 498.

38. *See* Dean Jaros and Robert I. Mendelsohn, "The Judicial Role and Sentencing Behavior," *MW. J. Political Science*, 11 (November, 1967), pp. 471–488.

39. Marvin E. Frankel, *Criminal Sentences* (New York: Hill and Wang), 1973, pp. 13–14.

40. For further discussion, *see* W. Anthony Fitch and Julian Tepper, "Structuring Correction and Decision-Making: A Traditional Proposal," *Catholic U. L. Rev.*, 22 (1973), p. 776.

41. *See* Douglas J. Hitchock, "The California Adult Authority — Indeterminate Sentencing and the Parole Decision as a Problem in Administrative Discretion," *U. Calif. at Davis L. Rev.*, 5 (1972), p. 373.

42. Procunier v. Martinez, 416 U.S. 396, 1974.

43. Holt v. Sarver, 300 F.Supp. 825, 1969.

44. Clutchett v. Procunier, 328 F.Supp. 767, 1971.

45. Banks v. Havener, 324 F.Supp. 27, 1964.

46. *See* Holt v. Sarver, *loc. cit.*

47. 418 U.S. 539, 1974.

48. V. O'Leary, M. Gottfredson and A. Gelman, "Contemporary Sentencing Proposals," *Crim. L. Bul.*, 11 (Sept.–Oct., 1975), pp. 555–586.

49. V. O'Leary and J. Nuffield, "Parole Decision Making Characteristics," *Crim. L. Bul.*, 8 (Oct., 1972), pp. 651–680.

50. Kenneth Culp Davis, *Discretionary Justice: A Preliminary Inquiry*, (Baton Rouge: LSU Press, 1969), p. 126.

51. 477 F.2d 278 5th cir 1973, p. 283.

52. Cagle v. Harris, 349 F.2d 404 8th cir 1965.

53. Escoe v. Zerbst, 295 U.S. 490, 1935. Other recent federal court decisions rejecting the extension of constitutional rights at parole hearings are *Menchino v. Oswald*, 430 F.2d. 403 2nd cir, 1970; *Barnes v. United States*, 445. F.2d. 260 8th cir, 1971; and Buchanan v. Clark, 446 F.2d. 1379, 5th cir 1971.

54. 397 U.S. 254, 1970.

55. 408 U.S. 471, 1972.

56. For a fuller treatment of problem in this area, *see* Plotkin, 1975.

57. "Report on the New York Parole: A Summary by Citizens' Inquiry on Parole and Criminal Justice," *Crim. L. Bul.*, 11 (May-June, 1975), pp. 273–303.

58. 408 U.S. 471, 1972.

2. DISCRETION, SEVERITY AND LEGALITY IN CRIMINAL JUSTICE

ARTHUR ROSETT

Southern California Law Review, Vol. 46, © 1973 by Arthur Rosett. Reprinted by permission.

■ How might abuses of discretionary power be controlled? Conceding that much of the use of discretion by public officials is inevitable, Rosett argues that judicial control and review, one of the frequently employed devices for managing discretionary abuse in the courtroom is inadequate because "even the tightest bureaucracy has chinks in its monolithic structure, and discretion operates in the cracks." Control of discretionary power in one agency, according to this author, is relatively meaningless because "the criminal justice system accommodates itself to rigid structuring" — "if squeezed in one spot it pops out in another." An alternative to judicialization that Rosett proposes is to control discretion by manipulating the severity of criminal sentences or, in other words, by making legal sanctions less severe and hence removing much of the energy that fuels discretionary abuse. Although this article addresses judicial control and review as means to control discretionary decisions, Rosett's careful explanation of the causes and effects of the use of discretion provides a strong foundation for the remaining articles in this volume. ■

If every policeman, every prosecutor, every court, and every post-sentence agency performed his or its responsibility in strict accordance with rules of law, precisely and narrowly laid down, the criminal law would be ordered but intolerable.[1]

If all the defendants should combine to refuse to plead guilty, and should dare to hold out, they could break down the administration of criminal justice in any state in the Union. But they dare not hold out, for such as were tried and convicted could hope for no leniency. The prosecutor is like a man armed with a revolver who is cornered by a mob. A concerted rush would overwhelm him. . . . The truth is that a criminal court can operate only by inducing the great mass of actually guilty defendants to plead guilty.[2]

THESE TWO FAMILIAR quotations describe the need to dispose of criminal cases outside the formal trial process and suggest that discretionary decision-making is both inevitable from the viewpoint of officials charged with administering the system and vital to the interests of individuals subjected to it. This article will explore the tangled connections between the pervasiveness of official discretion within the organizations that administer the criminal law and the severity of potential punishments and disabilities imposed on those ultimately condemned. Severity is a variable that can be manipulated to produce a less worrisome discretionary system. A judgment must be made, however, whether the reward of limiting discretion is sufficient to justify the costs that might attend reducing the severity of the criminal sanction. These costs are not limited to the time and expense of a ponderous formal process; they also include loss of potential deterrent effectiveness and interference with public demands for a punitive system. All of these costs must be considered in assessing the options available within the political context of lawmaking.

DISCRETION — ITS CAUSES AND EFFECTS

An appreciation for the severity and the discretionary selectivity of a process which subjects similarly situated individuals to disparate treatment is fundamental to an understanding of why discretion is viewed as a problem and why judicialization inevitably fails to provide an effective solution.

Selectivity and Discretion

Modern criminal justice is a highly selective process in which severe punishment is meted out to a few, while many other individuals who appear similarly situated escape with little or no punishment.[3] Each successive step in the legal process of charge, conviction, and sentence results in more fallout, so that, of every 100 adults arrested on felony charges in California, fewer than four will ever be confined in a penal institution.[4] At the same time, those who do pass through the sieve and are subjected to the full force of the process may experience dire consequences.

The selective operation of the criminal law is primarily determined by informal police decisions (made on the street and in the station house) regarding arrest and detention, by prosecutors' judgments as to which charge to file and guilty plea to accept, by judges' sentencing choices (usually made on recommendation of probation officers), and by decisions of correctional authorities fixing parole release, revocation, and discharge. Such decisions are discretionary in the sense that the official has the unfettered choice whether to act, and often how to act, in a given case. This free choice may arise from the explicit delegation of legal authority to the official, the absence of a rule prohibiting his acting, or the assertion of official power to act despite a governing rule.

Discretion usually is seen as normlessness, the absence of controlling substantive standards, but the term may have procedural connotations as well. In a procedural sense it may mean that the process used to reach decision is informal and provides opportunities for uncontrolled deviation from the governing norm. In a recent study of justified rule departures, Professors Kadish and Kadish emphasize discretion as a departure from announced substantive rules.[5] The prime example they draw upon is the phenomenon of the jury ignoring the judge's instructions and acquitting an apparently guilty criminal defendant. But jury nullification does not exist because there is no rule to govern the jury's decision (in most cases the jury is exhaustively instructed on the law by the judge), and certainly does not arise because there is a rule permitting them to ignore the rules. (They are instructed in most jurisdictions that the legal rules are binding on them as given.)[6] Rather, the key factor is the procedural setting in which the jury operates and in which the decision is reached. The jury has effective discretion because the jury room is outside the scrutiny and formality of the courtroom; what happens there is insulated by this procedural context from outside audit. Discretion, like so many other parts of the substantive law, has grown up largely in the interstices of procedure.

WHY DISCRETION IS A PROBLEM

Both the substantive and the procedural aspects of discretion make its prevalence worrisome. When discretion means substantive normlessness or the deviation from announced norms, it suggests that a process is ineffective, either because that process has not decided what it is trying to accomplish, or because, by operating contrary to standards, it is being counterproductive. Moreover, a system normless in its operation is unjust, applying pain randomly or arbitrarily and failing to give notice of the bases for its action to individuals who wish to plan their behavior.

Much of the dissatisfaction with the operation of the criminal process relates to the disparity in treatment of the individual that results in his being treated one way or another because of slight and sometimes random variations in circumstance. Some choices are undoubtedly dictated by an official's doubts as to whether the behavior is appropriately punishable, by flaws in the evidence relied upon to justify official action, or by the presence of compelling individual factors supporting mitigation of punishment. But many decisions cannot be persuasively explained on such grounds; they appear accidental or even venal.

The procedural aspects of discretion raise similar questions of justice and effectiveness. Our legal tradition demands that decisions be made dispassionately and rationally, pursuant to generally applicable rules. Idiosyncratic choice, whereby the individual's fate depends upon which official happens to be on duty that day, is repellent. Moreover, we place high value on the visibility of a process whose fairness is incarnate. Discretionary processes tend to operate invisibly — out of sight of the public, the reviewing judiciary, and often the parties affected by the decision. . . .

. . . Many discretionary decisions seem dominated by the need to keep the calendar moving or the desire to dispose of cases at the "going rate" for a particular violation, without attention to individual situations. The circumstances often must be con-

sciously distorted to fit the case into a desired category. Those who administer such a
system lose sight of broader goals. There is
sometimes an element of "let's pretend" as
inaccurate labels are placed on behavior and
officials engage in solemn charades they
know do not reflect the true state of facts.

Discretionary decision-making can actually serve to increase the costs and the size
of the total criminal justice system. The police, the prosecutor, and the court can be
viewed as a set of gates limiting the system's
intake by the narrowness of the passage
through which the cases flow. A constricting
and laborious process slows the system and
serves to prevent overcrowded prisons. But
the negotiated guilty plea and normless judicial sentencing discretion can create a bypass around these gates. Discretionary decision-making may permit economy at one
stage, but it is likely to do so by passing too
much work downstream to someone else and
increasing the total load on the system.

Reliance on discretion does not necessarily make an agency's caseload smaller than it
would otherwise be. Agencies develop a
vested interest in their workload. Discretionary decision-making, particularly in prisons,
hospitals and parole organizations, has been
associated with a prejudice in favor of retaining power over a client or inmate and
against release. The result can be institutions
filled with individuals who might well have
been released by a more demanding and less
flexible process.

Moreover, the prevalence of discretion
threatens the ability to channel and control
official behavior through law. The basic protections of the American criminal process
center on the court trial. Underlying the provisions of the Constitution and the codes of
procedure is the assumption that it is the job
of a judge, operating within the familiar setting of the common law trial, to decide
whether an individual shall be confined. If
the legality of the official process is chal-
lenged, it is a judge, typically in a proceeding for habeas corpus or a motion to suppress evidence, who is expected to test the
propriety of official action. But discretionary
processes tend to bypass these judicial protections. Cases are disposed of without full
and open hearings, and official behavior is
not subjected to judicial or public scrutiny.

Aside from the issues of effectiveness and
legality, there are other serious causes for
concern. Reliance on discretion vastly enhances the power of law enforcement and
correctional agencies, and is closely tied to
more generalized problems of governmental
bureaucracy. The absence of effective control on official behavior is not only a threat
to the personality of individuals subjected to
the process, it is also a political danger for
society as a whole. It places unbridled, coercive power in the hands of a group that has
an increasingly pronounced ideological identity. Because they dominate the discretionary processes, these officials have effective
control over the intake and outflow of the
agencies of criminal justice. Control over
their own workload and, therefore, over the
size of their agencies, enables these officials
to make sizeable and politically potent
claims for public funds. It influences the allocation of scarce local government reve-
nues in a field that consumes a major portion
of the resources of local government. It also
gives them power either to reinforce public
perceptions of the crime problem or to
"cure" that problem at will. The need to
bring discretion within acceptable limits is
more than a matter of technical neatness or
humanitarian sympathy for those subjected
to the system. It is a pressing political need.

JUDICIALIZATION — WHY IT DOES NOT ELIMINATE DISCRETION

The response of law-trained officials, particularly judges, when confronted with the
problem of discretion, has been dominated
by insistence upon pre-announced standards
and carefully defined procedures. The lawyer would reform procedure by requiring a
judicial hearing, rules of evidence and, most
importantly, counsel. But these techniques
of judicialization have proven to be of only
limited utility and often have only complicated the choreography of the criminal justice "ritual dance." The result of trying to
make a discretionary decision-making process look more like a trial has often been the
creation of a new discretionary process elsewhere. The criminal justice system accommodates itself to rigid structuring. If
squeezed in one spot it merely pops out in
another. New juvenile agencies appear that

are strikingly similar to the juvenile court; plea negotiators move their business out of the courtroom and into the hallway. Requiring the provision of counsel in a discretionary process is likely to result in the lawyer moving into an empty room; the important decisions already will have been made elsewhere. Uncritical reliance upon the hearing is likely to have little or no effect on how the decisions are actually made.

One clear effect of judicialization is to make the process of decision slower, more expensive and, ultimately, less certain. Procedural preoccupation reduces the capacity to decide cases and increases the incentive for officials to dispose of cases by discretionary or negotiated means. Overreliance on procedural safeguards tends to increase, rather than reduce, the ambit of discretion, as officials seek some way to get their job done.

THE INEVITABILITY OF DISCRETION

Judicialization is a dubious instrument of reform because it may leave untouched the most disturbing aspects of the system that call for change. If all lawyers' basic concerns were met, two crucial aspects of the existing system would persist quite unaffected. First, the consequences of the process and its potential for cataclysmic severity would persist; we would still act upon the condemned person with as much harshness as is presently employed. Second, the phenomenon of discretion would persist, because nothing in the lawyers' reforms removes the inherent and inevitable limitations that would continue to restrict the usefulness of the legal model. Many of these limitations are obvious, but it may be helpful to review briefly their most salient aspects.

The Limits of Definition

An inherent source of pervasive discretion is the difficulty of articulating definitions of crimes that can be applied to a variety of situations. Modern criminal codes represent a rather crude attempt to satisfy two aspects of the ideal of justice. One sense of justice demands that similarly situated people be treated alike; another demands that each man be treated according to his deserts.

The first sense of justice demands that definitions of crimes be stated generally and be applied to all similarly situated persons; the second demands that these general rules be flexible enough to allow for variations in individual circumstance. Eventually someone must give meaning to the words of the law, and that interpretation process inevitably involves substantial discretionary elements.

Factual Uncertainty

The confinement and severe loss of status that accompany criminal conviction should be imposed only when there is a high degree of certainty as to the circumstances. In many cases, however, such assurance is lacking, for human situations typically do not come in neat packages and circumstances often are indeterminate. Society does not expect a policeman to arrest, a prosecutor to charge, or a court to convict whenever there is a modicum of evidence of criminal behavior. At every stage in the criminal process, there must be a judgment, inevitably discretionary in nature, that there is sufficient persuasive evidence upon which a conviction can and should rest.

Untriable Questions

Discretion also arises out of the inherently limited usefulness of the formal trial process to reach some kinds of decisions. To the extent that cases turn on policy questions or therapeutic judgments, officials are forced to go outside the process to resolve them. If budgetary limitations or system overload demand that fewer criminal charges be brought, the responsible official will be forced to choose cases with circumstances that should be given special weight. This assignment of weight to circumstance can be only partially guided by rule and process. Ultimately, the judgment called for is discretionary in nature. Similarly, clinical choices involving therapeutic or diagnostic decisions cannot be determined in a trial setting. Doctors frequently testify in court as to judgments arrived at outside; but attempts to make the decision occur within the trial context distort both the legal and medical processes of decision-making. Doctors and judges simply do not make decisions in the same way.[7] This divergence leads to conflict that may be both substantive (contrast the medical concept of mental illness with the legal concepts of insanity and incompetence) and procedural (contrast the clinical casework file with the criminal trial record).

The Limits of Time, Talent and Money

The present criminal justice system is so dependent on discretionary processes to dispose of the workload that a fully formalized system seems only a remote possibility. Formal decisions require an expensive and potentially ponderous process. These costs are justified when important decisions like imprisonment are involved, but there are inevitable pressures to avoid the expense and foreshorten the decision process when there is no substantial dispute. This is more than a matter of monetary savings; there are programmatic advantages to the imposition of punishment or treatment soon after the offensive behavior. The likelihood of injustice from delay is greater than the likelihood of injustice from speedy disposition. The didactic impact of punishment on the offender and on society at large is also likely to be greater when the process moves quickly. In juvenile and mental health cases swift decisions are likely to be both a practical and a therapeutic necessity. In all situations it is silly to squander the scarce resources needed to make a full formal decision on a case in which it is not needed.[8]

DISCRETION AND ACQUIESCENCE

A remarkable aspect of the selective process is its emphasis on inducing the person subjected to it to acquiesce, if not actively cooperate, in the action taken against him. Many dubious aspects of the discretionary operation are tolerated, because they induce acquiescence. Police and prosecutors (and often, tacitly, courts) manipulate plea bargaining, overcharging, high statutory sentence limits, mandatory sentences and reduced charges to motivate an accused to cooperate in order to avoid a dire possibility. Even the threat of a death sentence may become permissible to motivate a guilty plea.

In the correctional system, indeterminacy of parole eligibility and discharge standards is similarly used to induce non-resistance. Means are used to obtain "consent" or at least a "waiver of rights" that would not conceivably be permissible in other areas of the law as an inducement to "voluntary action."[9]

Obviously there are strong functional virtues to acquiescence. If a fully judicialized model were adopted perhaps the defendants would not plead guilty. All phases of the process operate much more economically, promptly and smoothly without disruption caused by challenge. To the extent that the system is therapeutic in orientation, seeking to cure the malfunctioning individual, cooperating is a necessary precondition of treatment.

The system justifies its emphasis on acquiescence on grounds of efficiency and uses it to gain conviction when formal proof is lacking. Beyond its instrumental functions, however, acquiescence has intrinsic value in its own right. Even if there were adequate resources to convict every defendant after a contested trial, it is likely that the practice of seeking acknowledgment from the accused that condemnation and punishment are the "right" thing would continue. Our sense of justice is involved. We become uneasy when the system punishes a man who sincerely contests the legitimacy of his condemnation, and the best way to mollify our uneasiness is to gain a confession. The extent to which pressure is exerted on defendants to "go along" is not explainable solely in terms of efficiency or difficulty of proof. Confession as a virtue perhaps reflects an older system in which punishment was consciously used for the sacramental expiation of sin as well as the temporal punishment of the wrongdoer. The use of torture to obtain confession, *peine dur et forte* to obtain a plea is no longer permitted; nor is an abject and full confession demanded in all cases. A number of face-saving techniques have been established to enable an accused to acquiesce without formally consenting. But the need for legitimizing permission remains strong. This need poses a dilemma, for to meet the system's needs for acquiescence, practices are employed which intensify doubts as to the justice of the total process. Foremost among these is the threat of potentially severe punishment for those who resist.

DISCRETION AND UNDUE SEVERITY

Discretionary disposition of criminal charges is likely to be important to the individual official as the means by which he can avoid the unacceptably rigorous application of the letter of the law. Without such opportunities for leniency in compelling cases, conscientious men might hesitate to participate in the enforcement of the criminal law. Discretion to avoid excessive harshness is needed in any system to deal with the unusual case. It becomes a pervasive need in contemporary America because our criminal law is so harsh that its full application in all but aggravated cases would not only be cruel, but also expensive and socially destructive. Amelioration of the rigors of the written law is the norm, not the exception, in current practice. Virtually all of those who come to official attention on a criminal charge, whether or not they are arrested and prosecuted, are its "beneficiaries" to at least a limited degree.

However, discretionary amelioration does not affect the potential for severity of the penal code. It is true that the likelihood of that potential being exercised is decreased to the extent that procedural rules create what Professor Packer refers to as an "obstacle course in the path of conviction."[10] But the opportunity for non-judicial punishment by law enforcement officials remains. Good examples are pretrial detention and prosecutorial power over the charges to be filed. Both can be, and sometimes are, used to incarcerate individuals who are unlikely to be jailed as punishment after conviction, and to subject others to the trauma of prosecution and an indelible criminal record. Most of the individuals confined in California jails are in pretrial detention, suggesting that more people are punished by discretionary bail decisions before conviction than by the imposition of sentence after conviction.

Procedural complication also increases the pressure on officials to dispose of cases with the acquiescence of the accused. An ironic result of over-reliance on discretionary disposition is that, however compassion-ate its intent, the need to gain this acquiescence leads officials to place a heavy price in the form of enhanced severity on those who invoke the formal process but do not succeed in avoiding punishment. This can be seen in the operation of the negotiated guilty plea. In order to motivate acquiescence from others, an example occasionally must be made of the uncooperative individual who contests the case unsuccessfully. When opportunities to delay and defeat the process are introduced, there is a reciprocal tendency of officials to raise the gate and to increase the punishment given those who unsuccessfully contest the charge. In such a system it becomes permissible to impose the death sentence on the few in order to motivate the many to plead guilty and receive a lesser sentence.

From the viewpoint of the accused, the potential severity of the process also operates in a contradictory fashion. When the whole system is severe the accused is under great pressure to acquiesce and avoid a dire result, but he is also more fearful of acceding to the alternative punishment he is offered. Only a man very confident of his ultimate vindication would chance capital punishment, if such punishment is still permissible, rather than plead guilty. But, however tempted an individual may be to "pay the man the two dollars and go home," the path of nonresistance becomes less tempting as the alternative penalty increases. From the perspective of both the official and the subject, it is the unacceptable severity of the formal system that makes demands for discretionary escape mechanisms so urgent, just as it is the compelling demand to process cases by discretionary means that leads to undue harshness in some cases. The two aspects of the problem are inextricable.

DISCRETION AND THE DEMANDS OF BUREAUCRACY

A powerful limitation on the potential of judicialization is that discretion is the method of operation preferred by the bureaucratic organizations which administer the criminal justice system. Rules and codes of criminal procedure developed when professional police and prosecutors were much less important than they are today. Control has passed to agencies that are large, that are motivated by professional considerations and expertise, and in which organizational requirements shape the ways that decisions are made by operating officers.

The operations of bureaucratic organizations tend, over the long run, to be determined less by their external function (such as healing the ill or correcting offenders) and increasingly by strong pressures arising from the internal needs of the institution itself (*e.g.*, maintaining budgetary support or providing career opportunities for officials). Treatment programs, often vague from the outset, in time become further diluted and bent to support institutional control over inmates and to meet the day-to-day maintenance needs of institutions. These conflicting internal and external pressures force the official to respond by reaching for power to act outside the formal process.

We tend to think of bureaucratic organization as preoccupied with rules and procedures which limit choice to rigid and stifling channels. The bureaucrat creates the impression that he is merely a functionary, subject to rules governing his every action. But even the tightest bureaucracy has chinks in its monolithic structure, and discretion operates in the cracks. Many decisions present only

limited opportunities for control and supervision. Higher echelon police officials often are not in a position to control, or even to supervise, their subordinates' action or inaction in the field. It is particularly difficult to supervise the officer's choice to look the other way, not to file a report, or not to invoke his authority while on the beat. The man on the scene has immense decision-making power, not only because he is beyond the ears and eyes of his supervisors, but because he is the gatherer, evaluator, recorder and disseminator of the official facts upon which decision turns. By and large the judge or the parole board member learns only what the discretionary agent tells him, and can do little independent fact gathering. Strong social pressures operate upon the formal decision-maker, leading him to accept and agree with the judgments of a co-worker with whom he has a continuing and vital relationship; this pressure may be reinforced by the expert status of the discretionary field agent. Discretion and bureaucratic organization are closely associated because the individual official finds himself in a position in which his organizational role conflicts with the nominal job assigned. The only way to reconcile these conflicting pressures is through discretionary accommodation.

NOTES*

1. Breitel, "Controls in Criminal Law Enforcement," 27 *U. Chi. L. Rev.* 427 (1960) (hereinafter cited as Breitel).

2. H. Lummus, *The Trial Judge*, 46 (1937).

3. See F. Miller, *Prosecution* (1971); *Task Force on Administration of Justice, President's Comm. on Law Enforcement & Administration of Justice, Task Force Report: The Courts app. B (1967) (hereinafter cited as Courts);* H. Subin, *Criminal Justice in a Metropolitan Court (1966)*; M. Virtue, *Survey of Metropolitan Courts, Detroit Area* (1950); McIntyre, "A Study of Judicial Dominance of the Charging Process," 59 *J. Crim. L.C. & P.S.*, 463 (1968); "A Proposal for Reform of the Plea Bargaining Process," 119 *U. Pa. L. Rev.* 439 (1971).

4. BCS 1970, at note 4, p. 19 (table I-6). Many of the criminal events that occur in the community are absorbed without official attention. Of those

that become known to the police, only a small fraction result in arrest. Nor do all individuals officially accused of crime inevitably go to jail. Almost one-third of those arrested on charges of felony are released outright by the police or the district attorney without any court action.

5. Kadish & Kadish, "On Justified Rule Departures by Officials," 59 *Calif. L. Rev.* 905 (1971).

6. See *California Jury Instructions* § 1.00 at p. 2 (3d ed. 1970); 1 Devitt & Blackman, *Federal Jury Practice and Instructions* § 10.15 (2d ed. 1970).

7. Therapeutic questions are particularly difficult to fit into a court setting because they involve predictions as to the response of the patient to treatment. If it is hard to decide issues of historical fact with acceptable certainty, how much harder is it to make predictions as to the indeterminate future conduct of individuals? Consider, for example, the delicate issue of whether a person is a danger to

*This article has been abridged and its footnotes edited and renumbered.

himself or to others; that is, whether he is suicidal or assaultive. This is not as simple to determine as the issue of whether a defendant did in fact on a given date attempt suicide or assault another person.

8. It has been suggested that, beyond considerations of economy, the credibility of the total process depends on the relative rarity of its invocation.

So long as trials are the exception rather than the rule and are limited, by and large, to cases in which the defense offers a substantial basis for contesting the prosecutor's allegations, the defendant's presumption of innocence and the requirement of proof beyond a reasonable doubt are likely to remain meaningful to a jury. The very fact that the defendant contests the charges impresses upon the jurors the seriousness of their deliberations and the need to keep an open mind about the evidence and to approach the testimony of accus-ing witnesses with critical care and perhaps even a degree of skepticism. If contest becomes routine, jurors may likely direct their skepticism at the defense. Prosecutors too readily apply the overall, and overwhelming, statistical probability of guilt to individual cases; we do not want jurors to do the same. It makes some sense, then, to screen out those cases where there is no real dispute and encourage their disposition by plea, leaving for trial to the extent possible only those cases where there exists a real basis for dispute.

Emker, "Perspectives on Plea Bargaining," in *President's Comm. on Law Enforcement, Task Force Report: The Courts* 108, 112 (1967).

9. *See* Santobello v. New York, 404 U.S. 257, 262 (1971); Sutherland, "Crime & Confession," 79 *Harv. L. Rev.* 21, 36–37 (1965); Tigar, "Forward: Waiver of Constitutional Rights: Disquiet in the Citadel," 84 *Harv. L. Rev.* 1, 19–24 (1970).

10. H. Packer, *Limits of the Criminal Sanction*, 163 (1968).

3. DISCRETION

AMERICAN FRIENDS SERVICE COMMITTEE

From THE STRUGGLE FOR JUSTICE, Chapter 8, © 1971, by Hill and Wang. Reprinted by permission.

■ Discretionary power is anathema to many critics of the criminal justice system because it allows for deviation from a uniform application of legal sanctions. In a somewhat different vein than the article by Rosett, this selection argues that discretion is not inevitable and that, in fact, its existence serves to benefit the managerial and property classes. This excerpt from THE STRUGGLE FOR JUSTICE discredits the role of discretion in decision-making by examining the various justifications (as touched upon by Rosett) of its existence within the criminal justice process. ■

JUSTIFICATIONS FOR DISCRETION

TWO MAJOR JUSTIFICATIONS for discretion are the use of discretion for the purpose of implementing a system of individualized treatment and the use of discretion to restrain persons who have been identified as dangerous. In the case of the former, the conceptual underpinnings for an individualized treatment system of justice are either unconfirmed or totally invalid. Instead of promoting rehabilitation, the individualized system promotes inhumanity, discrimination, hypocrisy, and a sense of injustice. In regard to control of the dangerous, we argue that since there are no techniques for distinguishing which small number of a much larger class of individuals will continue to perform dangerous acts, holding the entire class in detention amounts to holding a majority of harmless people needlessly. Moreover, we suggest that this highly unjust practice is of minimal benefit to society because the number of unapprehended or unidentified lawbreakers in any given crime category is always much larger than those identified or in custody. Also, society has responded almost exclusively toward certain types of offenders, such as thieves, rapists, and murderers, but ignored almost completely larger numbers of persons who are much more dangerous, such as those who make and profit from war, unsafe automobiles, and contaminating pesticides.

TO INTERPRET THE LEGISLATIVE MANDATE

There are several other, more technical justifications for the existence of discretion that must be confronted before we examine its actual functions. One justification often submitted is that discretion is needed at the level of law enforcement because any law drafted and passed by a legislature is insufficiently specific. This argument suggests that it is impossible to anticipate in advance all the diverse situations in which the law might become applicable, and that there will always be a multitude of ambiguities in every law. Wayne La Fave, who has studied police discretion, commented:

The exercise of discretion in interpreting the legislative mandate is necessary because no legislature has succeeded in formulating a substantive criminal code which clearly encompasses all conduct intended to be made criminal and which clearly excludes all other conduct.[1]

We agree that written laws, particularly when they are first written, cannot spell out all the specific applications and ramifications of a law. This, however, is no justification for continued discretionary power in the hands of members of the criminal justice system. Exploring the ramifications of the law and specifying its applications is the role of the judiciary and is properly an ongoing and open process. Ideally, therefore, a recently enacted law would go through a process of open testing in the courts. In this way its specificities become part of common law. It is not necessary, in fact it is hypocritical and insidious, to operate with a vague law and to use its vagueness as a screen to conceal the other motives and practices of a discretionary system.

BECAUSE OF THE IMPOSSIBILITY OF ENFORCING ALL LAWS

Everyone attached to existing law enforcement agencies recognizes that it would be totally impossible to enforce all the laws all the time. The following statement is accurate here:

No policeman enforces all the laws of a community. If he did, we would all be in jail before the end of the first day.[2]

Our answer to this is that removal of discretion is, of course, not possible without other revisions in the criminal justice system. We are acutely aware that criminal law is passed on the assumption that great margins of discretion will be exercised. We presently have a system so overextensive that no one would want to see it fully enforced. This is exactly the state of affairs we object to. Let us end the legislative practice of passing laws as symbolic gestures with no intention that they be enforced, or passing purposely vague laws with the intention that something other than full enforcement be accomplished.

One of the basic principles we wish to promote is that of restraint. The goal throughout the system should be to reduce the extensiveness of the use of legal sanctions to govern our affairs. As this goal is approached, and the legislature only supports the laws they intend to be enforced, this justification for discretion will be removed.

The existence of vague laws and overextensive laws, which must be interpreted and enforced selectively at the lower echelons of the criminal justice system — at the level of the police — has given rise to a serious problem: the misuse of discretion by police. Following their unofficial mandate and utilizing the discretionary power granted to them, police in America do not primarily enforce the law. Instead they maintain order, often heavy-handedly. In accomplishing this goal they selectively enforce laws against individuals and classes whom they, or the dominant political and economic interests, see as threats to the social order. . . .

TO AVOID THE INTOLERABLE RIGIDITY OF LAW

Many persons argue strongly that a system of laws rigidly enforced would be intolerable, both to the persons enforcing the law and to the persons living under the law.

If every policeman, every prosecutor, every court, and every post-sentence agency performed his or its responsibility in strict accordance with rules of law, precisely and narrowly laid down, the criminal law would be ordered but intolerable. Living would be a sterile compliance with soul-killing rules and taboos. By comparision, a primitive tribal society would seem free, indeed.[8]

Ken Davis argues similarly that the existence of discretion has made the system more "equitable," particularly during periods when legal structures have become extensive and oppressive.[9] He quotes Morris R. Cohen on periods when systems of justice were particularly oppressive and were made less so by the use of discretion.

Legal history shows, if not alternating periods of justice according to law and justice without law, at least periodic waves of reform during which the sense of justice, natural law, or equity introduces life and flexibility into the law and makes it adjustable to its work. In course of time, however, under the social demand for certainty, equity gets hardened and reduced to rigid rules, so that, after awhile, a new reform wave is necessary.[10]

These arguments are misleading. They are based on a mistaken assumption and obscure the real problems of "rigidity" of the system.

As to the mistaken assumption, these writers seem to be suggesting that all facets of our lives are governed by legal norms. Though we agree that the areas presently being governed by legal norms are excessive, and that a principle of restraint should be observed in deciding what to prohibit by legal statute, even now most of our action and most of our choices are made free from penal restraints. Breitel's allusion to primitive tribal society is inaccurate here. Tribal society was rigid because of an excessively rigid *informal* system of controls. Our informal system of control is quite loose and discretionary and allows wide choice in possible courses of action. It does not follow that a formal (legal) system of control, particularly one governed by principles of restraint, would make life intolerably rigid. However, such a system would present other problems to the functionaries.

Aside from the false assumption that much of our lives would be governed by inflexible legal norms were it not for discretion, the thesis of the intolerability of a legal system without discretion is highly misleading in yet another manner. The writers above suggest that discretion allows functionaries to make exceptions to "rigid" legal norms and thereby lessen or remove the oppressiveness of the system. We must examine this more closely. By and large, the functionaries of a criminal justice system are either members of the politically and economically dominant classes of the society or totally subservient to these classes. Generally, these functionaries make exceptions only when they identify with the cultural values of the defendant, or when the defendant is not seen as a threat to the dominant political, moral, or economic systems, or when the defendant can exert power or influence on the political system. Moreover, the use of discretion, even when humanity, justice, equity, or expediency is served by doing so, has a negative side. That is, it increases the punishment of those for whom no exception is made. For instance, Charles Breitel suggests that few are dissatisfied with discretion that is intended to "ameliorate and qualify," such as the discretion of executive pardon, since "it can only save; it can never kill." We suggest that this is misleading. While a pardon that is granted can only save, the pardon application that is denied or ignored obviously does not save.

TRUE FUNCTIONS OF DISCRETION

The life of the ordinary citizen is not made intolerable by rigidly enforced legal sanctions. The power to make exceptions in the delivery of legal sanctions is humane only to those who gain the sympathy of the system or to those who have the power to merit special favor. Who then is hurt by a rigid system of justice and who benefits from a discretionary system? Is it not the functionaries of the criminal justice system, members of the dominant classes, and the political incumbents who gain by the operation of a discretionary system? Are these not the people who would find life less tolerable for themselves in a nondiscretionary system?

To prove this point we refer the reader to the area of property inheritance tax or business law or any area, for that matter, in which the affairs of the more powerful and rich segments are being regulated. In these areas the specificity of the law is extreme. Little margin is left for discretion. Two companies in a contract dispute or relatives contesting the division of property in a will would not tolerate a judge making a discretionary decision based on his conception of the "best interests of society and of all parties involved," even if these motives were those actually operating in a discretionary system. No, they insist that decisions be made on the basis of preestablished rules. In general, in any area of law where the persons being regulated have resources, there is practically no discretion operating. This is due in part to their ability and propensity to litigate their affairs. The powerful, monied classes not only manage with this "rigid" system, they insist upon it because they perceive that it is to their benefit.

If, as we suspect, the elimination of discretion would make the lives of the bulk of the clients of the criminal justice system more tolerable, then why do we have a discretionary system? Why is there such tenacious support of it? Is it not, as we have argued above, that life is made easier for those who run the system, the functionaries, and those they serve, the dominant classes of the society?

TO INCREASE MANAGERIAL EFFICIENCY

Governing by strict rules has always presented problems to those in authoritarian positions. It is easier for managers to make ad hoc decisions in each case upon criteria relating to efficiency and expediency. Consider private corporations as compared to government bureaucracies. It is generally agreed that private businesses can operate with greater efficiency because they are not restrained by so many rules and regulations limiting their discretionary power. For instance, when they decide to pick a person to fill a managerial position, they are not restrained by rules of tenure and seniority. They can ignore values of fairness to employees and operate solely on values of efficiency and expediency to promote the person they feel will do the company the most good.

An example of this efficiency norm operating to the extreme and to the detriment of other principles of justice is the plea-bargaining system, which dominates, with a few exceptions, every court operation in the country. Faced with more cases than can be tried with the resources available, the police, the judges, and the prosecuting attorney, operating with the assumption of guilt, charge a defendant with the maximum offense possible, and then bargain with him to accept a lesser charge if he pleads guilty. This is a highly unjust practice for many reasons. Parole boards with their margins of discretion are likely to informally reactivate the more serious charge. Poorer defendants who have to remain in jail are in a poorer bargaining position. No vigorous attempt is made to determine if the arrest was legal or if the defendant is actually guilty of the charges. However, it is efficient. Through its use 90 to 95 percent of the defendants found guilty plead guilty.

At every stage in the trial process, practically untrammeled discretion lubricates the urban court machinery, which must "process" dozens and even hundreds of cases every day. At the stage of indictment, bail is often set hastily and arbitrarily, with no consideration of ability to pay. In fact, bail is set punitively and repressively whenever the amount required exceeds ability to pay, as it often does. Half of the national county-jail population is composed of untried prisoners. An indigent person arrested for a minor offense does time under brutal and degrading conditions in a county jail even though not convicted of any crime. The pressures to plead guilty may be irresistible in such circumstances. . . .

FOR POLITICAL EXPEDIENCY

Discretionary power makes things considerably easier in the political sphere because it allows politicians to avoid some of the more difficult issues by passing the buck. As mentioned earlier, most legislation is enacted on the assumption that the administrative agencies and the judiciary operate with a great deal of discretion. When pressures are applied to the legislature from various segments of the citizenry, and when there are demands, often contradictory, that something be done, the politician can appear to respond by passing a law. He might have little or no intention of anything being done.

The classical example of this type of legislative maneuvering is the Prohibition Act, discussed in the preceding chapter. More recent examples of legislative buck-passing to solve problems of conflicting cross-pressures are many of the civil-rights laws passed under the Johnson Administration. Congress was somewhat assured that the full force of these laws would never be directed toward established practices or entrenched institutions, at least not in the near future. For the time being, they had their cake and ate it too.

TO DO THE PUBLICLY UNMENTIONABLE

Functionaries of the criminal justice system often find themselves in a position in which it seems necessary or to their best interest to take courses of action that are inconsistent with important publicly supported values. For example, they feel compelled to do this when they desire to control or coerce certain segments of society exhibiting characteristics or behavior that is not illegal, such as having long hair, being idle, being a hippy or a vagrant. The growth of vagrancy laws in England is a clear example of this. These laws were not directed merely at prohibiting idleness and loitering in English society. William Chambliss, who has studied the emergence of the English Vagrancy Laws, commented on the publicly less mentionable motives.

The foregoing analysis of the vagrancy laws has demonstrated that these laws were a legislative innovation which reflected the socially perceived necessity of providing an abundance of cheap labor to landowners during a period when serfdom was breaking down and when the pool of available labor was depleted.[14]

Because of discretionary power in the criminal justice system, a law against some specific or some vague behavior, such as vagrancy, can accomplish a publicly unmentionable goal.

This, of course, still occurs. In fact, it still occurs in the area of vagrancy laws, although these laws are being declared unconstitutional. Vagrancy laws now exist not because we are concerned specifically with persons hesitating or loitering in public places, since many do this, but for the purposes of controlling classes of people perceived as nuisances and potentially dangerous. For example, a city ordinance enacted in Carmel, California, aimed at removing a perceived nuisance to the city — the presence of hippies in public places.

We have observed an extraordinary influx of undesirable and unsanitary visitors to the city sometimes known as "hippies" and find that unless proper regulations are adopted immediately, the use and enjoyment of public property will be jeopardized, if not entirely eliminated. The public parks and beaches are, in many cases, rendered unfit for normal use by the unregulated and uncontrolled conduct of the new transients.[15]

This surprisingly honest law allows us to examine the intent of the controlling agencies. It spells out explicitly the intention of the city council to control classes of people rather than to prohibit acts. The law was subsequently declared unconstitutional. The more typical pattern of the controlling agencies is to pass a law that does not state the publicly inadmissible motive and to accomplish their intentions by enforcing the law selectively.

Another situation in which the criminal justice system feels compelled to accomplish the unspeakable through the use of discretion is when tensions exist from internal and external counterforces. For example, strikers often demand amnesty for all law and rule violations committed during a strike. In this case the power structure, because of the amount of counterpower the strikers possess, sees that it is to their advantage to make exception to normal practices. Note that this deviation from normal practices is not taken because of humanitarian concerns, but by and large for purposes of expediency. When the group that desires amnesty, for instance, is perceived to have insufficient power to cause trouble for the system, as with the University of California students arrested in the fall of 1964 in the administration building, no amnesty is given.

TO PROTECT ONE'S OWN KIND

One of the oldest problems ruling persons have had to face as societies moved toward legality — the principle of uniform nondiscretionary application of general rules — is that their ability to make exceptions for themselves and their kind becomes threatened. In the early development of legal structures in England between the twelfth and fifteenth centuries, the emerging criminal justice systems provided a variety of escape hatches for the aristocracy. These included such mechanisms as banishment, church asylum, and clerical immunity, all of which were open exclusively to upper-class persons. In our present systems the powerful and the influential classes still view this as an important need. Consequently, functionaries of the criminal justice system, who nearly all support or represent these classes, respond to this need through the exercise of discretion. Exceptions can be and are made for persons who share cultural identity or class position with the establishment.

TO INCREASE THE SENSE OF ADEQUACY

A final function that discretion serves for the functionaries of the criminal justice system is to infuse their jobs and their lives with a sense of adequacy. There is a strong need for this because these persons are regularly called upon to cope with intractable or insoluble problems, namely, the problems of crime and criminals and what to do about them. There is steady pressure from segments of the citizenry to "do something" about crime. There are simultaneous demands to stop crime, to punish criminals, and to transform them into decent citizens. These demands become especially pressing because of the strong American sentiment that anything can be accomplished if we put forth enough effort and resources. Or if we pass a law. In spite of American zeal, the problems in the area of criminal justice remain. Perhaps they will be with us eternally. Removing the margins of discretion might strip functionaries of some of their sense of adequacy or efficacy. We submit that even if this in fact would be the result, it is a small price to pay.

NOTES ON THE ELIMINATION OF DISCRETION

Our recommendations on the reduction or elimination of discretion in the criminal justice apparatus are tied to the present situation in our society, to discrimination, corruption, and the abuse of power. We are not legal philosophers working out rules for millennia to come. Today the evils of discretion far outweigh conceivable benefits, but this might not always be true. In today's world, however, we recommend the following to give the reader some idea of how a nondiscretionary criminal justice system would work.

Vagueness of laws as a source of discretion is to be eliminated. A person is to know in advance what the charge will be. Many laws are to be eliminated, such as those applying to crimes without victims. Some criminal matters are to be removed to tort law, in cases where the community has little interest and the matter can be put on a quantitative basis involving compensation for damage incurred by the victim.

Police discretion obviously can never be wholly eliminated. It is to be controlled via guidelines from the community or from the police department. These are to be public. Other limitations include measures for community accountability by police, easier false arrest suits, applicability of the law to police as well as to citizens.

Money bail is eliminated. Everyone awaiting trial is released except those few for whom there is heavy evidence that they will commit violent crime before trial; detention of these persons is not to be allowed to interfere with their preparation of a trial defense. Failure to bring the case to trial within a specified period of time results in dismissal of the case.

Plea-bargaining is abolished. Even guilty pleas go to trial. All charges bearing penalties are brought to court, with the provision that all felony cases are to be tried. The investigatory agencies of the state — crime labs, investigators — are at the disposal of both sides in the adversary process.

The facts are determined in a trial-like proceeding. The defendant if found guilty has access to a wide range of community services. Here is where the community gets its chance to show its concern for the individual. However it cannot coerce the individual into accepting such signs of concern and no penalty will be attached to failure to make use of such services.

If after a predetermined number of chances this community process fails to prevent law violations by one who has used these services, the offender is to be delivered to the punitive agency of the state. From this point on, all offenders in a broad class — such as type of crime, but not according to the unique characteristics of the individual — are to be treated alike.

Whatever sanction or short sentence is imposed is to be fixed by law. There is to be no discretion in setting sentences, no indeterminate sentences, and unsupervised street release is to replace parole.

The elimination of most discretion will shift many practices — such as sentencing and the supervision of street probation — out of the hands of administrative agencies and into a realm where the constitutional protections of due process and equal application of the law will apply.

NOTES*

1. *Arrest: The Decision to Take a Suspect into Custody* (Boston: Little, Brown, 1964), p. 68.
2. Dan Dodson, in a speech at Michigan State University, May 1955.
3. Quoted in Westly, *The Police: A Sociological Study of Law, Custom and Morality.* Unpublished doctoral dissertation, University of Chicago, 1951, p. 307.

4. *The Symbols of Government* (New Haven: Yale University Press, 1935), p. 153.
5. Carl Werthman and Irving Piliavin, "Gang Members and the Police." Unpublished typewritten manuscript, on file, Center for Study of Law and Society, University of California, Berkeley, p. 17.
6. "Patterns of Behavior in Police and Citizen

---

*This article has been abridged and its footnotes edited and renumbered.

Transactions," in the President's Commission on Law Enforcement and Administration of Justice Field Surveys, *Studies in Crime and Law Enforcement in Major Metropolitan Areas* (Washington, D.C.: U.S. Government Printing Office, 1967).

7. *Justice without Trial* (New York: Wiley, 1967), p. 129.

8. Charles D. Breitel, "Controls in Criminal Law Enforcement," *U. Chi. L. Rev.*, 1960.

9. *Discretionary Justice: A Preliminary Inquiry* (Baton Rouge: LSU, 1969).

10. Morris Cohen, *Law and Social Order: Essays in Legal Philosophy* (Hamden, Conn.: Archon Books, 1961), p. 261.

11. From the transcript of *People v. Wimberly*, City Court, Syracuse, N.Y., April 9, 1965, quoted in Patricia M. Wald, "Poverty and Criminal Justice," in *Task Force Report: The Courts*, President's Commission on Law Enforcement and the Administration of Justice, p. 142, n. 17.

12. *Federal Offenders in the United States District Courts*, 1963, Administrative Office of the U.S. Courts.

13. *Ibid.*, 1965.

14. *Crime and the Legal Process* (New York: McGraw-Hill, 1969), p. 61.

15. San Francisco *Chronicle*, March 28, 1970.

II. Arrest

4. POLICE DISCRETION NOT TO INVOKE THE CRIMINAL PROCESS

JOSEPH GOLDSTEIN

YALE LAW JOURNAL, 69:4, © 1960. Reprinted by permission.

■ Although legislatures draft criminal laws as if they were precise and unambiguous commands, there is considerable latitude for police to determine the actual contours of interpretation and enforcement. In this widely recognized article, Joseph Goldstein notes that police decisions *not* to invoke legal sanctions are frequently hidden from public view. In his description of police discretion, Goldstein adopts the concepts of total, full, and actual legal enforcement, each of which involves differing levels of police control of private behavior. The extent to which the police pursue a particular policy, Goldstein argues, depends upon the values of the particular community concerned. This selection demonstrates the enormous discretionary power exercised by the police and indicates that they often have as much influence in determining the effective substance of criminal law as does the legislature which officially drafted it. ■

POLICE DECISIONS not to invoke the criminal process[1] largely determine the outer limits of law enforcement. By such decisions, the police define the ambit of discretion throughout the process of other decisionmakers — prosecutor, grand and petit jury, judge, probation officer, correction authority, and parole and pardon boards. These police decisions, unlike their decisions to invoke the law, are generally of extremely low visibility and consequently are seldom the subject of review. Yet an opportunity for review and appraisal of nonenforcement decisions is essential to the functioning of the rule of law in our system of criminal justice. This article will therefore be an attempt to determine how the visibility of such police decisions may be increased and what procedures should be established to evaluate them on a continuing basis, in the light of the complex of objectives of the criminal law and of the paradoxes toward which the administration of criminal justice inclines.

I

The criminal law is one of many intertwined mechanisms for the social control of human behavior.[2] It defines behavior which is deemed intolerably disturbing to or destructive of community values and prescribes sanctions which the state is authorized to impose upon persons convicted or suspected of engaging in prohibited conduct.[3] Following a plea or verdict of guilty, the state deprives offenders of life, liberty, dignity, or property through convictions, fines, imprisonments, killings, and supervised releases, and thus seeks to punish, restrain, and rehabilitate them, as well as to deter others from engaging in proscribed activity. Before verdict, and despite the presumption of innocence which halos every person, the state deprives the suspect of life, liberty, dignity, or property through the imposition of deadly force, search and seizure of persons and possessions, accusation, imprisonment, and bail, and thus seeks to facilitate the enforcement of the criminal law.

These authorized sanctions reflect the multiple and often conflicting purposes which now surround and confuse criminal law administration at and between key decision points in the process. The stigma which accompanies conviction, for example, while serving a deterrent, and possibly retributive, function, becomes operative upon the offender's release and thus impedes the rehabilitation objective of probation and parole. Similarly, the restraint function of imprisonment involves the application of rules and procedures which, while minimizing escape opportunities, contributes to the deterioration of offenders confined for reformation. Since police decisions not to invoke the criminal process may likewise further some objectives while hindering others, or, indeed, run counter to all, any meaningful appraisal of these decisions should include an evaluation of their impact throughout the process on the various objectives reflected in authorized sanctions and in the decisions of other administrators of criminal justice.[4]

Under the rule of law, the criminal law has both a fair-warning function for the public and a power-restricting function for officials. Both post- and pre-verdict sanctions, therefore, may be imposed only in accord with authorized procedures. No sanctions are to be inflicted other than those which have been prospectively prescribed by the constitution, legislation, or judicial decision for a particular crime or a particular kind of offender. These concepts, of course, do not preclude differential disposition, within the authorized limits, of persons suspected or convicted of the same or similar offenses. In an ideal system differential handling, individualized justice, would result, but only from an equal application of officially approved criteria designed to implement officially approved objectives. And finally a system which presumes innocence requires that pre-conviction sanctions be kept at a minimum consistent with assuring an opportunity for the process to run its course.

But police decisions not to invoke the criminal process, except when reflected in gross failures of service, are not visible to the community. Nor are they likely to be visible to official state reviewing agencies, even those within the police department. Failure to tag illegally parked cars is an example of gross failure of service, open to public view and recognized for what it is. An officer's decision, however, not to investigate or report adequately a disturbing event which he has reason to believe constitutes a violation of the criminal law does not ordinarily carry with it consequences sufficiently visible to make the community, the legislature, the prosecutor, or the courts aware of a possible failure of service. The police officer, the suspect, the police department, and frequently even the victim, when directly concerned with a decision not to invoke, unlike the same parties when responsible for or subject to a decision to invoke, generally have neither the incentive nor the opportunity to obtain review of that decision or the police conduct associated with it. Furthermore, official police records are usually too incomplete to permit evaluations of non-enforcement decisions in the light of the purposes of the criminal law. Consequently, such decisions, unlike decisions to enforce, are generally not subject to the control which would follow from administrative, judicial, legislative, or community review and appraisal.

II

The police have a duty not to enforce the substantive law of crimes unless invocation of the process can be achieved within bounds set by constitution, statute, court decision, and possibly official pronouncements of the prosecutor. *Total enforcement*, were it possible, is thus precluded, by generally applicable due-process restrictions on such police procedures as arrest, search, seizure, and interrogation. *Total enforcement* is further precluded by such specific procedural restrictions as prohibitions on invoking an adultery statute unless the spouse of one of the parties complains, or an unlawful-possession-of-firearms statute if the offender surrenders his dangerous weapons during a statutory period of amnesty. Such restrictions of general and specific application mark the bounds, often ambiguously, of an area of *full enforcement* in which the police are not only authorized but expected to enforce fully the law of crimes. An area of *no enforcement* lies, therefore, between the perimeter of *total enforcement* and the outer limits of *full enforcement*. In this *no enforcement* area, the police have no authority to invoke the criminal process.

Within the area of *full enforcement*, the police have not been delegated discretion not to invoke the criminal process. On the contrary, those state statutes providing for municipal police departments which define the responsibility of police provide:

It shall be the duty of the police . . . under the direction of the mayor and chief of police and in conformity with the ordinances of the city, and the laws of the state, . . . to pursue and arrest any persons fleeing from justice . . . to apprehend any and all persons in the act of committing any offense against the laws of the state . . . and to take the offender forthwith before the proper court or magistrate, to be dealt with for the offense; to make complaints to the proper officers and magistrates of any person known or believed by them to be guilty of the violation of the ordinances of the city or the penal laws of the state; and at all times diligently and faithfully to enforce all such laws. . . .[5]

Even in jurisdictions without such a specific statutory definition, declarations of the *full enforcement* mandate generally appear in municipal charters, ordinances or police manuals. Police manuals, for example, commonly provide, in sections detailing the duties at each level of the police hierarchy, that the captain, superintendent, lieutenant, or patrolman shall be responsible, so far as is in his power, for the prevention and detection of crime and the enforcement of all criminal laws and ordinances. Illustrative of the spirit and policy of *full enforcement* is this protestation from the introduction to the Rules and Regulations of the Atlanta, Georgia, Police Department:

Enforcement of all Criminal Laws and City Ordinances, is my obligation. There are no specialties under the Law. My eyes must be open to traffic problems and disorders, though I move on other assignments, to slinking vice in back streets and dives though I have been directed elsewhere, to the suspicious appearance of evil wherever it is encountered. . . . I must be impartial because the Law surrounds, protects and applies to all alike, rich and poor, low and high, black and white. . . .

Minimally, then, *full enforcement*, so far as the police are concerned, means (1) the investigation of every disturbing event which is reported to or observed by them and which they have reason to suspect may be a violation of the criminal law; (2) following a determination that some crime has been committed, an effort to discover its perpetrators; and (3) the presentation of all information collected by them to the prosecutor for his determination of the appropriateness of further invoking the criminal process.

Full enforcement, however, is not a realistic expectation. In addition to ambiguities in the definitions of both substantive offenses and due-process boundaries,[6] countless limitations and pressures preclude the possibility of the police seeking or achieving *full enforcement*. Limitations of time, personnel, and investigative devices — all in part but not entirely functions of budget — force the development, by plan or default, of priorities of enforcement. Even if there were "enough police" adequately equipped and trained, pressures from within and without the department, which is after all a human institution, may force the police to invoke the criminal process selectively. By decisions not to invoke within the area of *full enforcement*, the police largely determine the outer limits of *actual enforcement* throughout the criminal process. This relationship of the police to the total administration of criminal justice can be seen in the diagram below on this page. They may rein-

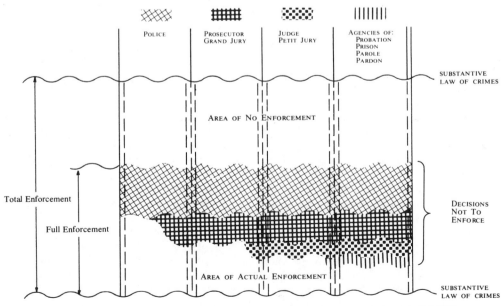

THE POLICE IN RELATION TO OTHER DECISIONMAKERS IN THE CRIMINAL PROCESS

force, or they may undermine, the legislature's objectives in designating certain conduct "criminal" and in authorizing the imposition of certain sanctions following conviction. A police decision to ignore a felonious assault "because the victim will not sign a complaint," usually precludes the prosecutor or grand jury from deciding whether to accuse, judge or jury from determining guilt or innocence, judge from imposing the most "appropriate" sentence, probation or correctional authorities from instituting the most "appropriate" restraint and rehabilitation programs, and finally parole or pardon authorities from determining the offender's readiness for release to the community.

III

Trading enforcement against a narcotics suspect for information about another narcotics offense or offender may involve two types of police decisions not to invoke fully the criminal process. First, there may be a decision to ask for the dismissal or reduction of the charge for which the informant is held; second, there may be a decision to overlook future violations while the suspect serves as an informer. The second type is an example of a relatively pure police decision not to invoke the criminal process while the first requires, at a minimum, tacit approval by prosecutor or judge. But examination of only the pure types of decisions would oversimplify the problem. They fail to illustrate the extent to which police nonenforcement decisions may permeate the process as well as influence, and be influenced by, prosecutor and court action in settings which fail to prompt appraisal of such decisions in light of the purposes of the criminal law. Both types of decisions, pure and conglomerate, are nonetheless primarily police decisions. They are distinguishable from a prosecutor's or court's decision to trade information for enforcement under an immunity statute, and from such parliamentary decisions as the now-repealed seventeenth and eighteenth century English statutes which gave a convicted offender who secured the conviction of his accomplice an absolute right to pardon. Such prosecutor and parliamentary de-

cisions to trade information for enforcement, unlike the police decisions to be described, have not only been authorized by a legislative body, but have also been made sufficiently visible to permit review.

In the municipality studied, regular uniformed officers, with general law enforcement duties on precinct assignments, and a special narcotics squad of detectives, with citywide jurisdiction, are responsible for enforcement of the state narcotics laws. The existence of the special squad acts as a pressure on the uniformed officer to be the first to discover any sale, possession, or use of narcotics in his precinct. Careful preparation of a case for prosecution may thus become secondary to this objective. Indeed, approximately eighty per cent of those apprehended for narcotics violations during one year were discharged. In the opinion of the special squad, which processes each arrested narcotics suspect, either the search was illegal or the evidence obtained inadequate. The precinct officer's lack of interest in carefully developing a narcotics case for prosecution often amounts in effect to a police decision not to enforce but rather to harass.

But we are concerned here primarily with the decisions of the narcotics squad, which, like the Federal Narcotics Bureau, has established a policy of concentrating enforcement efforts against the "big supplier."[7] The chief of the squad claimed that informers must be utilized to implement that policy, and that in order to get informants it is necessary to trade "little ones for big ones." Informers are used to arrange and make purchases of narcotics, to elicit information from suspects, including persons in custody, and to recruit additional informants.

Following arrest, a suspect will generally offer to serve as an informer to "do himself some good." If an arrestee fails to initiate such negotiations, the interrogating officer will suggest that something may be gained by disclosing sources of supply and by serving as an informer. A high mandatory minimum sentence for selling, a high maximum sentence for possession, and, where users are involved, a strong desire on their part to avoid the agonies of withdrawal, combine to place the police in an excellent bargaining position to recruit informers. To assure performance, each informer is charged with a narcotics violation, and final disposition is postponed until the defendant has fulfilled his part of the bargain. To protect the informer, the special squad seeks to camouflage him in the large body of releasees by not disclosing his identity even to the arresting precinct officer, who is given no explanation for release. Thus persons encountered on the street by a uniformed patrolman the day after their arrest may have been discharged, or they may have been officially charged and then released on bail or personal recognizance to await trial or to serve as informers.

While serving as informers, suspects are allowed to engage in illegal activity. Continued use of narcotics is condoned; the narcotics detective generally is not concerned with the problem of informants who make buys and use some of the evidence themselves. Though informers are usually warned that their status does not give them a "license to peddle," possession of a substantial amount of narcotics may be excused. In one case, a defendant found guilty of possession of *marijuana* argued that she was entitled to be placed on probation since she had cooperated with the police by testifying against three persons charged with sale of narcotics. The sentencing judge denied her request because he discovered that her cooperation was related to the possession of a substantial amount of *heroin*, an offense for which she was arrested (but never charged) while on bail for the marijuana violation. A narcotics squad inspector, in response to an inquiry from the judge, revealed that the defendant had not been charged with possession of *heroin* because she had been cooperative with the police on that offense.[8]

In addition to granting such outright immunity for some violations, the police will recommend to the prosecutor either that an informer's case be *nolle prossed* or, more frequently, that the charge be reduced to a lesser offense. And, if the latter course is followed, the police usually recommend to the judge, either in response to his request for information or in the presentence report, that informers be placed on probation or given relatively light sentences. Both the prosecutor and judge willingly respond to

police requests for reducing a charge of sale to a lesser offense because they consider the mandatory minimum too severe.[9] As a result, during a four year period in this jurisdiction, less than two and one-half per cent of all persons charged with the sale of narcotics were convicted of that offense.

IV

Another low visibility situation stems from police decisions not to invoke the felonious assault laws unless the victim signs a complaint.[10] Like the addict-informer, the potential complainant in an assault case is both the victim of an offense and a key source of information. But unlike him, the complainant, who is not a suspect, and whose initial contact with the police is generally self-imposed, is not placed under pressure to bargain. And in contrast with the informer program, the police assault program was clearly not designed, if designed at all, to effectuate an identifiable policy.

During one month under the nonenforcement program of a single precinct, thirty-eight out of forty-three felonious assault cases, the great majority involving stabbings and cuttings, were cleared "because the victim refused to prosecute."[11] This program, which is coupled with a practice of not encouraging victims to sign complaints, reduces the pressure of work by eliminating such tasks as apprehending and detaining suspects, writing detailed reports, applying for warrants to prefer charges and appearing in court at inconvenient times for long periods without adequate compensation.[12] As one officer explained, "run-of-the-mill" felonious assaults are so common in his precinct that prosecution of each case would force patrolmen to spend too much time in court and leave too little time for investigating other offenses. This rationalization exposes the private value system of individual officers as another policy-shaping factor. Some policemen feel, for example, that assault is an acceptable means of settling disputes among Negroes, and that when both assailant and victim are Negro, there is no immediately discernible harm to the public which justifies a decision to invoke the criminal process.[13] Anticipation of dismissal by judge and district attorney of cases in which the victim is an uncooperative witness, the police claim, has been another operative factor in the development of the assault policy.[14] A Policy Appraisal and Review Board, whose investigators had been specifically directed to examine the assault policy, should be able to identify these or other policy-shaping factors more precisely. Yet on the basis of the data available, a board could tentatively conclude that court and prosecutor responses do not explain why the police have failed to adopt a policy of encouraging assault victims to sign complaints, and, therefore, that the private value system of department members, as reflected in their attitude toward workload and in a stereotypical view of the Negro, is of primary significance.

Once some of the major policy-shaping factors have been identified, an Appraisal and Review Board might formulate and attempt to answer the following or similar questions: Would it be consistent with any of the purposes of the criminal law to authorize police discretion in cases of felonious assaults as well as other specified offenses? Assuming that it would be consistent or at least more realistic to authorize police discretion in some cases, what limitations and guides, if any, should the legislature provide? Should legislation provide that factors such as workload, willingness of victims or certain victims to sign a complaint, the degree of violence and attitude of prosecutor and judge be taken into account in the exercise of police discretion? If workload is to be recognized, should the legislature establish priorities of enforcement designed to assist the police in deciding which offenses among equally pressing ones are to be ignored or enforced? If assaults are made criminal in order to reduce threats to community peace and individual security, should a victim's willingness to prosecute, if he happens to live,[15] be relevant to the exercise of police discretion? Does resting prosecution in the hands of the victim encourage him to "get even" with the assailant through retaliatory lawlessness? Or does such a policy place the decision in the hands of the assailant whose use of force has already demonstrated an ability and willingness to fulfill a threat?

Can the individual police officer, despite his own value system, sufficiently respond to officially articulated community values to be delegated broad powers of discretion?[16] If not, can or should procedures be designed to enable the police department to translate these values into rules and regulations for individual policemen? Can police officers or the department be trained to evaluate the extent to which current practice undermines a major criminal law objective of imposing upon all persons officially recognized minimum standards of human behavior? For example, can the individual officer of the department be trained to evaluate the effect of decisions in cases of felonious assault among Negroes on local programs for implementing national or state policies of integration in school, employment, and housing, and to determine the extent to which current policy weakens or reinforces stereotypes which are used to justify not only police policy, but more importantly, opposition to desegregation programs? Or should legislation provide that the police invoke the process in all felonious assault cases unless the prosecutor or court publicly provide them in recorded documents with authority and guides for exercising discretion, and thus make visible both the policy of nonenforcement and the agency or agencies responsible for it?

Some of these issues were considered and resolved by the Oakland, California, Police Department in 1957 when, after consultation with prosecutors and judges, it decided to abandon a similar assault policy and seek *full enforcement*.[17] Chief of Police W. W. Vernon, describing Oakland's new program, wrote:

In our assault cases for years we had followed this policy of releasing the defendant if the complainant did not feel aggrieved to the point of being willing to testify. . . . [Since] World War II . . . our assault cases increased tremendously to the point where we decided to do something about the increase. . . .[18]

Training materials prepared by the Oakland Police Academy disclose that between 1952 and 1956, while the decision to prosecute was vested in the victim, the rate of reported felonious assaults rose from 93 to 161 per 100,000 population and the annual number of misdemeanor assaults rose from 618 to

2,630.[19] The materials emphasize that these statistics mean a workload of "nearly 10 assault reports a day every day of the year." But they stress:

The important point about these figures is not so much that they represent a substantial police workload, which they do, but more important, that they indicate an increasing lack of respect for the laws of society by a measurable segment of our population, and a corresponding threat to the rest of the citizens of our city. The police have a clear responsibility to develop respect for the law among those who disregard it in order to insure the physical safety and well-being of those who do.

We recognize that the problem exists mainly because the injured person has refused to sign a complaint against the perpetrator. The injured person has usually refused to sign for two reasons: first, because of threats of future bodily harm or other action by the perpetrator and, secondly, because it has been a way of life among some people to adjust grievances by physical assaults and not by the recognized laws of society which are available to them.

We, the police, have condoned these practices to some extent by not taking advantage of the means at our disposal; that is, by not gathering sufficient evidence and signing complaints on information and belief in those cases where the complainant refuses to prosecute. The policy and procedure of gathering sufficient evidence and signing complaints on information and belief should instill in these groups the realization that the laws of society must be resorted to in settling disputes. When it is realized by many of these people that we will sign complaints ourselves and will not condone fighting and cuttings, many of them will stop such practices.[20]

Following conferences with the police, the local prosecutors and judges pledged their support for the new assault program. The district attorney's office will deny a complainant's request that a case be dropped and suggest that it be addressed to the judge in open court. The judge, in turn, will advise the complainant that the case cannot be dismissed, and that a perjury, contempt, or false-report complaint will be issued in "appropriate cases"[21] against the victim who denies facts originally alleged.[22] The police have been advised that the court and prosecutor will actively cooperate in the implementation of the new program, but that every case will not result in a complaint since it is the "job [of the police] to turn in

the evidence and it's the Prosecuting Attorney's job to determine when a complaint will be issued."[23] Thus the role of each of the key decisionmaking agencies with preconviction invoking authority is clearly delineated and integrated.

With the inauguration of a new assault policy, an Appraisal and Review Board might establish procedures for determining how effectively the objectives of the policy are fulfilled in practice. A board might design intelligence retrieving devices which would provide more complete data than the following termed by Chief Vernon "the best evidence that our program is accomplishing the purpose for which it was developed. . ."[24] Prior to the adoption of the new policy, eighty per cent of the felonious assault cases "cleared" were cleared because "Complainant Refuses To Prosecute," while only thirty-two and two-tenths per cent of the clearances made during the first three months in 1958 were for that reason, even though the overall clearance rate rose during that period.[25] And "during the first quarter of this year Felony Assaults dropped 11.1 per cent below the same period last year, and in March they were 35.6 per cent below March of last year. Battery cases were down 19.0 per cent for the first three months of 1958."[26] An Appraisal and Review Board might attempt to determine the extent to which the police in cases formerly dropped because "Complainant Refused To Testify" have consciously or otherwise substituted another reason for "case cleared." And it might estimate the extent to which the decrease in assaults *reported* reflects, if it does, a decrease in the *actual* number of assaults or only a decrease in the number of victims willing to report assaults. Such follow-up investigations and what actually took place in Oakland on an informal basis between police, prosecutor, and judge illustrate some of the functions an Appraisal and Review Board might regularly perform.

V

The mandate of *full enforcement*, under circumstances which compel selective enforcement, has placed the municipal police in an intolerable position. As a result, non-enforcement programs have developed undercover, in a hit-or-miss fashion, and without regard to impact on the overall administration of justice or the basic objectives of the criminal law. Legislatures, therefore, ought to reconsider what discretion, if any, the police must or should have in invoking the criminal process, and what devices, if any, should be designed to increase visibility and hence reviewability of these police decisions.

The ultimate answer is that the police should not be delegated discretion not to invoke the criminal law. It is recognized, of course, that the exercise of discretion cannot be completely eliminated where human beings are involved. The frailties of human language and human perception will always admit of borderline cases (although none of the situations analyzed in this Article are "borderline"). But nonetheless, outside this margin of ambiguity, the police should operate in an atmosphere which exhorts and commands them to invoke impartially all criminal laws within the bounds of *full enforcement*. If a criminal law is ill-advised, poorly defined, or too costly to enforce, efforts by the police to achieve *full enforcement* should generate pressures for legislative action. Responsibility for the enactment, amendment, and repeal of the criminal laws will not, then, be abandoned to the whim of each police officer or department, but retained where it belongs in a democracy — with elected representatives.

NOTES*

1. "Invocation is the task of the officers concerned with law enforcement who . . . must provisionally assess whether a given act contravenes the . . . [criminal] code and initiate a demand for application." *Lasswell, The Decision Process* 3 (1956).
2. The criminal law may increase, decrease, or leave unaffected the impact on individual behavior, if any, of family, education, religion, "civil" law, the arts, science, freedom, mass communication, economic conditions, local, state, national, foreign and international governing bodies, and membership or nonmembership in many other formal and informal, large and small, groups including unions, country clubs, and gangs.
3. Sanctions are imposed by the state presumably against, or at least without regard to, the wishes of the individual being deprived. Implicit in the word "sanction," as used in this article, is involuntariness. In this context involuntariness is not treated as a psychological concept. Thus, for example, imprisonment is a sanction even if imposed on a person who commits a crime in order to be punished or in order to escape cold and hunger in the "warmth" of a jail.
4. Conflicts of purpose and function arise not only among the administrators of criminal justice within a single jurisdiction, but also between administrators in different jurisdictions.
5. *Mich. Stat. Ann.* § 5.1752 (1949); accord, *Ala. Code Ann.* tit. 54, § 5(4) (1941); *Alaska Comp. Laws Ann.* §§ 40-12-8 to -10 (cum. supp. 1958) (duties of territorial police); *Ark. Stat. Ann.* § 19-1705 (1956); *Colo. Rev. Stat. Ann.* § 139-75-5

(1954); *Hawaii Rev. Laws* § 31-5 (1955) (duties of high sheriff as head of territorial police); *Ill. Rev. Stat.*, Ch. 38 § 655 (1957); *Ind. Stat. Ann.* §§ 48-6107, 48-6110 (1950); *Iowa Code Ann.* § 748.4 (1950); *Me. Rev. Stat. Ann.* Ch. 15, § 2 (1954) (state police); *Mass. Laws Ann.* Ch. 41, § 98 (1952); *Mo. Stat. Ann.* § 74.203 (1952) (duties of chief of police); *Neb. Rev. Stat.* § 29-401 (1948); *Ohio Rev. Code Ann.* § 737.11 (Page 1954); *Tenn. Code Ann.* § 6-2129 (1955); *Utah Code Ann.* § 10-6-66 (1953); *Va. Code Ann.* § 15-557 (1956); *W. Va. Code Ann.* § 509 (1955); *Wis. Stat. Ann.* § 62.09(13) (1957); *Wyo. Stat. Ann.* § 7-12 (1959). The *full enforcement* mandate is reinforced in such states by local police manuals. *E.g., Boston Mass., Police Dept. Rules & Regs.* foreword, rules 10, § 2; 24 § 1; 35 § 5(d) (1950); *Cincinnati, Ohio, Police Division Manual* §§ 00.673(h), 01.09 (1959); *Detroit, Mich., Rev. Police Manual* Ch.1 § 9, Ch. 2 § 1, Ch.3 § 142 (1958); *Milwaukee, Wis., Police Dept. Rules & Regs.* introduction at VII, rules 1, § 3; 5, § 2; 6, § 2; 7, §§ 4, 8, 49; 11, § 1; 14, § 1; 28, §§ 3, 24 (1932); *Nashville, Tenn., Police Dept. Rules & Regs.* 9; §§ 14, 33 (1955); *New Bedford, Mass., Police Dept. Rules & Regs.* rules 1; 4, § 2; 14, § 11; 15, § 3 (1957); *Salt Lake City, Utah, Police Manual* foreword at 3; Ch. III, §§ 3, 5, 7; Ch. IV, §§ 3, 9; Ch. VI, § 1 (1951); *Sioux City, Iowa, Police Dept. Manual* pp. 20, § 1; 24, § 2; 26, § 2; 29, § 2; 31, § 2; 42, § 1 (1956); *Wheeling, W. Va., Police Dept. Rules & Regs.* §§ 3, 5 [undated].
6. Ambiguities in substantive definition, assuming no procedural ambiguities, may cause events actu-

---

*This article has been abridged and its footnotes edited and renumbered.

ally within the *full enforcement* area to appear to be beyond the boundary of *total enforcement*. Ambiguities in procedural limitations, assuming no substantive ambiguities, may cause events actually within the *full enforcement* area to appear to be within the *no enforcement* area between *total* and *full enforcement*. See diagram at *p. 35 infra*, in which these ambiguities are indicated by the wavy boundary lines dividing enforcement areas.

7. See *Staff of Subcomm. on Narcotics, House Comm. on Ways and Means, 84th Cong., 2d Sess., Illicit Traffic in Narcotics, Barbiturates, and Amphetamines in the United States* 11 (Comm. Print 1956).

Upon questioning individuals on the street, the police are frequently told "I'm working for the Bureau" or "I'm working for Sergeant ———'s crew." For example, the officers of a cruiser car stopped a car to question the occupants. The driver told the officers that he was working for the Narcotics Squad and was trying to make a purchase from the other person in the car. The other person, who was questioned separately, told the officers that he, too, was an informer — but for the Federal agency, and that he was associating with the driver in hopes that he would obtain some information relating to the sale of narcotics.

8. On imposing a sentence of two to ten years, the judge said that her cooperation in the heroin offense did not place any moral obligation on him or the police department as to her sentence for the marijuana charge. Had she been charged and convicted on both counts, the maximum could have been twenty years. A third conviction for possession would carry a mandatory twenty years minimum with a possible maximum of forty years.

9. The police work under specific instructions from the judges to notify them of those cases in which they wish to have imposed the heavy mandatory sentences prescribed by statute.

10. Police decisions not to invoke the criminal process in assault cases involving a willing or insistent complainant are not examined. The frustrated victim may make such decisions visible for example, by complaining to the prosecutor or grand jury or by seeking to initiate newspaper or crime commission investigations. See 7 *W. Res. L. Rev.* 203, 204–05 (1956); 1957 *Chicago Crime Comm. Ann. Rep.* 37–39.

The exercise of police discretion in misdemeanor assaults is not discussed. In such cases, the police similarly avoid what they view to be their problem by placing the burden of initiating criminal prosecution on the victim. Unless the assault occurs in the officer's presence, he does not have authority in this jurisdiction to arrest the offender without a warrant and can cite this lack of authority as a basis for his decision not to pro-

ceed. Of course, this does not fully explain his decision, for he might further investigate the case and obtain a warrant for arrest. The victim is usually referred to detectives who will assist in obtaining a warrant. Experience has indicated that the victim rarely will take the initiative necessary to contact the detectives in order to bring criminal charges.

11. The police are frequently made aware of the offense by victims apparently more anxious to obtain ambulance service to the hospital than to initiate apprehension and prosecution of an assailant. If hospitalization is required, the police arrest the offender even though the complainant may not wish to prosecute. When such arrests are made, the police conduct a "minimum type" investigation to assure that the basic facts will be available should the victim die and murder or manslaughter become the more appropriate charge for the state, as complainant, to lodge against the offender. The police decision to arrest, however, does not reflect any intention to further invoke the process because of the seriousness of the injury inflicted. For soon after the disturbing event, in an effort to close the case, the police will ask the hospitalized victim to decide whether prosecution should be initiated. Though his condition may cast doubt about his competence to understand and respond to such an inquiry, in at least one case the victim demonstrated complete awareness. Shortly before his death for which the assailant was subsequently charged with murder, he replied from his hospital bed, "I want to see whether or not I live first."

The police will also make arrests, even if the complainant does not wish to prosecute, if the suspect has offered to pay off the complainant or if the suspect is a "known criminal" whom the police wish to get off the street. The decision to invoke the process in these cases is equally a reflection of the private value system of the police. In these cases the state acts as complainant and the victim is subpoenaed to appear at trial. See Miller, "The Compromise of Criminal Cases," 1 *So. Cal. L. Rev.* 1, & nn. 3–5 (1927) (on compounding crime as a separate offense).

12. A decision to arrest may be influenced by the time an offense occurs and the time the police officer is scheduled to go off and return to duty. An officer assigned to the vice squad explained, for example, that officers will not make an arrest on Saturday night if they can avoid it since court appearance is likely to be scheduled for their day off. And no matter what the duration of his court appearance, the officer receives credit for only two hours work.

13. In such cases the police do not attribute their unwillingness to act on any legal restriction placed upon them or any particular difficulty which they may encounter in taking the case to court. Other

expressions of private and possibly community value systems are found in police decisions, for example, not to proceed against an elderly gentleman for larceny of a ham ("You are 74 years old — for crying out loud we don't want to lock you up for something like that . . ." the lieutenant said), or to take home an upper class drunk while locking up a "drunken bum."
14. The courts dismiss or prosecutors decline to proceed with these cases possibly to reduce their workload as a means of "system maintenance."

Anticipated court responses manifest themselves in other police decisions to enforce or not to enforce. The police may decide not to enforce particular offenses if the judge assigned to the criminal docket is "known" to be lenient re the specific offense. Another view, on paper at least, is to be found in the following catechism from *New Bedford, Mass., Police Dept. Rules & Regs.* 38, (1957): "Of what interest is it to a policeman if a complaint against a prisoner is dismissed by the court? None whatever; a policeman's duty is accomplished when he brings his prisoner to the station, and presents his case in court."
15. See note 11.
16. The police officer is confronted with a most difficult task. . . . He must bring under control his personal sentiments and prejudices and subordinate them in a truly professional spirit. . . . He must refrain from expressing private notions in discharging the duties of office. This entails a capacity to distinguish between his own right as a private citizen to his private convictions and his responsibilities as a police officer.

Lohman, *The Police and Minority Groups* 5 (1947) (manual prepared for use in the Chicago Park District Training School).
17. Police Academy, Oakland, Calif., *Police Dept., Instructors' Material*, Vol. 6, Bull. No. 35, 1957.
18. Letter From W. W. Vernon to Joseph Goldstein, Sept. 24, 1958.
19. Police Academy, Oakland, Cal., Police Dept. at note 71, p. 3:

Felony Assaults	Reported to Police	Arrests	Charged
(For year 1956)	618	350	67
(1st 6 mos. of 1957)	394	197	62
Misdemeanor Assaults			
(For year 1956)	2631	941	454
(1st 6 mos. of 1957)	1322	522	not available

(Note the difference between the number arrested and the number charged. *The difference is attributed to the fact that the type of people involved do not prosecute in physical assault cases*.) (Emphasis added.)

20. See Hall, "Police and Law in a Democratic Society," 28 *Ind L. J.* 133, 153 (1953):
Discriminatory law enforcement, including the failure to protect Negroes from the aggression of other Negroes, aggravates tendencies toward criminal behavior. Equal enforcement of law by the police would have a curative, morale building effect which would be of the greatest value in critical situations.
21. Police Academy, Oakland, Cal., Police Dept. at note 23.
22. *Cal. Penal Code Ann.* §§ 118, 118a (perjury), 166(6) (contempt), 148.5 (false report of criminal offense) (Supp.).
23. Police Academy, Oakland, Cal., Police Dept., at note 23.
24. Chief W. W. Vernon, Assault Cases Memorandum to All Line-Ups, May 9, 1958.
25. Ibid. "In 1956 86.5% of the reported Misdemeanor Assaults were cleared, and 53.4% of these Clearances were on the basis of non-cooperation of complainants. In the first quarter of 1958 the Clearance Rate was up to 92.9% and only 15.9% of these cases were cleared as Complainant Refuses to Prosecute." Ibid.
26. Ibid.

5. SOME FACTORS IN POLICE DISCRETION AND DECISION-MAKING

JAMES FINCKENAUER

JOURNAL OF CRIMINAL JUSTICE, Vol. 4, © 1976 by Pergamon Press. Reprinted by permission.

■ Professor Finckenauer in this selection is concerned with the variables which affect police discretion — under what circumstances, in other words, is discretionary action most likely to occur? The author offers an empirical investigation of police response to several hypothetical situations. His study shows that each particular situation the police confront determines how — and to what extent — police will exercise discretionary power to make an arrest. His data also show that the boundaries of police discretion are affected by the patrolman's perception of what the community's values are concerning, specifically, gambling, drunkenness, welfare fraud, prostitution, and juvenile offenses. ■

POLICE DISCRETION IS an important but controversial topic. Joseph Goldstein (1960) recognized its importance in one of the earliest serious efforts to confront and define the issues surrounding the police decision-making role in the administration of criminal justice. Goldstein said: "Police decisions not to invoke the criminal process largely determine the outer limits of law enforcement. By such decisions, the police define the ambit of discretion throughout the process of other decision makers — prosecutor, grand and petit jury, judge, probation officer, correction authority, and parole boards." More recently, Bittner (1970), among others, has pointed out that police officers "have, in effect, a greater degree of discretionary freedom in proceeding against offenders than any other public official." In the *Report on Police*, the National Advisory Commission on Criminal Justice Standards and Goals (1973) comments on police discretion as follows: "The police in the United States exercise considerable discretion. The decisions they make largely define the limits of the criminal justice process and have a profound effect upon the overall administration of justice. . . ."

The existence of police discretion is often denied because it means that police officers may decide for themselves, in a "low-visibility" manner, what laws should and should not be enforced and what the level of enforcement should be. Few police administrators are willing to publicly acknowledge that discretion is being exercised although a strong case can be made for it. Limited police resources, the moral and legal ambiguities concerning the behavior circumscribed by certain criminal statutes, conflicting and changing public expectations, and the whims of public officials to whom the police are accountable all lead to a situation in which there is and must be less than full enforcement of all the criminal laws.

This study does not address the question of whether or not there should be police discretion, but instead accepts its exercise as a necessary circumstance in the real world of modern police work. This is not meant to convey an acceptance of unbridled police discretion without guidelines, supervision, and evaluation, but simply to delimit the research effort here undertaken. In order to better understand how the criminal justice system functions — or does not function — it is necessary to study it at the point where the basic and fundamental determination of whether or not a person is to be subject to the criminal process is made — at the initial point of contact with the police.

The problems addressed in this study include: How do the police exercise that discretion they are acknowledged to possess? What factors in individual discretionary situations influence their decision making? And, what characteristics of individual police officers influence their use of discretion? These questions relate to what Pepinsky (1975) has defined as the central research question on police decision-making ". . . how the police decide to respond to information as though an offense has occurred, given legitimate ambiguity on the point. From this perspective, the exercise of police discretion is fundamentally a matter of deciding how to treat ambiguous information, not one of ignoring what are already known to be offenses or of failing to find unknown ones.''

The relationship of ambiguity to police discretion has been discussed in the literature. Herman Goldstein (1963) points out that, "the need for resolving ambiguities in the criminal law frequently places the police in the position of having to determine the forms of conduct which are to be subject to the criminal process." The double standards of morality within which the police must operate serve to increase the ambiguity involved in police decision-making. Some laws are simply intended to put the community on record as opposing a form of conduct, but are not meant to be fully enforced. When a serious felony offense such as murder, armed robbery, or burglary has occurred, the alternatives available to the police in the decision-making process are much more clearly defined than they are in most of the other more numerous situations with which they are confronted. For example, the President's Crime Commission's (1967) *Task Force Report: The Police* indicates:

When criminal activity involves a "willing buyer" and a "willing seller," a somewhat different pattern of problems is present. Widespread community support for some forms of gambling activity or an ambivalent community attitude toward some forms of sexual conduct require that a police agency decide what constitutes an appropriate level of enforcement.

It would seem then that one factor characterizing individual discretionary situations that might influence the police decision-making process is ambiguity, both legal and moral. Another related factor might be ambivalence on the part of the police officer torn between competing values — his own and those of a suspected offender, and those of the society as a whole. The police officer's idiosyncratic intrepretation of a particular behavior and the circumstances surrounding that behavior is assumed to be an important factor in police discretion and decision-making.

On the issue of individual police officer characteristics that could influence their use of discretion, Banton (1964) identified the sources from which police officers draw their ideas as to the way in which they should exercise their discretionary powers as: training, the example of their colleagues, advice or instruction from their supervisors, a knowledge of what cases the courts will accept, and a sense of judgment arising from an awareness of the public's point of view. With the exception of training, these sources would all be developed during the process of gaining practical police experience.

Without identifying specifically what personal characteristics are particularly relevant, James Q. Wilson (1968b) states that the handling of what he defines as citizen-invoked order maintenance situations will vary considerably, and that this variation will depend more on the personal characteristics of the police officer and the citizen participants than on departmental policies. (Order maintenance situations are those involving a dispute in which the law must be interpreted, standards of right conduct determined, and blame assigned — in other words, situations that are likely to be high in ambiguity and ambivalence.)

A previous study by this author entitled "Higher Education and Police Discretion" concluded that college-educated police officers seem to respond differently from non-college-educated police officers to certain discretionary situations. Their responses differ in that those with college educations are less likely to advocate invoking the criminal process in such situations than are non-college-educated officers.

This research will explore how police officers react to ambiguous situations and what characteristics govern those reactions.

METHOD

The 209 subjects tested were all police recruits undergoing basic training at one of the police training academies in New Jersey. In order to test the subjects' decision-making and use of discretion, a number of illustrative situations were borrowed from Wayne R. LaFave's *Arrest: The Decision to Take a Suspect into Custody* (1965).

The recruits were asked to read each of the incident descriptions and to indicate in writing for each case their agreement or disagreement with the police response described, and what their own response would have been. These responses are classified into the following three categories: (1) would make an arrest or take other official action, e.g., issue summons, issue complaint, etc.; (2) would take action not involving invocation of the criminal process, e.g., explain, advise about making complaint, refer to another agency or department, take report, etc.; or (3) would do nothing.

In the analysis of responses to each of the discretionary situations, three primary questions provide the analytical framework:

1. How would they exercise their discretion? Would they make an arrest or take other official action? Would they take another action? Or, would they do nothing?

2. What factors in the situation seem to influence their use of discretion? What reasons or rationale are offered by them for taking the action indicated?

3. Do certain personal characteristics (age, education, and experience) influence their decision-making, and if so, how? (Age was not a significant factor in any of the cases; therefore, this variable was deleted from the discussion of the results.)

RESULTS

GAMBLING

Gambling is a multi-faceted problem for the police. There is a moral ambivalence about gambling in the public mind that is reflected in police attitudes toward the enforcement of gambling laws. Large segments of the population want to gamble, and some forms of gambling have been legalized in some jurisdictions. Partial legalization of gambling creates or reinforces conflicts in the public and police minds about the criminal nature of gambling activity.

Another facet of the gambling problem is its possible or suspected relationship to organized crime. The individual police officer is caught in a difficult position when known or suspected gambling is affiliated with an organized crime operation. Decisions about investigating and apprehending the participants in such an operation may then be determined, not by sound law enforcement policy making, but by being responsive to political pressures that can influence police discretion.

A third facet in this picture is the actual or perceived relationship between gambling and police corruption. Gambling is a large and profitable enterprise in which gambling figures are willing, if necessary, to pay well to ensure that the police will be less than vigilant in their pursuit of gambling operations. There have been numerous investigative reports over the years that have indicated that the police have been involved in gambling pay-offs. The public is well aware of this form of police corruption, and as a result may tend to suspect the worst in a non-enforcement-against-gambling situation. Such a situation, including the police response, is illustrated in the following incident:

The police were aware of the operation of a private card game in which there was no house "cut." Since this operation therefore qualified as mere social gambling, no action was taken against the offenders. However, the operators of the game made no attempt to conceal the operation, and it was soon apparent to the general public that the police must be aware of it. Realizing this, the police arrested the gamblers.

A majority of all groups would make an arrest or take other official action in this situation, but recruits with no college and no previous experience are the most likely to invoke the criminal process.

The key factor in the situation, which was most often reported as influencing decision-making, was the public awareness of the gambling. This was more often cited as a reason to make arrests than the illegality of the gambling itself.

RESPONSE:
I see nothing wrong with the boys getting together for a poker game especially if its [sic] getting away from the old lady. But since the public was aware

and complaining and the offenders were too ignorant to conceal it, I can see no other course of action but to arrest them. Unless you don't like your job.

RESPONSE:
After being apparent to the general public I felt it was necessary to make the arrest. It goes back to the old saying that taxpayers pay our salary and to the fact that some of us do have a certain amount of pride in our job. To become the laughing stock and lose any control over a situation would be bad for ourselves as well as the public. Most people look to the police for everything at one time or another. We command the people as well as their respect.

There were, on the other hand, those in the sample who simply reacted to the criminality factor in the situation.

RESPONSE:
Why did the police wait so long to act? The situation should have been arrested long before this stage. The police became fearful of the citizens' opinions so they had to save face. I would have put a halt to it before it ever got this far. The police in this situation were abusing their role prescribed by the community and hence were failing the system.

The analysis indicates that as the amount of experience increases, the likelihood of arrest or other official action tends to decrease. The correlation is small, but the indications are that the most experienced police recruits, i.e., those with at least four months on the job, are slightly more likely to take some other action and are considerably more likely to simply do nothing. The factors mentioned by Banton as influencing police discretion would seem to be operative here. This is particularly true of the sense of judgment arising from an awareness of the public's point of view.

DRUNKENNESS

Drunkenness is a resource- and time-consuming problem for the police. This is evidenced by the fact that the police report making approximately two million arrests for simple drunkenness annually. In most communities an unnecessarily large allocation of scarce police resources must be devoted to this problem because of the absence of other agencies or programs that are able and willing to assume responsibility for what is more properly a sociomedical problem than a criminal justice problem. Until statutes decriminalizing public drunkenness are adopted and provisions are made for diverting drunks from the criminal justice system, the police must continue to try coping with the problem, ill-equipped and ill-prepared though they may be.

In most cases the objective of the police is the protection of the individual drunk — who may or may not be an alcoholic — from the consequences of his own behavior, and the protection of others from those consequences as well. The down-and-out drunk is a potential target for a mugging, and the drunken driver is a serious menace to all in his path. The following example illustrates a common occurrence as far as the police are concerned. In this particular example, no police action was taken.

A patrolman came upon a man staggering down the street. The man was clearly intoxicated but, while his gait was unsteady, he was able to walk without any great risk of falling. Upon questioning the man, the patrolman learned that he was on his way home and that he lived about a block away. No arrest was made.

Only one recruit in the sample would take official action in this case. Other action included seeing that the man got home safely and possibly counseling him and his family about his drinking. This course of action was recommended by a majority of all respondents.

The personal conflict experienced in reacting to this situation is evidenced in the following statement from one of the recruits.

RESPONSE:
At one time or another everyone ties one on. We as police officers do as well. If the man seemed to be in no great danger or a menace to anyone else, I feel the officer was justified. If it made him feel better the officer could have taken him home himself.

The element of danger or risk to the offender or to others, mentioned above, was the most influential criterion on the use of discretion as evidenced in these excerpts.

RESPONSE EXCERPT:
He was apparently not harming anyone so an arrest was not necessary.

RESPONSE EXCERPT:
As long as he was walking and bothering no one there is just about nothing you can do.

RESPONSE EXCERPT:
The intoxicated man was in a sense violating the law, however he was on his way home, only a short distance away and causing no other person any harm or danger including himself.

RESPONSE EXCERPT:
A person who is intoxicated to the extent of personal injury to himself or that of another would be a totally different story.

RESPONSE EXCERPT:
Would have made sure he got home safely. . . .

The actions recommended in this case are consistent with general police practices that make use of warnings rather than arrests where minor violations of this type are concerned. As LaFave (1965:108–110) indicates, drunkenness is an offense that occurs frequently but is not subject to full enforcement. Occasional drunks are not considered serious cases, and since habitual drunks are not deterred or rehabilitated by the criminal justice process, an arrest in these cases is seen as accomplishing little or nothing.

Education and experience made no significant difference in the recruits' responses when these variables were analyzed individually.

WELFARE FRAUD

Another example of both moral and legal ambiguity is found in the efforts of the police to enforce certain sexual and social standards. As with too many other laws, there is selective enforcement depending upon the socioeconomic status of the offender. This occurs not solely because the police choose to use their discretion in such a selective fashion, but because the community, or at least the so-called power structure of the community, wants the police to enforce certain laws against certain people only. The laws themselves, which are not made by the police, reflect this community desire for selective enforcement. The incident that follows is an example of such a situation, but in this case one in which the police used their discretion not to take any action.

A local welfare director presented positive proof to the police that a local welfare recipient was engaging in an adulterous relationship. Notwithstanding a repetition of the complaint on another occasion, the police refrained from taking any action against the violator.

Reasons offered by the recruits for taking some official action included such criteria as a belief that the behavior described constituted welfare fraud; that a morals charge might be appropriate; that there may be children involved who would be adversely affected; and that the taxpayer should not have to support welfare recipients who are enjoying themselves at the taxpayers' expense.

Reasons offered for doing nothing included such things as a belief that the question of with whom a person sleeps is not an appropriate police matter; that the police must consider the relative acceptance of such behavior in the community and the present attitudes toward sexual behavior; and that an arrest is not likely to result in a successful prosecution.

The last two reasons again show the influence of an awareness of public attitudes and a working knowledge of the courts, both gained through increased experience.

The remarkable conclusion from this is that so few (one) of those recruits with the most experience would invoke the criminal process. A great majority of this same group would opt to do nothing. The rank order correlation indicates that the likelihood of arrest decreases as experience increases. This is consistent with the first case as far as the influence of experience is concerned.

PROSTITUTION

Police officers are sometimes confronted with situations in which the victim of an offense has himself been involved in criminal conduct when the victimization occurred. Typical examples of this type of situation occur in the so-called victimless crimes when an individual willingly engages in illegal conduct such as gambling, prostitution, or purchasing drugs, and in turn may be victimized by having his money stolen or by being assaulted. The police must use discretion in determining what offense, if any, to pursue in these cases. They must also decide whether another action might be appropriate or whether it is best to simply do nothing.

The illustration which follows is meant to typify the problems confronting the police in such situations.

A man entered a precinct station and complained that he had just been cheated of $20. Asked to explain, he said that he had given the money to a prostitute who had agreed to meet him at a certain time and place, but that she had failed to appear. The police, although familiar with this kind of racket, subjected the complainant to some ridicule, suggested that he had learned his lesson, and sent him on his way.

Informal police policy in cases of this kind is often to take no official action. Although it is possible to arrest the victim for his own involvement and to conduct an investigation in an effort to find and arrest the prostitute in question, neither is likely to result in a successful prosecution because of the nature of the case.

Forty-three of the police recruits in this study indicated that they would be likely to either arrest the complaining victim or endeavor to find and arrest the prostitute. The noncollege group is much more likely to take some official action through invoking the criminal process. In general, the "toughest" group in this situation, i.e., those most likely to make an arrest, are the non-college police officers with previous police experience. The "softest" group, i.e., those most likely to simply advise or to do nothing, is the college-educated recruits with no experience.

Analysis of the individual statements reveals that a majority of the sample in general felt that the complainant should not have been subjected to any ridicule, action which LaFave (1965:124) indicates may be taken purposely in an attempt to shame the victim out of desiring police action.

Examples of the rationale supporting each of the three decision choices made by the recruits follow.

Arrest

RESPONSE:
The man was cheated and a complaint should be signed. This was not a victimless crime.

RESPONSE:
I would ask him if he would recognize her again, if so try and locate this person and arrest her for prostitution and fraud.

RESPONSE:
I would try to get a description of the prostitute and have him sign a complaint against her. Also, I would sign a complaint against the man for soliciting to the prostitute.

Another Action

RESPONSE:
This is not a victimless crime but a flim flam where he was really cheated of his $20. Ridicule came from the fact that he is a violator of the law, however he feels a piece of ass is worth $20 if he gets it. In this case I would have taken a report to make the man feel better and also advised him prostitution is illegal — but not ridicule.

RESPONSE:
I don't think I would have ridiculed the man. I would have taken his complaint and tried to show an interest in his problem, even though I do think he was a dumb ass for giving the broad the money for services not received. I'd explain all the legalities involved in signing the complaint if he wanted to do that, and also all the embarrassment he would cause himself. If he wanted to go through with it, I'd take the appropriate action.

Do Nothing

RESPONSE:
Obviously the man deserved to be sent on his way. Prostitution is illegal and he was a willing participant. Losing his $20 just might have taught him a good lesson.

RESPONSE:
Again, laws are made to aid people in learning a lesson. This man got cheated but knew he was going to take part in an illegal activity. He learned his lesson.

RESPONSE:
The question mentions precinct which signifies an urban area. Here prostitution and vice are commonplace and police are aware of the various attitudes toward prostitution. I would feel the man had been made wiser, but would not take legal action because of the social differences of the area.

The primary factor influencing decision-making in this case is the fact that fraud or cheating was involved in addition to prostitution. Some recruits cited this as a reason for taking some official action, whereas others cited it as a good learning experience for the would-be client.

Analyzing separately the relationship of each of the variables to the police response indicated, it was found that experience made no significant difference in their responses, but that education showed a small correlation. As the level of education increases, the likelihood of arrest or other official action tends to decrease. The correlation is weak, but is in the direction of supporting the idea that college-educated police officers may tend to react less punitively in certain discretionary situations.

JUVENILE OFFENSE

Another area of deviant behavior that causes considerable ambivalence on the part of the police is that involving children and youths. Nathan Goldman's (1963) study of the police handling of juveniles indicates that the police were influenced in their use of discretion partly by the act of the offender, but also by the idiosyncratic interpretation of this act, and the degree of pressure applied by the community on the police. Piliavin and Briar (1964) found in their study that many police officers felt that the juvenile court failed to rehabilitate offenders, so they were reluctant to turn youths over to it. In instances of minor delinquencies, they found that police decisions tended to be influenced by the personal characteristics of the youths rather than by their offenses.

James Q. Wilson's (1968a) study of the police handling of juveniles in "Western City" and "Eastern City" indicates that the police who reacted most severely toward juveniles were the ones who verbalized non-punitive and less moralistic views of offenders, while those who spoke harshly about lawbreakers were the ones who handled them informally outside the framework of the juvenile court. The more "professionalized" department of "Western City" exerted pressure upon officers to take formal action in juvenile cases, whereas the "fraternal" department of "Eastern City" stressed the use of personal judgment and a more personalized, informal enforcement of the law.

The situation that follows is intended to typify the kind of minor offense involving a juvenile with which the police are frequently confronted, and in which they must use their discretion with little clear direction from either the law or from policy guidelines. It is this type of case that complicates police decision-making and forces the police officer to depend upon factors other than the offense in order to make a judgment.

A traffic officer stopped a car that had been going 15 m.p.h. over the speed limit. The driver was a youth, but he had a valid driver's license. Although the 15 m.p.h. excess was beyond the ordinary toleration limit for speeding violations, the officer only gave the youth a severe warning. The officer knew that the law required suspension of the license of a juvenile driver for any moving violation.

The composite picture of the responses indicates that, with the exception of those four recruits who failed to respond, no one would "do nothing" in the situation described. The issue posed was not really one of whether or not to make an arrest, but rather one of whether or not to issue a summons that would represent invoking the criminal process in this case. The noncollege recruits with experience would be the most likely to issue a summons. A typical response from this group is the following.

SAMPLE RESPONSE:
He would definitely be ticketed and have his license pulled because he's not only endangering himself but other people especially and possibly myself.

In the college group with no experience, few would take official action. An example of their rationale is as follows:

SAMPLE RESPONSE:
Because of the law requiring suspension of the youth's drivers license, I feel a severe warning would have accomplished the same as the suspension, possibly more considering youth-police relations.

The concern reflected in the above statement for police-juvenile relations seemed to be the primary determining factor in the use of discretion in this case. The following excerpts also reflect this concern.

RESPONSE EXCERPT:
I feel the police role on youths is extremely impor-

tant as it leaves a lasting mark in the way the matter was handled.

RESPONSE EXCERPT:
By taking his license he would have embedded a hatred of police in the youth's mind — the violation wasn't that serious.

RESPONSE EXCERPT:
Discretion is a broad term. Here it applies to the fact that the point was gotten across possibly without any later feeling of animosity toward the police.

As the level of education increases, there is a tendency for the likelihood of official action to decrease. As in the previous case, the college-educated recruits seem to be less punitive.

The relationship of experience to the responses indicates that those with the most experience tend to be the most punitive and those with no experience tend to be the most lenient. The influence of experience is again apparent, but in this case its effect is the opposite of that in the earlier cases. An interesting twist concerning the handling of this situation that is reflective of the ambivalence involved was the fact that a number of recruits who indicated that they would issue a summons also indicated they would probably write one for less than the 15 m.p.h. exceeding the speed limit.

SUMMARY AND CONCLUSIONS

Based upon the five discretionary situations illustrated, the police response was very definitely inclined toward taking actions other than invocation of the formal criminal process. In four of the five cases (the exception being the gambling case) a majority would not make an arrest or take other official action. The police recruits were also generally not inclined to ignore the situations — in only one case would a majority do nothing. Other actions are thus very much the preferred response, and it is this particular course of action which requires the greatest imagination and innovation in solving police problems. The two extremes in the universe of possible decisions, arrest or do nothing, are generally much simpler and more clearly defined, but they are also generally all or nothing decisions. Rather

than opt for one of these approaches, the respondents most often selected from among the various shades of gray. It is in these instances that the police have the greatest latitude to impose their own sense of justice.

The primary factor characterizing all the situations which seemed to influence the exercise of discretion was the desire on the part of the respondents to maintain a certain public image of the police role. There was a clear sensitivity to community attitudes, beliefs, and expectations. The recruits seemed to react in accordance with a certain preconceived notion of what the appropriate police action should be, but these reactions were not so much governed by a legal definition of what must be done as by a personal definition of the situation. The reactions were determined by a judgment of what the police should do in each case in order to fulfill a particular role expectation. Bittner (1967) has pointed out that enormous discretion is inevitable in the peace-keeping role of the police since that role is so very vague and ambiguous. He states further that it is the exigencies of a situation, and not a technical violation of the law, that determines the police decision to arrest; peace-keeping involves the discretion to use alternatives to strict enforcement through arrest. The findings here lend support to that conclusion.

The decision that the public's awareness of the social gambling would lead to an expectation that the police should take some action, the decision that the drunk was not in any danger and wasn't endangering anyone else, the decision that the adulterous welfare recipient was not engaging in conduct which was publicly intolerable and needed no police action, the decision that the would-be "John" had learned a valuable lesson from his experience, and the decision to give the juvenile driver a break in the interest of better police-juvenile relations — all were decisions in accordance with certain preconceived notions or situational stereotypes. Each of these cases involved criminal violations, but in only one did a majority feel that they were compelled to take official action.

These unique definitions of the situations that influenced police decision-making were most apparent in the gambling case and the case of the youthful driver, but also in the others as illustrated in the following.

Drunkenness

RESPONSE:
The police stop showed his concern to the public. He should have taken subject home, this is where police get good culture traits [sic] and society in the various towns get good rapport, and reputation of the department is high!

Welfare Fraud

RESPONSE:
The police do not have the time to get involved in who is having an affair with another just because the party is on welfare. However they should have taken the information from the welfare director just to keep him aware that the police are doing their job, but do not have time to get involved.

Prostitution

RESPONSE:
The information should have been taken from the man and he should not have been ridiculed even though it was his fault because this man will have little respect for the police because he would be of the opinion that the police are so much better than he is.

The concern for public image and for community awareness is obvious in each of the above quotations. This characteristic police reaction was described by Goldman (1963: 106–107) in his discussion of the necessity for maintaining respect for police authority in the community:

As a social and political organization existing for the purpose of social control the police must maintain "face" or prestige in the community. The police officer is concerned with the proper recognition of his authority. An assault on his self-esteem will lead quickly to punitive action. . . . The police must also maintain some semblance of prestige in their own professional circles. The loss of face in the eyes of a fellow policeman cannot be tolerated.

Age did not seem to influence the recruits' decision-making, but the amount of education and particularly the amount of experience did make some difference in how they responded. The failure to find any strong evidence that having a college education leads to better or even different use of discretion leaves open this important question for further research.

The influence of experience on the use of discretion seems to result from an accumulation of so-called "street wisdom." Stereotypes learned by police officers in the course of their careers become clearer as their experience increases (Rubinstein, 1973). The importance of experience as a primary factor influencing police discretion implies that the belief in more and better training and more education (college-level) as the way to improve basic police decision-making must be viewed cautiously as being perhaps simplistic. It may be that "street wisdom" ameliorates the effect of some of the training and of the education, at least at the street-cop level. It may be that the police role and functions capture the individual to such an extent as to counteract the liberalizing effects of education. Police role analysis would seem to be a prerequisite to identifying the training and educational needs of the police.

The influence of experience is also closely related to the concern for public image and community expectations. It shows the importance of a two-way communications process between the police and the community. The police are the agents of formal social control in the community — they have a monopoly over the use of legitimate coercion. This coercion is legitimate only so long as it is consistent with community expectations. It is therefore incumbent upon the community and its representatives to make known to the police what their expectations are. This study shows that the police need to be receptive to such communications because it is this knowledge that guides and influences how they use their discretion. If the police are more aware of and responsive to community attitudes and expectations, not only will their actions be given greater legitimacy and police-community relations be improved, but the ambiguity in the exercise of police discretion should be reduced.

REFERENCES

Banton, M. (1964). *The Policeman in the Community* (New York: Basic Books, Inc.).

Bittner, E. (1967). "The Police on Skid Row: A Study of Peace-Keeping," *Am. Soc. Rev.* 32:699–715.

_____ (1970). *The Functions of the Police in Modern Society*, Chevy Chase, Maryland: Center for Studies in Crime and Delinquency. Public Health Service Publication 2059:107.

Goldman, N. (1963). *The Differential Selection of Juvenile Offenders for Court Appearance*. National Council on Crime and Delinquency, 44 East 23rd Street, New York, New York 10010, p.132.

Goldstein, H. (1963). "Police Discretion: The Ideal vs. the Real," *Pub. Adm. Rev.* 23:148–156.

Goldstein, J. (1960). "Police Discretion Not To Invoke the Criminal Process: Low-Visibility Decisions in the Administration of Justice, *Yale Law Journal* 69:543–588.

LaFave, W. (1965). *Arrest: The Decision to Take a Suspect Into Custody* (Boston: Little, Brown and Co.), pp. 108–110.

National Advisory Commission on Criminal Justice Standards and Goals (1973). *Report on Police.* (Washington, D.C.: U.S. Government Printing Office), p. 107.

Pepinsky, H. E. (1975). "Police Decision-Making," in D. M. Gottfredson (Ed.), *Crime and Delinquency Issues: A Monograph Series*. Chevy Chase, Maryland: Center for Studies in Crime and Delinquency.

Piliavin, I., and Briar, S. (1964). "Police Encounters with Juveniles," *Am. J. Soc.* 70:206–214.

President's Commission on Law Enforcement and Administration of Justice (1967). *Task Force Report: The Police.* (Washington, D.C.: U.S. Government Printing Office), p. 14.

Rubinstein, J. (1973). *City Police* (New York: Farrar, Straus and Giroux, Inc.).

Siegel, L. J., Sullivan, D. C., and Green, J. R. (1974). *Decision Games Applied to Police Decision-Making — An Exploratory Study of Information Usage, Journal of Criminal Justice* 2:131–146.

Wilson, J. Q. (1968a). *The Police and the Delinquent in Two Cities.* In S. Wheeler (Ed.), *Controlling Delinquents* (New York: John Wiley and Sons).

_____ (1968b). *Varieties of Police Behavior* (Cambridge, Mass: Harvard University Press), pp. 83–90.

*This article has been abridged.

6. POLICE DISCRETION

JAMES Q. WILSON

HARVARD UNIVERSITY PRESS, © 1968. Reprinted by permission.

■ In every case of suspected crime, the police weigh a range of factors to decide whether and when to intervene, and whether or when to arrest a suspect. The degree of responsibility left to the individual officer varies with type of offense, the type of offender and the policies of different police departments. These policies in turn, are influenced, as Finckenauer's empirical study suggests, by the values and interests of the local communities in which they serve and by the attitudes of courts — both of which may greatly affect the intensity and direction of law enforcement and the ways in which police discretion is controlled and exercised. In this excerpt, police-invoked law enforcement is examined in relation to victimless crimes. ■

THOUGH THE LEGAL and organizational constraints under which the police work are everywhere the same or nearly so, police behavior differs from community to community. First, the conduct with which the police must cope varies from place to place. Both crime and disorder are more common in low-income areas than in high-income ones. How frequently the police intervene in a situation, and whether they intervene by making an arrest, will depend in part on the number and seriousness of the demands the city places on them. Second, some police behavior will be affected by the tastes, interests, and style of the police administrator. Finally, the administrator's views of both particular problems and the general level and vigor of enforcement may be influenced, intentionally or unintentionally, by local politics. . . .

THE DETERMINANTS OF DISCRETION

The patrolman's decision whether and how to intervene in a situation depends on his evaluation of the costs and benefits of various kinds of action. Though the substantive criminal law seems to imply a mandate, based on duty or morality, that the law be applied wherever and whenever its injunctions have been violated, in fact for most officers there are considerations of utility that equal or exceed in importance those of duty or morality, especially for the more common and less serious laws. Though the officer may tell a person he is arresting that he is "only doing his duty," such a statement is intended mostly to reduce any personal antagonism (that is, psychic costs to the officer incurred by being thought a bad fellow). Whatever he may say, however, his actual decision whether and how to intervene involves such questions as these: Has anyone been hurt or deprived? Will anyone be hurt or deprived if I do nothing? Will an arrest improve the situation or only make matters worse? Is a complaint more likely if there is *no* arrest, or if there *is* an arrest? What does the sergeant expect of me? Am I getting near the end of my tour of duty? Will I have to go to court on my day off? If I do appear in court, will the charge stand up or will it be withdrawn or dismissed by the prosecutor? Will my partner think that an arrest shows I can handle things or that I can't handle things? What will the guy do if I let him go?

The decision to arrest, or to intervene in any other way, results from a comparison, different perhaps for each officer, of the net gain and loss to the suspect, the neighborhood, and the officer himself of various courses of action. Under certain circumstances, the policy of his department may set the terms of trade among these various considerations or alter the scales on which these values are measured. Such policies may in some cases make arrest (or no arrest) so desirable that, for all practical purposes, the patrolman has no discretion: he is doing what the department wants done. In other cases departmental policies may have little or no effect, and thus such discretion as is exercised is almost entirely the officer's and not the department's.

To explain fully the uses of discretion many factors would have to be considered.

For simplicity, two major determinants (major in the sense that they explain "enough" of the variation) suffice: whether the situation is primarily one of *law enforcement* or one of *order maintenance* and whether the police response is *police-invoked* or *citizen-invoked*. To repeat the difference between law enforcement and order maintenance, the former involves a violation of a law in which only guilt need be assessed; the latter, though it often entails a legal infraction, involves in addition a dispute in which the law must be interpreted, standards of right conduct determined, and blame assigned. A police-invoked response is one in which the officer acts on his own authority, rather than as the agent of a citizen who has made a specific verbal or sworn complaint (though citizens "in general" may have complained about "the situation"); a citizen-invoked response is one in which the officer acts on the particular complaint or warrant of the citizen. Although some situations cannot be neatly placed in any category, enough can, I hope, so that we can imagine four kinds of situations in which discretion is exercised, as illustrated by the figure below.

CASE I: POLICE-INVOKED LAW
ENFORCEMENT

In this situation the police themselves initiate the action in the specific instance, though sometimes in response to a general public concern over the problem, and whatever action they take is on their own authority. If there is an arrest, the officer is the complaining witness. Many crimes handled in this way are "crimes without victims" — that is, no citizen has been deprived and thus no citizen has called the police. Such calls as the police may get are from "busybodies" — persons who dislike "what is going on" but who themselves are not participants. Enforcement of laws dealing with vice, gambling, and traffic offenses are of this character. The rate and form of police interventions in these situations can be strongly influenced by the policy of the administrator. He can apply a performance measure to his subordinates, though (to introduce a further distinction) that measure differs with the particular offense. With respect to certain forms of vice and gambling, his measure will be whether a brothel or a bookie operates; if they do, his men are "not performing" and the administrator, if he is so inclined, will urge them to greater efforts. His performance measure is *goal-oriented* — that is, it is based on his observation of whether the substantive law enforcement goal has been attained. Accordingly, not only does the administrator have substantial control over his officers, but the community (the mayor, the city council, the newspapers), being able to make the same observations, has substantial opportunity to control the administrator. With regard to traffic enforcement, however, the administrator's measure will be how many traffic tickets the officers have written, not how safe the streets are or how smoothly traffic flows. He cannot judge his men, except perhaps in the extreme case, on these substantive grounds because he knows that writing traffic tickets has only a small effect on actual traffic conditions. Accordingly, his performance measure will be *means-oriented*, and as a result,

Figure 1. Four kinds of discretionary situations

Basis of police response

		Police-invoked action	Citizen-invoked action
Nature of situation	Law enforcement	I	II
	Order maintenance	III	IV

Each case offers a different degree of discretion for the patrolman, the department, or both.

the community will be less able to hold him responsible for traffic conditions. Should they accuse him, which is unlikely, of letting the accident rate rise, he can reply reasonably that, unlike police attitudes toward brothels, police attitudes toward traffic law enforcement are not the sole or even the major determinant of whether there will be accidents.

CASE II: CITIZEN-INVOKED LAW ENFORCEMENT

Here a citizen is the victim of a crime and he or she complains to the police. The vast majority of crimes with victims are those against property — larceny, auto theft, and burglary — and the vast majority of these are crimes of stealth for which the suspect is unknown. As a result, only a small percentage are solved by an arrest. The patrolman in these circumstances functions primarily as a report taker and information gatherer except when the suspect is still on the scene or has been caught by the victim or an onlooker. This is often the case, for example, with shoplifting. Here the patrolman must decide whether to make an arrest, to tell the citizen that it is up to him to handle the matter by getting a complaint and taking the suspect to court himself, or to encourage him to effect a citizen's arrest on the spot. The police department in turn may insist that prosecutions once started, either by an officer or a citizen, may not be dropped; conversely, it may make it easy for the arresting party to change his mind and forget the whole thing. The patrolman's attitude and departmental policy are amenable to some control by the administrator, especially since a majority of the suspects are likely to be juveniles.[1] The police are formally and legally vested with considerable discretion over juveniles (any person in New York under the age of sixteen and in California and Illinois under the age of eighteen). They can decide, if not *whether* to intervene (that is decided for them by the citizen who invokes the law), at least *how* to intervene (to arrest, take into temporary custody, warn and release, and so forth). The police administrator can influence the use of that discretion significantly, not, as with Case I, by observing substantive outcomes or by measuring the output of individual of-

ficers, but by setting guidelines on how such cases will be handled and by devoting, or failing to devote, specialized resources (in the form of juvenile officers, for example) to these matters.

CASE III: POLICE-INVOKED ORDER MAINTENANCE

In this instance the police on their own authority and initiative intervene in situations of actual or potential disorder. The most common charges are drunkenness, disorderly conduct, or breach of the peace. Not all drunk or disorderly arrests, of course, result from a police-invoked response — some, to be discussed below, are police ways of handling disorderly situations to which the police have been called by the citizen. Because the police invoke the law, the administrator has some control over patrolmen's discretion. He can urge them to "keep things quiet" but he cannot, as in traffic enforcement, judge each officer's "production" by how many arrests he makes on the assumption that there is an almost inexhaustible supply of disturbances to go around. Nor can he insist, as he might with cases of shoplifting, that an arrest is always the best way to handle the situation. In short, discretion in these cases is more under the control of the patrolman and can be modified only by general incentives to be "more vigorous" or to "take it easy." The administrator can boost drunk arrests but only by ordering his officers to treat drunks as problems of law enforcement rather than order maintenance: arrest on sight a man intoxicated in a public place even if he is bothering no one. In this case, a drunk arrest falls under Case I and accordingly is subject to the same relatively high degree of control.

CASE IV: CITIZEN-INVOKED ORDER MAINTENANCE

In this last case, a citizen calls for police assistance because of a public or private disorder. But for some reason, being of assistance is often not an easy matter. In almost every department, such a citizen call must be followed by a police response to avoid the charge of "doing nothing"; however, the way the patrolman handles these situations will depend on his assessment of them and on the extent to which the participants are inclined to be tractable and victims prepared to sign a formal complaint. Thus, although the handling of these situations will vary considerably, that variation will depend more on the personal characteristics of the officer and the citizen participants than on departmental policies. Young college-educated patrolmen in a pleasant suburb may handle these matters in one way; older, working-class officers in a racially mixed central city may handle them in another.

In sum, in Cases I and IV the patrolman has great discretion, but in the former instance it can be brought under departmental control and in the latter it cannot. In Case II the patrolman has the least discretion except when the suspects are juveniles and then the discretion is substantial and can be affected by general departmental policies and organization. Case III is intermediate in both the degree of discretion and the possibility of departmental control. In the remainder of this chapter, such evidence as exists will be introduced to indicate the extent to which departments differ in handling these four police situations and the degree to which those differences are intended by the administrator. Because the amount of police activity and the way that police discretion is used will depend in part on the character of the community, it is first necessary to describe the eight communities in which the observations were made.

THE EIGHT COMMUNITIES

Five of the communities in this study are industrial, working-class cities with a median family income that is below the state average, a declining downtown business district, and a population that is at least one fourth of foreign stock; four of the five (Albany, Newburgh, Oakland, and Syracuse) have in addition a large and growing Negro population. The fifth, Amsterdam, was bypassed by the northward migration of Negroes and, because the city has lost much of its industrial base and thus many of its low-skill jobs, Negroes are not likely to start arriving. The other three communities are well-to-do suburban areas; one, Brighton, is a town near Rochester; a second, Highland Park, is a city near Chicago; and a third, Nassau, is an urbanized county adjacent to New York City. These suburbs have all experienced rapid population growth in the last decade or two. There are virtually no Negroes in Brighton or Highland Park; only about 4 per cent of the Nassau population is nonwhite. . . .

THE USES OF DISCRETION

CASE I: POLICE-INVOKED LAW ENFORCEMENT

The rate at which traffic tickets are issued varies enormously among the eight police departments and this variation is primarily the result of the policies of the administrator, not the characteristics of the community. Table 1 shows the rate per thousand population at which tickets were issued in 1965. In Syracuse, the rate was ten times that in Albany, though the social composition and street pattern of the two cities are quite similar. Highland Park's police department issued half again as many tickets as the department in Brighton, though the two communities are almost identical upper-status suburbs. Both Oakland and Nassau County are criss-crossed with major high-speed highways connecting large cities to their suburbs, yet the Oakland police issued four times as many tickets as the Nassau police.

These findings are in every respect similar to those of Gardiner, who in his studies of the cities and towns of Massachusetts and of over five hundred cities in all parts of the country found that only a small part of the great differences in traffic enforcement levels could be explained by differences in the character of the community (income, education, ethnic composition, population mobility, or the like) but could be explained by the policies of the chief.[2]

The chief may influence traffic law enforcement by creating specialized units for that purpose, or by inducing officers in or out of that unit to "produce" tickets, or both. In Amsterdam and Newburgh, special-

Table 1.   Tickets issued for moving traffic violations, and rates per thousand population, 1965.[a]

City	Tickets for moving violations	
	Number	Rate per 1,000
Albany	1,368	11.4
Amsterdam	460	16.4
Newburgh	1,226	40.9
Brighton	1,829	61.0
Nassau County	68,375	61.0
Highland Park	2,933	97.8
Syracuse	23,465	109.1
Oakland	90,917	247.7

[a]Ticket rate based on 1965 population estimates.

ization occurred but without strong inducements to produce. In 1964, both departments purchased a radar speed detector and trained officers in its use. Because of the new technology and the fact that during its use the cars and men assigned did nothing else, traffic ticket rates in both cities more than doubled in one year. In Amsterdam, however, the equipment is used only sporadically, and hence traffic ticket production varies erratically. In a recent year, only six tickets were issued in February and seven in November, but eighty-eight were issued in April and one hundred and five in May. Newburgh has two units rather than one and uses its radar more regularly; thus its ticketing rate is not only twice that of Amsterdam's, but more constant from month to month.

With or without specialization, the chief has various means of inducing officers to "produce." One is the quota system. Almost no police administrator will admit he sets a traffic ticket quota (the one who came closest insisted on calling it a "norm"), but several use devices that are quotas in everything but name. In Brighton the chief expects all his men (there is no specialized traffic unit) to write at least two tickets per man per week, and in 1966 fourteen of his twenty-one full-time patrolmen did. In Oakland, the members of the traffic division are expected to write two tickets per man *per hour*. For a six-week period selected at random, the thirteen men assigned to one shift worked 1,266 hours and wrote 2,505 tickets

for a rate of 1.97 per man per hour and ten of the thirteen men came within plus or minus 0.3 tickets per hour of the standard rate of 2.0 — striking testimony to a large organization's ability to achieve uniform behavior among its members when the objectives are clear and quantitative performance criteria are available.

Syracuse and Highland Park have not had exact numerical quotas, but careful records have been kept of each man's performance and superiors have examined these records regularly to let the men know if they were "falling behind." A senior officer in the Syracuse traffic division described how he ran his unit:

Nobody likes to talk quotas, but that's what is in the back of everybody's mind. We don't tell the men they have any quota, but the deputy chief is always onto me about enforcement, enforcement, enforcement, and I'm always onto the lieutenant about the same thing, and he gets to the sergeant and the sergeant gets to the men. We have a daily report on how many tickets each man writes, how many tickets each platoon writes, and how many tickets are written for each of the various moving offenses. This is put on my desk and on the chief's desk every day. We can glance down here and see how the men are doing . . . if somebody is falling off, we can go around and talk to him and ask him why he isn't pulling his share of the load.

Additional evidence of the ability of the administrator to determine policy in this area can be adduced from the changes some have achieved. When a "reform" police chief came to Syracuse in 1963, he announced that he expected all officers — in and out of the traffic division — to enforce traffic laws. By the end of 1964, ticket production had increased 58 per cent and between 1964 and 1965 it increased another 18 per cent. After a new chief arrived in Highland Park in the mid-1950's, the number of tickets issued tripled during his first two years in office.[3] Though no quota existed, any officer who "was below the average" for a particular month was called in by the chief and, according to one lieutenant, "had to explain why."

Indeed, pressure more than specialization seems to account for the very high rates of some departments. The Nassau police, for example, have a large traffic division that operates sixteen cars (two equipped with radar) and twelve two-wheel motorcycles, but they write tickets at a rate no greater than that in Brighton — largely because there is no quota for traffic officers and no strong pressure for nontraffic patrolmen to write tickets at all. Albany also has a specialized traffic unit with forty-five men and fifteen vehicles assigned to it but the men are used primarily to direct traffic at intersections and the vehicles to aid in enforcing parking regulations (over thirty thousand parking tickets but only a few hundred moving violation tickets were issued in the first half of 1966).

The combined effects of specialization and pressure can be seen in Figure 2, which suggests that pressure is more important than specialization: the four departments in the right hand column (experiencing strong pressure from the chief) are as high or higher

than any other department in ticketing rates, but are evenly divided between those that are specialized and those that are not.

Police policies towards gambling and vice are also strongly subject to the control of the police administrator, but unlike traffic law enforcement these policies are also constrained by community characteristics. The social composition of the city is one determinant both of the potential market for illicit services and of the degree to which public opinion will tolerate activities that serve that market. In almost all cities with a substantial lower class and in almost all large cities whatever their class composition, there will be a demand for vice and gambling that will be served by those residents who find such enterprises profitable. In small, upper-status communities, on the other hand, whatever demand exists will be served, if at all, only with great difficulty. Being small, any activity that requires the regular coming and going of customers can be easily detected; being upper-income, not many residents are likely to find the money profits of prostitution and gambling worth the social costs and most potential customers would probably prefer to avail themselves of such services more anonymously in the nearby central city. Finally, in any city other agencies of law enforcement in addition to the police must act before vice and gambling can be curtailed. Prosecutors must prosecute, judges must convict, and sentences must be imposed that are severe enough to raise the cost of doing business above what the market for such services will support.

In short, the widespread opinion that gambling and prostitution could not exist in

Figure 2. The influence of specialization and administrative norms on traffic ticket rates in eight communities, 1965

| | | Use of pressure or norms | | |
		None	Traffic unit only	Department-wide
Specialized traffic unit	No	Amsterdam (16.4)	—	Brighton (61.0) Highland Park[a] (97.3)
	Yes	Albany (11.4)	Newburgh (40.9) Nassau (61.0)	Oakland (247.7) Syracuse (109.1)

[a]Highland Park traffic enforcement policy changed after 1964.

a city unless the police tolerated them is not generally or simply true. The level of vice depends on the character of the community and the legal resources available to the police (primarily the ability to impose certain and severe sanctions) as well as on police competence and honesty. To impose such sanctions, the police must have evidence. Unlike a traffic infraction, an act of prostitution or gambling is not easily detected; moreover, gathering evidence admissible in court — by actually placing a bet, or seizing betting slips, or having a girl accept money to commit an act of prostitution — is difficult, especially when professional gamblers and prostitutes know police vice officers by sight. Under prevailing rules of evidence, judges are not easily convinced and even when they are they tend to impose penalties that are modest in proportion to the earnings of the gambler. Nassau County, with 1.4 million persons, has gamblers partly because the cost of being arrested for gambling is not high. In 1965, 104 cases involving gambling were disposed of by the Nassau District Court. In 14 per cent of them the charge was dismissed or the defendant was acquitted; in another 19 per cent the defendant received a suspended sentence. Half the defendants were fined, the typical fine being $250; only 15 per cent of the defendants went to jail, most for less than 45 days.[4] A $250 fine, even if imposed twice a year, is a small fee to pay for a lucrative business — less than what it would cost in taxes and fees to own a liquor store legally. A prostitution conviction is rarely more serious.

Arrest and prosecution are not the only ways the police can deal with vice, of course. They can follow a strategy of harassment whereby buyers or sellers or both are kept under obvious surveillance, picked up for frequent interrogations, and arrested on lesser charges (public intoxication, disorderly conduct, breach of the peace, or the like). Certain forms of illegal commerce are more vulnerable than others to such methods. Brothels, for example, can be put out of business by periodic raids or even by merely stationing a police officer outside to take the names of customers, even though no individual prostitute is seriously penalized. Gamblers in "horse rooms" can likewise be kept under such heavy pressure

that, though they may not go out of business, they must so severely restrict their clientele to friends and persons with the right introductions that it becomes, in effect, private gambling rather than a service available to anybody in the market. On the other hand, streetwalkers in a big-city slum or call girls in the downtown business district are elusive prey even for a dedicated vice squad. They operate alone without houses to be raided (hotel rooms, bars, or even parking lots suffice), they must (if streetwalkers) be approached in public or (if call girls) through friends and intermediaries, and they can quickly and easily disappear into the neighborhood or change their area of operations. Police activity can raise the cost of information to the potential customer to the extent that only the most persevering girl hunter will find what he wants, but it cannot put big city prostitution out of business altogether.

Thus, the relevant question is not, "Is there vice in this city?" but "Given the characteristics of the community, has or has not vice been reduced to the level one would expect from intensive police activity and prevailing judicial penalties?" Intensive police activity should produce a highly decentralized industry that utilizes least-risk communications systems and avoids fixed locations, the production of physical evidence, or dealings with strangers.

Because of these considerations, the police administrator has some ready-made excuses if he should decide for any reason to tolerate a certain amount of vice and gambling. Wherever researchers for this study found illegal enterprises, the police responded by saying that it is "small-scale stuff," that "We can't put them out of business" because "they know all our men," "You can't get evidence," "The courts won't issue search warrants or authorize wire taps," and "The judges let them off with a slap on the wrist anyway." The police claimed that such inhibitions were more constraining than in fact they were, but there was some truth in all their arguments.

In upper-income suburbs such as Brighton and Highland Park, there was no vice, at least of the sort run by professionals. The Brighton police on at least one occasion found bookies attempting to set up business in a motel on the outskirts of town but, with the cooperation of the State Police, they raided them and put them out of business. In another case, a woman complained that her husband was losing money gambling at a veteran organization's picnic; the police closed the game down. In one of the towns, the chief admitted he had been offered a large bribe by a big-city gambler eager to move in, but he turned it down (there is no reason to doubt him). If organized gambling or vice were discovered in such towns, there would be a scandal and the police know it. Residents would expect that "In a town like this" the police could "keep that element out," and they would be right.

In small industrial towns such as Amsterdam and Newburgh, it is another story. With many bars and dance spots and a working-class population, there are many opportunities for illegal businesses and little, if any, pressure from public opinion to eliminate it altogether. Unlike in Brighton and Highland Park, the gamblers would not be "outsiders" seeking to bribe or sneak their way in, but locals running local businesses for local customers. As they are members of the community, they cannot be kept out and, so long as they are reasonably discreet, they will not be harassed. In any case, as locals they know by sight every police officer and thus, should the police want to crack down, it would be hard to gather the kind of evidence (for example, actually placing a bet) that the courts increasingly require. The issue in such cities, then, is not whether there will be illegal businesses, but only on what scale they will operate.

In Amsterdam, they are small scale and confined mostly to gambling. In 1961 the State Police raided and made arrests at four-teen gambling spots, in 1964 city police made three arrests at a numbers game, apparently because of complaints the game was not honest, and in 1966 the State Police raided ten places and arrested thirteen persons. In at least the last instance, the State Police were called in by local authorities but only to "keep the situation under control" not to "end gambling in Amsterdam."

In Newburgh, on the other hand, vice is a major industry and, at least for college boys and servicemen, a principal tourist attraction. There are at least two brothels,[5] but as of 1966 there had not been a single arrest for prostitution since 1958, and that year there were only four. There have been gambling arrests almost every year — especially in 1963 and 1964, when there were some State Police raids — but rarely more than four or five, and these men usually reopen business at the same locations.[6] Prostitutes solicit openly in some of the city's thirty-three bars. One girl told an interviewer how the system worked:

A lot of these bartenders let us come in to pick up men. Sometimes if a guy is looking for a girl, the bartender will phone us and tell us to come on over, there's somebody they want us to meet. They never ask for money. Of course, they expect that we will have a few drinks in their place before leaving. It's all nice and friendly. . . . We don't let outside girls come in. I was raised right here in Newburgh and I would talk to some people if any girl from New York tried to operate here. . . . The police let us alone and they don't try to shake us down as long as we're quiet and don't try to rob some guy.

An important political leader in New-burgh accepted this situation matter-of-factly. He told an interviewer: "I'm too old to be interested in that sort of thing myself, but everybody says that Little Lil's place [pseudonym] down in the colored section has twenty or thirty cars parked out in front of it on Saturday night. I don't know much about it . . . but it's common gossip."

More and better-organized illegal businesses are tolerated in Newburgh than in Amsterdam. The extent to which these differences are simply the result of police policies and the extent to which they represent political decisions is partly a matter of conjecture, but interviews with Newburgh politicians suggest that they at least consent to the existence of a conspicuous vice industry. It is important to bear in mind, however, that the major difference between the two cities is in the level of prostitution and that in Newburgh most, but certainly not all, the prostitutes are Negro. There are very few lower-income Negroes in Amsterdam; if there were more, vice there might not be so very different from in Newburgh. As will be suggested in a later chapter, the police strategy in such cities is based in part on standards of public morality that vary for different racial groups.

In the larger communities, the police

have more resources to devote, if they wish, to vice suppression. They have more men, they can create specialized units to deal with vice, and they can enlist as allies civic associations and newspapers that either do not exist at all in the small town or that feel their mission is to boost and defend, rather than criticize or investigate, the community. At the same time, the big city's vice industry has more resources with which to resist suppression — urban anonymity makes concealment easier and talented criminal lawyers can usually be hired to oppose prosecutors and the police.

The four large communities included in this study show almost the full range of police policies. In three of the four places, there have been significant changes in these policies since the 1940's. In Nassau County, for example, a major gambling scandal in the police department in the 1940's led to the appointment of a "reform" police commissioner, and since that time a tough policy on vice has been followed, complicated only by some rivalry between the NCPD and the District Attorney over control of the vice squad. The twenty-man squad, now part of the NCPD, conducts a vigorous program of surveillance on bookies and prostitutes; court-authorized wiretaps are used to get information on the former, undercover men to get evidence on the latter. In 1965 the police made 479 vice arrests — 115 for bookmaking, 101 for operating a policy racket, 73 for running a dice game, 42 for prostitution, 26 for distributing pornographic materials, and the rest for assorted offenses. There have been in addition, several major gambling and prostitution raids.[7] The State Police, frequently active in other New York communities, have not had occasion to intervene in Nassau County.

Syracuse has also changed, but because it is a large industrial city with a substantial Negro and other lower-income population, reducing vice and gambling to the relatively low level found in suburban Nassau is much harder. The present policy dates from the report of the Temporary Commission of Investigation of the State of New York (popularly known as the "SIC") issued in February 1963, which condemned the Syracuse Police Department in the strongest language: "In summary, the investigation disclosed police corruption; unchecked gambling, prostitution and violations of the liquor laws; 'tip-offs' by Detectives of impending police raids; and improper police associations with criminals."[8]

The report contained excerpts from testimony and extracts from wiretaps confirming that money and "Christmas gifts" were given police officers, that leading gamblers held frequent meetings with detectives, that rookie officers who made gambling arrests without departmental approval were rebuked or given no support, that the police chief never took effective steps to initiate an anti-gambling investigation, and that high political figures intervened with the chief to help certain officers, including some close to gamblers, to win promotions.[9] At almost the same time that the report appeared, a newly elected mayor appointed a new chief and deputy chief of police. A strong effort was made by the new leadership to close down gambling and prostitution, which they discovered existed, but not as flagrantly as the SIC report had suggested. The Syracuse department in 1965 made 116 gambling arrests, producing an arrest rate five times higher than that in Albany or Newburgh. Most bookies and card game operators seem to have been put out of business or at least driven behind the closed doors of "private clubs" where they deal only with persons known to themselves. The level of prostitution is harder to evaluate, but interviewers could find no bars where open solicitation occurred nor were bartenders and the like able or, if able, willing to give the addresses of brothels.

Because resources in any police department are limited, some aspects of vice are emphasized more than others. Before the new police administration took over, there were only three men on the Syracuse vice squad. As a present member of the squad told an interviewer, "Those three men had to spend their time on after-hours places and on prostitution because those were the things that got the church groups excited." The new police chief enlarged and reorganized the squad into a ten-man "organized crime division," which increased gambling arrests by more than 25 per cent during the first year of its operation. Even so, gambling continues to exist and these men know it. Of

58 gambling cases disposed of by the Syracuse City Court during 1964, over half (59 per cent) were dismissed or the defendant was acquitted; none resulted in a jail sentence. One judge told an interviewer that this happened both because of the nature of the case and because of the attitude of the judges:

Most of the gambling cases that are brought before us are weak cases. There are very difficult technical motions on rules of evidence, search and seizure procedures, and the like that the judge must consider. But above all, I don't believe gambling constitutes a serious crime. The judge has to reflect community attitudes. What else can he do? He's a human being. . . Seventy-five per cent of the public gambles. . . I know the police chief here is death on gambling, but I can't understand why . . . It's not a great sin in my eyes. I simply cannot get too excited about it.

The police are aware of this and resent it. If they fail to arrest gamblers, the public will suspect them of being corrupt or incompetent; if they do arrest them, no serious penalty ensues and the effort seems pointless. As a result the police try to harass the gamblers. An officer in the organized crime division told an interviewer:

We keep on these gamblers because we feel that's our job. We mug 'em, we print 'em, we book 'em. And what happens after that is not our business. We have to keep reminding ourselves of that or we would get discouraged. Basically, we are harassing the gamblers and even though all we're doing is arresting them and bringing them in here, we're hurting them plenty. . . We're at least forcing them to hire a lawyer and we're breaking up their operations and we're making life tough for their customers.

Oakland also was once a more tolerant city. Before the reform police administration came to power in the mid 1950's, gambling was widespread, including regular games in the basement of a major labor union headquarters and in the Chinese district. The churches ran bingo contests. A long-time member of the vice squad told an interviewer about the change:

The police tolerated these things because the community wanted them tolerated. Nobody complained and nobody demanded the police do anything about it. About fifteen years ago, a new chief and city manager came in and decided to close it

down. They were closed down and they've been closed down tight ever since. . . . There is no lottery; the labor temple has been closed down tight. We had to write a letter to all the churches . . . telling them that bingo was not going to be allowed anymore. I almost got myself excommunicated! I had to go around and see all those priests and tell them I was closing up their carnivals, but it stuck.

In a series of raids beginning in 1955, gambling was hit hard, not only at labor headquarters and among the Chinese tongs, but at churches and civic organizations.[10] Individuals and organizations with carnival-style gambling, normally immune from police action, were not exempted. The police raided a bingo game run by a seventy-year-old lady at a women's fraternal organization, a gambling carnival run for charity, it was claimed, at a local Lion's club, and a wheel-of-fortune game at two separate Catholic church bazaars.[11] (There are limits to police zeal in these matters. A member of the vice squad told an interviewer that a "friendly poker game" in a home or at a lodge or club would not be bothered unless there was evidence it was being run by professionals or the house was taking a profit from the pots.) The pressure has continued. In 1965 Oakland police made 415 gambling arrests, mostly by the eighteen-man vice control division. This arrest rate was over ten times that of Albany and Newburgh and twice that of Syracuse. Very few of the arrests are of bookies, mostly because serious bookmaking has been all but eliminated in the city.[12]

Prostitution arrests are also numerous — 295 in 1965 — but the industry flourishes nonetheless. The police deny there are brothels in the city, and no informant or researcher could find one, but the police do not deny — indeed, they complain about — the large number of predominantly Negro streetwalkers, especially in and around the bars on the lower-class east side. It is difficult under the law to make a good pinch that does not also involve entrapment, that is, unlawfully inducing a person to commit an illegal act.[13] Men, mostly white, drive slowly through the Negro area on East Seventh Street; girls hail them and they negotiate through the open car window; if a bargain is struck, the girl gets in the car and directs the driver to a rendezvous — sometimes in a hotel room, sometimes in a parking lot. The practice is called "trolling." To stop it, the Oakland vice squad officers — often using new recruits or others as undercover "special employees" — troll also and spar verbally with the girls until one takes the step that makes a legal arrest on a prostitution charge possible: offering on her own initiative to commit an act of prostitution for a stated sum of money. Prostitutes are still easily found because, in the opinion of the police, the courts "do nothing" with the girls after they are arrested. One vice squad officer told an interviewer:

There are lots of whores here. They come in from Los Angeles, San Francisco, Fresno, from all over. They come in because the heat's on in these other places. Down in Los Angeles, judges have been giving 30, 45, 90, and 180 day jail sentences. Over in San Francisco, the police have been rousting them — picking them up on weak holding charges and shipping them out of town. . . The reason we make so many arrests is because the girls are back out on the street before the officer can finish making out his report. We've had cases of girls being busted twice in the same night for prostitution. . . [Some] judges are just not locking these people up. They've told me flat out they don't believe prostitution is really wrong. But we have to do our job and they have to do theirs, and we just have to try to forget about what happens after we've done our job.

Albany has changed also, but not in response to a scandal or the advent of a reform administration and not with the intention of reducing the level of vice and gambling to a minimum. Rather, the changes have been made by the police and the city government to adjust the level of illegal business to new conditions of demand and public tolerance. Until the 1960's, Albany was famous for its "Gut" — several blocks of bars packed with B-girls and interspersed with brothels. One officer who used to walk that beat told an interviewer a few years later that "when things were going good" in that area "there were forty or fifty gin mills, most of them with girls hustling in them, just in the two-block area next to police headquarters." Another officer told an interviewer that when the Gut was flourishing, prostitutes paid off to party headquarters at the rate of $20 each per week but that most patrolmen were

themselves forbidden to take anything but "small favors." In the spring of 1961, investigators for the State Liquor Authority (SLA) charged twenty-six Albany bars, mostly in the Gut, with a total of 140 violations of the liquor code for allegedly permitting gambling on the premises and allowing B-girls to loiter and solicit for immoral purposes.[14] The police made little effort to close down these places.

Not long afterward, the Republican administration of Governor Rockefeller tore down the Gut in order to make way for a new, 100-acre state office building complex (and also, one suspects, to weaken the power and lessen the income of the Democratic administration that runs the city). With a few exceptions, the bars and brothels that were torn down never reopened. At least one well-known brothel still operates in the area (though staffed with Negro girls it is for white men only) and several girls continue to work the streets or hustle in bars, mostly in the Negro section; some of the street girls, but none of those in the brothel, are occasionally arrested. To the casual visitor, Albany is now a quiet, even dull, city. Girls are available, but one must search a bit to find them — their presence is no longer advertised by the bright lights and loud noises of honky-tonk bars — which is, one imagines, just the way the police now want it.

Gambling continues to flourish but also more circumspectly. In June 1964 agents of the U.S. Internal Revenue Service arrested twenty-nine persons in Albany on charges of failing to purchase a $50 federal wagering tax stamp.[15] The Albany police chief answered "no comment" when reporters asked whether he knew of the gambling and, if so, why he had not ended it. The Internal Revenue Service spokesman said the Albany police had not been informed of the raid and their cooperation had not been sought.[16] Most of those arrested were eventually fined sums ranging from $150 to $1,250. Two years later, the State Police raided the Albany area again, arresting twenty-six persons on gambling charges, mostly for bookmaking.[17] This time the Albany police participated in the raid but those arrested managed to escape punishment. . . .

NOTES*

1. Property crimes — burglary, larceny of items valued over $50, and auto theft — accounted in 1965 for 82 per cent of the major crimes ("Index Crimes") reported to the FBI and 84 per cent of the causes of victimization reported by respondents in the Crime Commission household survey. About 21 per cent of these three crimes were, according to police reports to the FBI, "cleared by arrest." About 57 per cent of those arrested for these offenses (and those arrested, of course, may not be a representative sample of those who committed the crimes) were under the age of eighteen. See President's Commission on Law Enforcement and Administration of Justice, *Crime and Its Impact — An Assessment* (Washington: Government Printing Office, 1967), p. 17; and Federal Bureau of Investigation, *Uniform Crime Reports, 1965* (Washington: Government Printing Office, 1965), pp. 97, 112. A study by the Oakland Police Department in 1963 showed that 74.6 per cent of all persons processed by the police for shoplifting were juveniles, that is, under the age of eighteen. Most of these cases came from retail stores with security guards and only a few stores accounted for most of the arrests. Between January 1962 and October 1963, 2,394 shoplifting cases were reported by 453 stores; over half came from 57 stores, 29 per cent came from only 4 stores, and 10 per cent came from just one store. Oakland Police Department, "An Analysis of the Shoplifting Problem in Oakland, 1962 and 1963," (mimeograph, November 1963). See also Walter B. Miller, "Theft Behavior in City Gangs," in Malcolm W. Klein, *Juvenile Gangs in Context* (Englewood Cliffs: Prentice-Hall, 1967), pp. 25–37.

2. John A. Gardiner, "Police Enforcement of Traffic Laws: A Comparative Analysis," in James Q. Wilson, ed., *City Politics and Public Policy* (New York: John Wiley & Sons, 1968). Of all the demographic variables, only population mobility was correlated with ticket rates.

3. Data before 1956 are very scanty; the threefold increase is an estimate based on magistrate's records.

4. Calculated from the docket of the Nassau County District Court, Vols 43–48. Many gambling cases were adjourned into the next calendar year, so the totals do not correspond to police arrests in 1965.

5. The adage that a sociologist is a man who needs a $50,000 grant to find a whorehouse is either untrue or inapplicable to political scientists.

6. See accounts of gambling raids in the Newburgh *Evening News*, June 20 and December 8, 1963; May 4 and December 20, 1964; and March 9 and July 15, 1965.

7. In May 1966 ninety NCPD officers conducted gambling raids on twenty-eight homes in the North Shore area, arresting twenty-eight persons on bookmaking charges. *New York Post*, May 12, 1966. Earlier, a tavern owner was arrested for trying to bribe the vice squad commander in an effort to squelch a gambling investigation. And before that, Nassau County received national publicity for breaking up what was erroneously described as a "housewives prostitution ring." (In fact, it consisted, not of suburban housewives earning pin money while their husbands were away, but of professionals operating out of motels and bars.) Two Nassau County police officers were apparently involved in the ring, one of whom allegedly checked the license plate numbers of customers to make certain none was an NCPD detective.

8. Temporary Commission of Investigation of the State of New York, *Summary of Activities During 1962* (New York: 1963), p. 47. A 1947 grand jury report had censured the Syracuse police department for its "complete lack of police work in respect to gambling." During the period 1947–1962, state police and U.S. Internal Revenue agents made a total of twenty-seven gambling raids in the city, arresting 47 persons. After — but rarely before — each raid, the Syracuse police would also make some arrests.

9. Ibid., pp. 84–90, 98–100, 102–107, 110–114.

10. In October 1955 thirteen persons were arrested in a police raid on the American Federation of Labor Temple in Oakland. The police stated that gambling had been going on there for twenty-two years, producing a monthly revenue of $3,000 for the Temple. In June 1956 fifty-eight persons were arrested on gambling charges at another fraternal order. And in April 1959 fourteen persons were arrested in a raid at the Boilermakers' Union, Local 10. See *Oakland Tribune*, October 11, 1955; June 23, 1965; April 22, 1959. The organized gamblers did not give up easily. In 1959 the police arrested five Chinese, including the leader of a local ring, for attempting to bribe top Oakland police officers in order to obtain police consent to operating two gambling centers with six card tables each; every table was to pay off $50 to $90 per day, or a total of $18,000 a year, to the police. *Oakland Tribune*, March 10, 1959. In 1965 Oakland police arrested a patrolman on charges of accepting bribes to protect a poker game. Another patrolman believed to have been involved killed two men he thought were informants and then tried to commit suicide. *Oakland Tribune*, December 8, 1965.

11. *Oakland Tribune*, November 30, 1960; March 11, 1961; October 23, 1961.

*Footnotes have been abridged, edited, and renumbered.

12. The market for certain forms of gambling in Oakland may be reduced, and therefore the pressure on the police eased by the fact that draw-poker casinos are legal in the neighboring city of Emeryville.

13. Jerome H. Skolnick, *Justice Without Trial* (New York: John Wiley & Sons, 1966), p. 96–106, has an interesting account of prostitution arrests in a California city.

14. *Knickerbocker News*, March 14, 1961, and Albany *Times-Union*, April 20, 1961. The police chief told a reporter that such matters were the responsibility of the SLA, adding that "anytime a crime is committed in the presence of a police officer an arrest is made and proper action is taken." *Times-Union*, April 25, 1962. In 1960, the year before the SLA investigation, the Albany police made thirty arrests on prostitution charges, but this had little effect on business.

15. *Knickerbocker News*, June 10, 11, 12, and 13, 1964.

16. Ibid., June 11, 1964.

17. *Times-Union*, July 17, 1966.

III. Prosecution

7. DISCRETION AND PUBLIC PROSECUTION

LEON FRIEDMAN

From SOCIAL PSYCHOLOGY AND DISCRETIONARY LAW, edited by Lawrence Abt and Irving Stuart. © 1979 by Van Nostrand Reinhold Co. Reprinted by permission of the publisher.

■ After an arrest has been made, the next stage of the criminal justice process that entails considerable discretion is the decision to prosecute. The circumstances which allow this discretion to exist are varied. Leon Friedman reviews several of these, such as separation of powers and the vagaries of the laws to be enforced. Obviously, the decision of whether or not to prosecute, as well as the selective intensity of enforcement, are but two aspects of a prosecutor's discretion. Friedman notes the problems associated with this inherent discretion. Moreover, he suggests some of the ways in which selective enforcement and intensity of enforcement can have important policy and political consequences. ■

THE PROSECUTOR HAS more control over life, liberty, and reputation than any other person in America."[1] So wrote Attorney General (later Supreme Court Justice) Robert H. Jackson in 1940. His candid analysis of the range of prosecutorial discretion in our criminal justice system is still the starting point for any serious discussion of the subject.

His discretion is tremendous. He can have citizens investigated and, if he is that kind of person, he can have this done to the tune of public statement and veiled or unveiled intimations. Or the prosecutor may choose a more subtle course and simply have a citizen's friends interviewed. . . . He may dismiss the case before trial, in which case the defense never has a chance to be heard. . . . [A] prosecutor stands a fair chance of finding at least a technical violation of some act on the part of almost anyone. . . . It is in this realm — in which the prosecutor picks some person whom he dislikes or desires to embarrass, or selects some group of unpopular persons and then looks for an offense, that the greatest danger of abuse of prosecuting power lies.[2]

Prosecutors in continental Europe are professional civil servants owing their allegiance to and under the responsibility of the judiciary rather than the executive department. In theory they have no discretion — they must prosecute all cases that the evidence allows to the fullest extent possible. And they have little if any role in the decision on sentencing. Recent studies have cast some doubt on the lack of discretion in the European systems,[3] but there is no question that American prosecutors have far greater decision-making power, and that the American system permits — indeed requires — that crucial decisions at all stages of the process be left in the hands of the public prosecutors with little if any supervision, control, or standards to guide them.

The reasons for this wide range of discretion are varied and complex:

1. *Separation of Powers*. Unlike the European systems, in the Amercian system we consider the lack of control of prosecutors by the courts to be a virtue rather than a shortcoming. Each arm of government is supposed to be separate and distinct, with no control by one over the other. The power to prosecute belongs to the executive department. Under the Constitution, the President must execute the laws; that is, he must prosecute those who disobey them. If the different phases of the process — investigation, charging, granting immunity, prosecuting, plea bargaining — were supervised by the courts, the commingling of functions would raise serious due process problems. In addition, since many prosecutors are elected or chosen through the political process, they are, for good or bad, subject to popular pressures. Thus the democratic process that we all applaud requires some flexibility in what has been looked upon as a political office.

2. *Range and Vagueness of the Laws*. A wide range of penal laws are in force, which reach many phases of the day-to-day lives of citizens. These include prohibitions against intoxication, certain kinds of sexual behavior, almost any form of gambling, and more recently certain drug offenses — crimes that many people do not consider

immoral. The tax laws prohibit any intentional falsification of returns, however small. Licenses or permits are necessary for many business activities, and the failure to secure the right document may lead to criminal charges. Bad check and non-support laws exist in every jurisdiction. In the business field, laws against securities violations, price-fixing, market-sharing, conflict of interest, or trading with the enemy are in force. Many Americans are unclear about what conduct is forbidden and may regularly violate such laws, in part because they do not feel their conduct is morally reprehensible. In addition, some of the criminal statutes are so loosely written, vague, or ambiguous on the one hand, or so complex and incomprehensible on the other, that it is often difficult to determine what behavior they cover. Legal prohibitions exist against many types of inchoate crimes (conspiracy, attempts, solicitation, aiding and abetting) and existing legal rules make these crimes applicable to what appears to laymen to be innocent behavior. All of this gives a prosecutor the opportunity to apply the criminal codes selectively.

3. *Lack of Institutional Controls.* In theory there are a number of institutional controls over a prosecutor that can limit his discretion. In practice they are seldom if ever applied. The grand jury, consisting of 23 citizens, is supposed to investigate a crime, call witnesses in front of it, question them, and determine whether to indict. In fact, it is the prosecutor who makes such decisions. In the rare cases in which a grand jury does not indict, it is usually because a prosecutor does not want any action taken. Any honest prosecutor will admit that the grand jury takes direction from him. Even if an exceptional grand jury asserted itself against a prosecutor, he could always bring the matter before a second grand jury, since the double jeopardy clause does not apply to grand jury actions.[4] The fiction of an independent grand jury in fact plays into a prosecutor's hands. Since in theory the grand jury is reviewing what a prosecutor does, and itself consists of ordinary citizens who would protect other citizens being investigated, it seems permissible to grant a grand jury enormous powers of investigation. But those powers

are being usurped by the prosecutor, giving him even more power than he had previously. A prosecutor's discretion is also limited in theory by a magistrate who can decide in a preliminary examination that a prosecution lacks merit. But the legal rules allow the preliminary examination to be eliminated if the grand jury has returned an indictment. Even when a grand jury has not acted, magistrates will not dismiss an indictment if there is any legal evidence presented that could lead a jury to convict even if the magistrate is himself dubious about the evidence. Thus there are no effective institutional controls over a prosecutor's decision to bring a criminal action.

4. *Discretion as Mercy.* Discretion is a two-way street. In the same way that discretion may be used to prosecute someone based on little if any evidence, discretion may also be applied not to prosecute someone, despite the fact that he is clearly guilty of a crime. Our criminal justice system encourages its participants to use their discretion mercifully — that is, in favor of the defendant — at all stages. Thus a district attorney may decide not to prosecute a youthful offender for stealing a car because it was his first offense, because he was under the influence of others, because the car was returned, and so on, even though technically the offender is just as guilty as the others. Other offenders may not be prosecuted because the evidence was secured illegally, or the offender had a compassionate reason for doing what he did, or he has already been punished in other ways (by losing his job, having his reputation tarnished). Still others may not be prosecuted because they have agreed to testify against their co-conspirators. We applaud prosecutors who take such actions. But they can do so only if they are given wide latitude in their decision to prosecute. Thus we have established and maintained a system that gives prosecutors great discretion at both ends of the spectrum.

The prosecutor's powers are enormous and almost unreviewable. If he decides to investigate a particular individual, he does not have to give any reason for doing so. Jonathan Goldstein, the former United States Attorney for New Jersey, developed an enviable reputation for his prosecution of fraud and white-collar crime. He has publicly stated that his investigations often began on a "hunch." If he heard about a particular municipal contract being signed, he might subpoena all the bank records of the participants without their knowing about it. (The Supreme Court has held that bank records of a depositor are owned by the bank, and therefore the depositor has no right to complain if bank records about him are subpoenaed.) Phone records and credit card records might also be secretly subpoenaed. Thus a prosecutor can build up an enormous file on a person and on his business and political activities. The prosecutor also decides whom to call before a grand jury, whom to grant immunity to, and whom to cite for contempt if he feels their answers are inadequate. Since the grand jury's powers are so sweeping and far-ranging, the courts seldom if ever put limits on what is done in the grand jury's name.

If a prosecutor decides not to bring a case, his decision is not reviewable. In the early days of the civil rights drive in the deep South, civil rights workers tried to force the federal government (particularly Robert F. Kennedy, as Attorney General) to bring federal criminal action against Mississippi sheriffs and police officers who were violating the rights of blacks and civil rights workers. They offered an impressive number of affidavits by the victims of these crimes, showing that civil rights violations had occurred. Nevertheless, the courts refused to order Kennedy to do anything.[5] Similarly, some of the victims of the state troopers who use excessive force in their recapture of Attica prison in 1971 tried to obtain a federal court order requiring prosecution of the state troopers. They were refused relief.[6]

The reluctance of the courts to order prosecution is understandable. After all, the prosecutor is in charge of the case when it reaches the courts. If he does not want to bring a prosecution, it is doubtful that he will enthusiastically press the charges. Thus the case is likely to be lost anyhow. Only in rare instances is it possible to appoint a special prosecutor, as when a conflict of interest is present. In addition, ordering a prosecutor to bring a case is inconsistent

with the mercy we want him to show wherever possible.

The only time the courts have become involved in the decision not to prosecute is if the decision is based upon racial or other class-motivated grounds. In 1976 the NAACP brought a case against Attorney General Edward Levi charging that the FBI would not fully investigate charges of police brutality against blacks in Arkansas. This "the plaintiffs claim, was arbitrary and racially discriminatory conduct by federal officials." The federal judge hearing the case held that the complaint stated a good cause of action and that the plaintiffs "should be afforded an opportunity to support these allegations."[7]

However, even if the plaintiffs won such a case, the most they would receive is a court order requiring the prosecutors to exercise their discretion in a racially neutral manner. The courts would still not order a prosecutor to bring a particular case against a particular individual because of the impossibility of supervision and the other reasons noted above.

We have had a long history in this country of what now appear to be politically motivated trials.[8] A prosecutor may bring criminal charges on the flimsiest of grounds against representatives (often the leaders) of opposition groups to suppress their political activities or at the least to shed unfavorable light on their political efforts. Opponents of the existing regime, or dissident groups challenging the existing order, or even specific individuals who oppose one or more policies of the government, have been targets of elusive and ambiguous criminal laws, which focus primarily on their open political actions. The following examples are familiar to most students of American law and politics:

1. In the period from 1798 to 1800 the Federalist party used the Alien and Sedition Acts to indict a number of their political opponents in the Jeffersonian-Republican party merely for voicing criticism of the government.

2. Union members in the early part of the nineteenth century were indicted for organizing other workers, striking, or picketing in violation of common law conspiracy laws.

3. In the period before the Civil War it was made a crime in all the southern states to be a member of an abolition society or to suggest that owners had no property rights in slaves.

4. Eight anarchist leaders were indicted for conspiracy to murder after the Haymarket bombing of 1886 when eight policemen were killed. Five of the defendants were not even present at the meeting where the bombing occurred, but all were tried and found guilty, since they had advocated the use of violence in labor disputes.

5. During World War I, leading members of the IWW and the Socialist party were indicted for interfering with the recruitment of men for the Army because they said in public speeches that the war was a capitalist war and was not in the interests of the working man.

6. In 1941, the leaders of a Minneapolis teamster union, leaders of a dwindling Trotskyite faction, were indicted under the recently enacted Smith Act for conspiring to plot the violent overthrow of the government. The indictments were instigated by national teamster leaders who had important influence with the Roosevelt administration and applauded by the Communist party, to whom the Trotskyites were anathema.

7. During the civil rights drive of the early 1960s, many black activists and their supporters were casually arrested by southern authorities on charges of disturbing the peace for distributing voter registration information or protesting or demonstrating in any way.

8. During the Vietnam war, Benjamin Spock and four other were indicted for conspiring to counsel young men not to enter the armed forces. The charges were based entirely on their meetings and printed manifestos opposing the war and supporting young draft resisters. The prosecutions grew out of a dispute between the Justice Department and General Lewis Hershey of the Selective Service System, who insisted that action be taken.[9]

It is doubtful that a single one of the criminal charges outlined above would hold up under the current state of the law. Except for the Haymarket affair, no one was accused of violence against persons or property, and the defendants' open political activity was the basis of the charges. There is little question that the primary offense of the defendants was that they were political opponents of the party in power, and the government saw some political gain for itself in bringing the cases. The vagueness and overbreadth of the criminal laws and the existing legal rules granting prosecutors such broad discretion allowed the prosecutors to select a politically unpopular group of defendants for criminal action.

With the rise of public protest over the Vietnam war, the problem of selective enforcement of the law came into the courts with greater frequency. One of the first cases involved a group of Quakers who held a peace worship service in the Pentagon.[10] They were prosecuted for making loud and unusual noises in government buildings. In their defense they showed that an Army band had played in exactly the same place where they had held their service and no action had been taken against the players. There were 16 other meetings in the same place with no complaint from the authorities. The court of appeals threw out the prosecution.

In another case, arising in Hawaii, the government prosecuted a young man for refusing to answer questions for the 1970 census. He was a vocal opponent of the census and had urged other citizens not to cooperate with the census takers. He held press conferences, distributed leaflets, and appeared on radio shows protesting against snooping by the government into a citizen's private life. He and three associates were investigated by the government as "hardcore resisters," and eventually criminal charges were brought. The court of appeals threw out his conviction: "We conclude that Steele demonstrated a purposeful discrimination by census authorities against those who had publicly expressed their opinion about the census."[11]

The law of selective enforcement is now firmly established in American law. Although the courts have retreated from the ready acceptance of the defense that followed the Falk case, they have now established legal standards for testing the defense and institutional procedures for determining whether it is validly invoked. The acceptance of the defense should not seriously interfere with the legitimate activities of prosecutors. A defendant must show a general policy of non-enforcement of a particular law. Even then, if a prosecutor can show some valid reason for applying the law, the courts will approve his actions. Thus if he resurrects a law that had been generally ignored and announces that it will be enforced again, the courts will probably decide that a legitimate law enforcement purpose is being served. If he carefully selects a case to test a new law, that will be considered permissible. In short, almost any activity that shows an intent to enforce the law on a wide scale will pass muster.

As for proving improper motive, the defendant has the burden of showing either that the prosecution was based on improper classification by the government or that it acted to chill his exercise of constitutional rights. The courts will not readily accept such claims, since they start with a premise that the government usually acts in good faith.

Nevertheless we have advanced far from the days when a prosecutor's actions were considered unreviewable. He was the last government official whose discretion became subject to check. Yet he was the one, as Robert Jackson said almost 40 years ago, who had the greatest control over our day-to-day lives.

NOTES*

1. Jackson, Robert H., The federal prosecutor. *Journal of American Judicature Society 24:* 18, 19 (1940).
2. Ibid.
3. See Goldstein, Abraham S., and Marcus, Martin, The myth of judicial supervision in three "inquisitorial" systems: France, Italy and Germany. *Yale Law Journal 87:* 240 (December 1977); Davis, Kenneth, *Discretionary Justice in Europe and America* Urbana, Ill. (1976).
4. In the nineteenth century, the grand jury played a truly independent role — investigating political corruption and setting itself apart from the prosecutor. There are a number of reported cases in which the grand jury would exclude the prosecutor from their operations. But in this century that independence has disappeared. The legal rules became more complex and beyond the scope of the most lay grand jurors. A prosecutor can assert his point of view because of his superior knowledge of the law. In addition, grand jurors were more selectively chosen and came to reflect the law-and-order position of the prosecutor. In general, the population has simply become more pliant when dealing with persons in authority.
5. Moses v. Kennedy, 219 F. Supp. 762 (D.D.C. 1963).

6. *Inmates of Attica v. Rockefeller*, 477 F.2d 375 (2d Cir. 1973). In the summer of 1977, a group representing "battered wives" brought an action against New York City police personnel and Family Court personnel for refusing to apply the criminal law against husbands who beat up their wives. A New York Supreme Court Justice stated that "this court has the power to compel the Police Department defendants to perform the duty imposed upon them by law to exercise their discretion, and to exercise it in a reasonable, non-arbitrary manner" [Bruno v. Codd, 46 L.W. 2042 (N.Y. Sup. Ct. July 6, 1977)]. No prosecutors were involved in the case since the police rarely made arrests that could lead to prosecution.
7. NAACP v. Levi, 418 F. Supp. 1109 (D.D.C. 1976).
8. See Friedman, Leon, Political power and legal legitimacy: A short history of political trials, *Antioch Review 30:* 157 (Summer 1970).
9. Mitford, Jessica, *The Trial of Dr. Spock* (New York, 1969).
10. United States v. Crowthers, 456 F.2d 1074 (4th Cir. 1971).
11. United States v. Steele, 461 F.2d 1148, 1152 (9th Cir. 1972).

*Footnotes have been abridged, edited, and renumbered.

8.   SANTOBELLO V. NEW YORK

The Supreme Court on Prosecutorial Discretion and Plea Bargaining: *Santobello v. New York, Blackledge v. Allison*, and *Bordenkircher v. Hayes*.

■ Plea bargaining has been the focus of considerable criticism by legal scholars and practitioners alike. It would be erroneous to presume, however, that plea bargaining is without its supporters. While it would be obvious to identify prosecutors as one source of support, it might be less apparent that courts have also condoned its existence, although more often than not in a tacit rather than explicit manner. The *Santobello, Blackledge* and *Bordenkircher* decisions, decided by the United States Supreme Court in 1971, 1977 and 1978 respectively, suggest some of the parameters that have been imposed upon prosecutorial discretion. While these decisions, particularly *Santobello* and *Bordenkircher*, support plea bargaining, it is also clear that the Court will impose reasonable restraints upon prosecutorial decision-making. The facts of *Santobello* appear in the body of the case. In *Blackledge*, discussed in the text of *Bordenkircher*, the defendant had pleaded guilty to breaking and entering allegedly upon the understanding that the prosecutor would recommend, and that the judge would impose, a ten year sentence. The trial judge in fact imposed a sentence of 17–21 years. Bordenkircher had been indicted under a Kentucky statute for uttering a forged instrument. *Bordenkircher v. Hayes* raised the issue of whether a prosecutor can carry out a threat to indict a defendant who pleads not guilty on a charge more serious, in this instance mandatory life imprisonment under the Kentucky habitual offender law, than what would be imposed had the defendant cooperated with the prosecutor and had pleaded guilty. ■

WHEN A GUILTY PLEA rests in any significant degree on a promise or agreement of the prosecutor, so that it can be said to be part of inducement or consideration, such promise must be fulfilled. Fed.Rules Crim.Proc. rule 11, 18 U.S.C.A.

Mr. Chief Justice BURGER delivered the opinion of the Court.

We granted certiorari in this case* to determine whether the State's failure to keep a

*35 A.D. 2d 1084, 316 N.Y.S. 2d 194.

commitment concerning the sentence recommendation on a guilty plea required a new trial.

The facts are not in dispute. The State of New York indicted petitioner in 1969 on two felony counts, Promoting Gambling in the First Degree, and Possession of Gambling Records in the First Degree, N. Y. Penal Law, McKinney's Consol. Laws, c. 40, §§ 225.10, 225.20. Petitioner first entered a plea of not guilty to both counts. After negotiations, the Assistant District Attorney in charge of the case agreed to permit petitioner to plead guilty to a lesser-included offense, Possession of Gambling Records in the Second Degree, N. Y. Penal Law § 225.15, conviction of which would carry a maximum prison sentence of one year. The prosecutor agreed to make no recommendation as to the sentence.

On June 16, 1969, petitioner accordingly withdrew his plea of not guilty and entered a plea of guilty to the lesser charge. Petitioner represented to the sentencing judge that the plea was voluntary and that the facts of the case, as described by the Assistant District Attorney, were true. The court accepted the plea and set a date for sentencing. A series of delays followed, owing primarily to the absence of a pre-sentence report, so that by September 23, 1969, petitioner had still not been sentenced. By that date petitioner acquired new defense counsel.

Petitioner's new counsel moved immediately to withdraw the guilty plea. In an accompanying affidavit, petitioner alleged that he did not know at the time of his plea that crucial evidence against him had been obtained as a result of an illegal search. The accuracy of this affidavit is subject to challenge since petitioner had filed and withdrawn a motion to suppress, before pleading guilty. In addition to his motion to withdraw his guilty plea, petitioner renewed the motion to suppress and filed a motion to inspect the grand jury minutes.

These three motions in turn caused further delay until November 26, 1969, when the court denied all three and set January 9, 1970, as the date for sentencing. On January 9 petitioner appeared before a different judge, the judge who had presided over the case to this juncture having retired. Petitioner renewed his motions, and the court again rejected them. The court then turned to consideration of the sentence.

At this appearance, another prosecutor had replaced the prosecutor who had negotiated the plea. The new prosecutor recommended the maximum one-year sentence. In making this recommendation, he cited petitioner's criminal record and alleged links with organized crime. Defense counsel immediately objected on the ground that the State had promised petitioner before the plea was entered that there would be no sentence recommendation by the prosecution. He sought to adjourn the sentence hearing in order to have time to prepare proof of the first prosecutor's promise. The second prosecutor, apparently ignorant of his colleague's commitment, argued that there was nothing in the record to support petitioner's claim of a promise, but the State, in subsequent proceedings, has not contested that such a promise was made.

The sentencing judge ended discussion, with the following statement, quoting extensively from the pre-sentence report:

"Mr. Aronstein [Defense Counsel], I am not at all influenced by what the District Attorney says, so that there is no need to adjourn the sentence, and there is no need to have any testimony. It doesn't make a particle of difference what the District Attorney says he will do, or what he doesn't do.

"I have here, Mr. Aronstein, a probation report. I have here a history of a long, long serious criminal record. I have here a picture of the life history of this man. . . .

" 'He is unamenable to supervision in the community. He is a professional criminal.' This is in quotes. 'And a recidivist. Institutionalization —'; that means, in plain language, just putting him away, 'is the only means of halting his anti-social activities,' and protecting you, your family, me, my family, protecting society. 'Institutionalization.' Plain language, put him behind bars.

"Under the plea, I can only send him to the New York City Correctional Institution for men for one year, which I am hereby doing."

The judge then imposed the maximum sentence of one year.

This record represents another example of an unfortunate lapse in orderly prosecutorial procedures, in part, no doubt, because of the enormous increase in the workload of the often understaffed prosecutor's offices. The heavy workload may well explain these episodes, but it does not excuse them. The disposition of criminal charges by agreement between the prosecutor and the accused, sometimes loosely called "plea bargaining," is an essential component of the administration of justice. Properly administered, it is to be encouraged. If every criminal charge were subjected to a full-scale trial, the States and the Federal Government would need to multiply by many times the number of judges and court facilities.

Disposition of charges after plea discussions is not an essential part of the process but a highly desirable part for many reasons. It leads to prompt and largely final disposition of most criminal cases; it avoids much of the corrosive impact of enforced idleness during pre-trial confinement for those who are denied release pending trial; it protects the public from those accused persons who are prone to continue criminal conduct even while on pretrial release; and, by shortening the time between charge and disposition, it enhances whatever may be the rehabilitative prospects of the guilty when they are ultimately imprisoned.

[1–4] However, all of these considerations presuppose fairness in securing agreement between an accused and a prosecutor. It is now clear, for example, that the accused pleading guilty must be counseled, absent a waiver. Fed.Rule Crim. Proc. 11, governing pleas in federal courts, now makes clear that the sentencing judge must develop, *on the record*, the factual basis for the plea, as, for example, by having the accused describe the conduct that gave rise to the charge.[1] The plea must, of course, be voluntary and knowing and if it was induced by promises, the essence of those promises must in some way be made known. There is, of course, no absolute right to have a guilty plea accepted. A court may reject a plea in exercise of sound judicial discretion.

[5] This phase of the process of criminal justice, and the adjudicative element inherent in accepting a plea of guilty, must be attended by safeguards to insure the defendant what is reasonably due in the circumstances. Those circumstances will vary, but a constant factor is that when a plea rests in any significant degree on a promise or agreement of the prosecutor, so that it can be said to be part of the inducement or consideration, such promise must be fulfilled.

[6] On this record, petitioner "bargained" and negotiated for a particular plea in order to secure dismissal of more serious charges, but also on condition that no sentence recommendation would be made by the prosecutor. It is now conceded that the promise to abstain from a recommendation was made, and at this stage the prosecution is not in a good position to argue that its inadvertent breach of agreement is immaterial. The staff lawyers in a prosecutor's office have the burden of "letting the left hand know what the right hand is doing" or has done. That the breach of agreement was inadvertent does not lessen its impact.

[7] We need not reach the question whether the sentencing judge would or would not have been influenced had he known all the details of the negotiations for the plea. He stated that the prosecutor's recommendation did not influence him and we have no reason to doubt that. Nevertheless, we conclude that the interests of justice and appropriate recognition of the duties of the prosecution in relation to promises made in the negotiation of pleas of guilty will be best served by remanding the case to the state courts for further consideration. The ultimate relief to which petitioner is entitled we leave to the discretion of the state court, which is in a better position to decide whether the circumstances of this case require only that there be specific performance of the agreement on the plea, in which case petitioner should be resentenced by a different judge, or whether, in the view of the state court, the circumstances require grant-ing the relief sought by petitioner, *i. e.*, the opportunity to withdraw his plea of guilty.[2] We emphasize that this is in no sense to question the fairness of the sentencing judge; the fault here rests on the prosecutor, not on the sentencing judge.

The judgement is vacated and the case is remanded for reconsideration not inconsistent with this opinion.

Mr. Justice DOUGLAS, concurring.

I join the opinion of the Court and add only a word. I agree both with The Chief Justice and with Mr. Justice MARSHALL that New York did not keep its "plea bargain" with petitioner and that it is no excuse for the default merely because a member of the prosecutor's staff who was not a party to the "plea bargain" was in charge of the case when it came before the New York court. The staff of the prosecution is a unit and each member must be presumed to know the commitments made by any other member. If responsibility could be evaded that way, the prosecution would have designed another deceptive "contrivance.". . .

These "plea bargains" are important in the administration of justice both at the state[3] and at the federal[4] levels and, as the Chief Justice says, they serve an important role in disposition of today's heavy calendars. . . .

I join the opinion of the Court and favor a constitutional rule for this as well as for other pending or oncoming cases. Where the "plea bargain" is not kept by the prosecutor, the sentence must be vacated and the state court will decide in light of the circumstances of each case whether due process requires (a) that there be specific performance of the plea bargain or (b) that the defendant be given the option to go to trial on the original charges. One alternative may do justice in one case, and the other in a different case. In choosing a remedy, however, a court ought to accord a defendant's preference considerable, if not controlling weight inasmuch as the fundamental rights flouted by a prosecutor's breach of a plea bargain are those of the defendant, not of the State.

NOTES*

1. Fed.Rule Crim. Proc. 11 provides:

   "A defendant may plead not guilty, guilty or, with the consent of the court, *nolo contendere*. The court may refuse to accept a plea of guilty, and shall not accept such plea or a plea of *nolo contendere* without first addressing the defendant personally and determining that the plea is made voluntarily with understanding of the nature of the charge and the consequences of the plea. If a defendant refuses to plead or if the court refuses to accept a plea of guilty or if a defendant corporation fails to appear, the court shall enter a plea of not guilty. The court shall not enter a judgment upon a plea of guilty unless it is satisfied that there is a factual basis for the plea."

2. If the state court decides to allow withdrawal of the plea, the petitioner will, of course, plead anew to the original charge on two felony counts.

3. In 1964, guilty pleas accounted for 95.5% of all criminal convictions in trial courts of general jurisdiction in New York. In 1965, the figure for California was 74.0%. *President's Commission on Law Enforcement and Administration of Justice, Task Force Report: The Courts* 9 (1967).

4. In 1964, guilty pleas accounted for 90.2% of all criminal convictions in United States district courts. *Ibid.*

*This decision has been abridged, footnotes edited and renumbered, and citations omitted.

9. BORDENKIRCHER V. HAYES

434 U.S. 357; 98 S.Ct. 663, (1978).

III

[1, 2] WE HAVE RECENTLY had occasion to observe: "[W]hatever might be the situation in an ideal world, the fact is that the guilty plea and the often concomitant plea bargain are important components of this country's criminal justice system. Properly administered, they can benefit all concerned." *Blackledge v. Allison*, 431 U.S. 63. The open acknowledgment of this previously clandestine practice has led this Court to recognize the importance of counsel during plea negotiations, *Brady v. United States*, 397 U.S. 742, the need for a public record indicating that a plea was knowingly and voluntarily made, *Boykin v. Alabama*, 395 U.S. 238, and the requirement that a prosecutor's plea-bargaining promise must be kept, *Santobello v. New York*, 404 U.S. 257. The decision of the Court of Appeals in the present case, however, did not deal with considerations such as these, but held that the substance of the plea offer itself violated the limitations imposed by the Due Process Clause of the Fourteenth Amendment. Cf. *Brady v. United States, supra*, 397 U.S., at 751 n. 8. For the reasons that follow, we have concluded that the Court of Appeals was mistaken in so ruling.

IV

This Court held in *North Carolina v. Pearce*, 395 U.S. 711, that the Due Process Clause of the Fourteenth Amendment "requires that vindictiveness against a defendant for having successfully attacked his first conviction must play no part in the sentence he receives after a new trial." The same principle was later applied to prohibit a prosecutor from reindicting a convicted misdemeanant on a felony charge after the defendant had invoked an appellate remedy, since in this situation there was also a "realistic likelihood of 'vindictiveness.' " *Blackledge v. Perry*, 417 U.S., at 27.

In those cases the Court was dealing with the State's unilateral imposition of a penalty upon a defendant who had chosen to exercise a legal right to attack his original conviction — a situation "very different from the give-and-take negotiation common in plea bargaining between the prosecution and defense, which arguably possess relatively equal bargaining power." *Parker v. North Carolina*, 397 U.S. 790 (opinion of Brennan, J.). The Court has emphasized that the due process violation in cases such as *Pearce* and *Perry* lay not in the possibility that a defendant might be deterred from the exercise of a legal right, see *Colten v. Kentucky*, 407 U.S. 104; *Chaffin v. Stynchcombe*, 412 U.S. 17, but rather in the danger that the State might be retaliating against the accused for lawfully attacking his conviction. See *Blackledge v. Perry, supra*, 417 U.S., at 26–28.

[3] To punish a person because he has done what the law plainly allows him to do is a due process violation of the most basic sort, see *North Carolina v. Pearce, supra*, 395 U.S., at 738 (opinion of Black, J.), and for an agent of the State to pursue a course of action whose objective is to penalize a person's reliance on his legal rights is "patently unconstitutional." *Chaffin v. Stynchcombe, supra*, 412 U.S., at 32–33, n. 20. See *United States v. Jackson*, 390 U.S. 570. But in the "give-and-take" of plea bargaining, there is no such element of punishment or retaliation so long as the accused is free to accept or reject the prosecution's offer.

[4] Plea bargaining flows from "the mutuality of advantage" to defendants and prosecutors, each with his own reasons for wanting to avoid trial. *Brady v. United States, supra*, 397 U.S., at 752. Defendants advised by competent counsel and protected by other procedural safeguards are presumptively capable of intelligent choice in response to prosecutorial persuasion, and unlikely to be driven to false self-condemnation. 397 U.S., at 758. Indeed, acceptance of the basic legitimacy of plea bargaining necessarily implies rejection of any notion that a guilty plea is involuntary in a

constitutional sense simply because it is the end result of the bargaining process. By hypothesis, the plea may have been induced by promises of a recommendation of a lenient sentence or a reduction of charges, and thus by fear of the possibility of a greater penalty upon conviction after a trial. See ABA Project on Standards for Criminal Justice, Pleas of Guilty § 3.1 (App. Draft 1968); Note, Plea Bargaining and the Transformation of the Criminal Process, 90 Harv. L. Rev. 564 (1977). Cf. *Brady v. United States, supra*, at 751; *North Carolina v. Alford*, 400 U.S. 25.

[5] While confronting a defendant with the risk of more severe punishment clearly may have a "discouraging effect on the defendant's assertion of his trial rights, the imposition of these difficult choices [is] an inevitable" — and permissible — "attribute of any legitimate system which tolerates and encourages the negotiation of pleas." *Chaffin v. Stynchcombe, supra*, 412 U.S., at 31. It follows that, by tolerating and encouraging the negotiation of pleas, this Court has necessarily accepted as constitutionally legitimate the simple reality that the prosecutor's interest at the bargaining table is to persuade the defendant to forgo his right to plead not guilty.

[6–11] It is not disputed here that Hayes was properly chargeable under the recidivist statute, since he had in fact been convicted of two previous felonies. In our system, so long as the prosecutor has probable cause to believe that the accused committed an offense defined by statute, the decision whether or not to prosecute, and what charge to file or bring before a grand jury, generally rests entirely in his discretion.[8] Within the limits set by the legislature's constitutionally valid definition of chargeable offenses, "the conscious exercise of some selectivity in enforcement is not in itself a federal constitutional violation" so long as "the selection was [not] deliberately based upon an unjustifiable standard such as race, religion, or other arbitrary classification." *Oyler v. Boles*, 368 U.S. 448. To hold that the prosecutor's desire to induce a guilty plea is an "unjustifiable standard," which, like race or religion, may play no part in his charging decision, would contradict the very premises that underlie the concept of plea bargaining itself. Moreover, a rigid constitutional rule that would prohibit a prosecutor from acting forth-rightly in his dealings with the defense could only invite unhealthy subterfuge that would drive the practice of plea bargaining back into the shadows from which it has so recently emerged. See *Blackledge v. Allison*, 431 U.S., at 76.

There is no doubt that the breadth of discretion that our country's legal system vests in prosecuting attorneys carries with it the potential for both individual and institutional abuse. And broad though that discretion may be, there are undoubtedly constitutional limits upon its exercise. We hold only that the course of conduct engaged in by the prosecutor in this case, which no more than openly presented the defendant with the unpleasant alternatives of forgoing trial or facing charges on which he was plainly subject to prosecution, did not violate the Due Process Clause of the Fourteenth Amendment.

Accordingly, the judgment of the court of Appeals is

Reversed.

Mr. Justice POWELL, dissenting.

The plea-bargaining process, as recognized by this Court, is essential to the functioning of the criminal-justice system. It normally affords genuine benefits to defendants as well as to society. And if the system is to work effectively, prosecutors must be accorded the widest discretion, within constitutional limits, in conducting bargaining. This is especially true when a defendant is represented by counsel and presumably is fully advised of his rights. Only in the most exceptional case should a court conclude that the scales of the bargaining are so unevenly balanced as to arouse suspicion. In this case, the prosecutor's actions denied respondent due process because their admitted purpose was to discourage and then to penalize with unique severity his exercise of constitutional rights. Implementation of a strategy calculated solely to deter the exercise of constitutional rights is not a constitutionally permissible exercise of discretion.

---

*This decision has been abridged, footnotes have been omitted and citations edited.

10. CONFINING, STRUCTURING, AND CHECKING PROSECUTING POWER

KENNETH CULP DAVIS

From DISCRETIONARY JUSTICE, © 1971 by the University of Illinois Press. Reprinted by permission.

■ Professor Davis has long been an advocate of checking discretionary power in administrative rule-making. In this selection, he discusses some of the broad assumptions that are often imposed upon analyses of prosecutorial decision-making. Using examples of structured prosecutorial power, one from West Germany, the other from a limited American context (the National Labor Relations Board), Davis argues that checking prosecutorial discretion is neither impossible to achieve nor alien to the American system of justice. His question, "if *some* abuses of *some* prosecutors are reviewable in some courts, why should not *all* abuses of *all* prosecutors be reviewable in some court?" by its very simplicity, deserves an answer. ■

MUST THE PROSECUTOR'S DISCRETIONARY POWER BE UNCONTROLLED?

VIEWED IN BROAD perspective, the American legal system seems to be shot through with many excessive and uncontrolled discretionary powers but the one that stands out above all others is the power to prosecute or not prosecute. The affirmative power to prosecute is enormous, but the negative power to withhold prosecution may be even greater, because it is less protected against abuse.

The prosecuting power is not limited to those who are called prosecutors; to an extent that varies in different localities the prosecuting power may be exercised by the police, and a goodly portion of it is exercised by regulatory agencies, licensing agencies, and other agencies and officers. The prosecuting power is not limited to the criminal law; it extends as far as law enforcement extends, including initiation of proceedings for license suspension or revocation, and even to enforcement of such provisions as those requiring that rates or charges be reasonable.

Even though the many prosecuting powers at all levels of government obviously vary widely in the extent and manner of confining, structuring, and checking, the major outlines are almost always governed by a single set of universally accepted assumptions. The principal assumptions are that the prosecuting power must of course be discretionary, that statutory provisions as to what enforcement officers "shall" do may be freely violated without disapproval from the public or from other officials, that determinations to prosecute or not to prosecute may be made secretly without any statement of findings or reasons, that such decisions by a top prosecutor of a city or county or state usually need not be reviewable by any other administrative authority, and that decisions to prosecute or not to prosecute are not judicially reviewable for abuse of discretion.

Why these various assumptions are made is not easy to discover; the best short answer seems to be that no one has done any systematic thinking to produce the assumptions, but that the customs about prosecuting, like most other customs, are the product of unplanned evolution. Whatever caused the assumptions to grow as they did, prosecutors usually assert that everybody knows that they are necessary.

But I wonder: Why should a prosecutor — say, a county prosecutor — have discretionary power to decide not to prosecute even when the evidence of guilt is clear, perhaps partly on the basis of political influence, without ever having to state to anyone what evidence was brought to light by his investigation and without having to explain to anyone why he interprets a statute as he does or why he chooses a particular position on a difficult question of policy? Why should the discretionary power be so unconfined that, of half a dozen potential defendants he can prove guilty, he can select any one for prosecution and let the other five go, making his decision, if he chooses, on the basis of considerations extraneous to justice? If he finds that A and B are equally guilty of felony and equally deserving of prosecution, why should he be permitted to prosecute B for felony but to let A off with a plea of guilty to a misdemeanor, unless he has a rational and legal basis for his choice, stated on an open record? Why should the vital decisions he makes be immune to review by other officials and immune to review by the courts, even though our legal and governmental system elsewhere generally assumes the need for checking human frailities? Why should he have a complete power to decide that one statute duly enacted by the people's representatives shall not be enforced at all, that another statute will be fully enforced, and that a third will be enforced only if, as, and when he thinks that it should be enforced in a particular case? Even if we assume that a prosecutor has to have a power of selective enforcement, why do we not require him to state publicly his general policies and require him to follow those policies in individual cases in order to protect evenhanded justice? Why not subject prosecutors' decisions to a simple and general requirement of open findings, open reasons, and open precedents, except when special reason for confidentiality exists? Why not strive to protect prosecutor's decisions from political or other ulterior influence in the same way we strive to protect judges' decisions?

The unthinking answer to such questions as these is that the prosecutor's function is merely to do the preliminary screening and to present the cases, and that the decisions that count are made on the basis of the trial. But public accusation and trial often leave scars which are not removed by proof of innocence. Mr. Justice Jackson was talking realism when he said, as Attorney General:

The prosecutor has more control over life, liberty, and reputation than any other person in America. His discretion is tremendous. He can have citizens investigated and, if he is that kind of person, he can have this done to the tune of public state-

ments and veiled and unveiled intimations. Or the prosecutor may choose a more subtle course and simply have a citizen's friends interviewed. . . . He may dismiss the case before trial, in which case the defense never has a chance to be heard. . . . If the prosecutor is obliged to choose his cases, it follows that he can choose his defendants. . . . [A] prosecutor stands a fair chance of finding at least a technical violation of some act on the part of almost anyone. . . . It is in this realm — in which the prosecutor picks some person whom he dislikes or desires to embarrass, or selects some group of unpopular persons and then looks for an offense, that the greatest danger of abuse of prosecuting power lies. It is here that law enforcement becomes personal. . . .[1]

Mr. Justice Jackson was discussing what a prosecutor does affirmatively; the damage done by public accusation may be permanent even when innocence is proved in a later proceeding. What a prosecutor does negatively is almost always final and even less protected — withholding prosecution, nol pros of a case, acceptance of a plea of guilty to a lesser offense — even when such decisions are irrational or improperly motivated and even when the result is unjust discrimination against those who are not similarly favored. The notion that the tribunal that holds the trial corrects abuses of the prosecuting power is obviously without merit.[2]

Nor will the other usual justification for uncontrolled discretionary power of prosecutors stand analysis — that the intrinsic nature of the prosecuting function is such that the only workable system is uncontrolled discretion. True, the habit of assuming that *of course* the prosecutor's discretion must be uncontrolled is so deeply embedded that the usual implied response to questions as to whether the prosecuting power can be confined or structured or checked is that the questioner must be totally without understanding. Inability of those who are responsible for administering the system to answer the most elementary questions as to the reasons behind the system is itself a reason to reexamine.

Lawyers all over the continent of Europe know that a prosecuting system can be viable without uncontrolled discretion. A quick look at a prosecuting system in one such country will show that the basic assumptions Americans have long made about the prosecuting power are not the only possible ones.

THE PROSECUTING SYSTEM IN WEST GERMANY

Some knowledge of continental attitudes about the prosecuting power is useful, not because those attitudes should be transplanted to America, but because Americans need to realize that the assumptions on which our system is built are not inevitable.

Alexander Pekelis, who, with a European background, examined in depth both European and American legal institutions, observed that:

. . . under the American system criminal prosecution is simply a right and never a duty of the federal or state attorney. Its exercise is wholly within the discretion of the prosecuting officers and the grand jury. In Italy . . . prosecution [is] a duty of the attorney general; in France and in Germany the prosecuting agency had but a slight degree of discretion, and this pertained to minor offenses and was subject to review by the court. . . . Thus the practical administration of criminal justice [in the United States], at least in its negative aspect, becomes an administrative rather than a judicial activity. . . . In brief, then, comparative investigations thus far seem to reveal that in the administration of justice the common-law countries have traditionally relied upon a wide exercise of discretionary power to an incomparably greater extent than any civil-law country in Europe.[3]

Although no two continental systems of prosecuting are the same, all stand in contrast with the Anglo-American systems in the fundamental attitude about discretionary power of prosecutors. The continental countries seem in general to reflect the Pekelis background remark that "the European Rechtsstaat was planned and organized with the very purpose of reducing the human element in the administration of justice to its imaginable minimum. . . . The less discretion, the more justice."[4] British and American attitudes seem the opposite: Uncontrolled discretionary power of prosecutors is simply assumed.

American assumptions that a prosecutor must in the nature of things have a broad and largely uncontrolled discretionary power run so deep that I have found extreme skepticism on the part of any Americans to whom I have tried to explain the European attitudes about prosecuting. The almost universal reaction is along this line: "The prosecuting power intrinsically involves broad discretion because (1) in the nature of things all law can't be enforced, (2) the prosecutor has to interpret uncertain statutory provisions, and (3) the prosecutor has to exercise discretion in deciding whether the evidence is sufficient." But the plain fact is that viable systems exist in which prosecutors have almost no discretionary power. Let us look more closely at one of them, that of West Germany.

Like the realities of the American prosecuting power, the realities of the German prosecuting power are beyond the statutes and the published reports of cases. The crucial element is the customary practices of prosecutors. To get the facts, I have sought help from five informants, all of whom have a German legal education and experience in the German system, and two of whom have had experience in prosecuting German cases: A distinguished legal scholar in comparative law who has worked in America since 1933,[5] a judge of the Supreme Administrative Court,[6] a young legal scholar in a German university who has taught as a visiting professor in two American law schools,[7] and two younger legal scholars who have come to America from Germany.[8] In the facts I am about to relate, the five are unanimous; omitted from my description is one facet about which they are not unanimous.

A German lawyer who is asked whether or not a German prosecutor has discretionary power is likely instinctively to say no. This is because students in German law schools are taught that prosecutors do not have discretionary power. The practice for the most part conforms to the theory that is taught, although some deviations from the theory can be found.

The American will immediately ask: "How on earth can a prosecutor interpret vague or ambiguous statutes and pass upon sufficiency of evidence without exercising discretionary power?" The German answer to that question is one that deserves to be understood by Americans. A crucial part of the answer is that some of the discretion exercised by American prosecutors is exercised by German judges.

The most important difference between the German system and the American system is this: *Whenever the evidence that the defendant has committed a serious crime*[9] *is reasonably clear and the law is not in doubt, the German prosecutor, unlike the American prosecutor, is without discretionary power to withhold prosecution. This means that selective enforcement, a major feature of the American system, is almost wholly absent from the German system.* The German prosecutor does not withhold prosecution for such reasons as that he thinks the statute overreaches, that justice requires withholding enforcement because of special circumstances, that the statute ought to be enforced against some violators and not others, that he lacks time for bringing a marginal prosecution, or that he finds political advantage in not prosecuting. Hence, the German prosecutor never has discretionary power to engage in plea bargaining.

The German and American systems also differ when the evidence or the law or both seem to the prosecutor to be doubtful. When a doubt seems to require a discretionary choice, the German prosecutor does not resolve the doubt; he almost always presents a doubtful case to the judge, who determines the sufficiency of the evidence and the proper interpretation of the law. Of course, in America the prosecutor makes a discretionary determination in every doubtful case, either to prosecute or not to prosecute.

Even when the prosecutor finds prosecution of a suspect clearly inappropriate, the German system, unlike the American system, provides protection against abuse of power. When a crime is reported by the police or by a private party, a file is opened and registered; the file can be traced at any time. A German prosecutor can never simply forget about the case as his American counterpart may do. The file cannot be closed without a statement of written reasons, which in important cases must be approved by the prosecutor's superior, and which must be reported to any victim of the crime and to any suspect who was interrogated. Every prosecutor is supervised by a superior in a hierarchical system headed by the Minister of Justice, who is himself responsible to the cabinet. The supervision is real, not merely a threat; files are in fact often reviewed. Availability to victims of crimes of procedure to compel prosecution constitutes still another check.

Departures from the theory that prosecutors lack discretionary power in Germany are few and slight. Determining whether to make an investigation of a suspect, or whether to investigate further, or whether innocence is so clear that the case should not be presented to the judge may involve some element of discretion. And a little play in the joints is probably inevitable. One of my German informants has the impression, for instance, that the statute against homosexual practices is not fully enforced in Hamburg, but he thinks that the method of withholding prosecution is usually by finding the evidence insufficient; if his impression is correct, some discretionary power even about policy may in fact be exercised. During the Weimar Republic, the Minister of Justice, with Cabinet approval but in violation of the statutes, openly refused to prosecute for certain political crimes. Although a statute makes it a crime not only to perform an abortion but for a woman to have one performed, women are seldom prosecuted for having abortions performed. But these examples of deviations from the theory are highly exceptional. With respect to the great bulk of crimes, the German prosecutor ordinarily has no power of selective enforcement. In this he stands in contrast with his American counterpart, who, with respect to the great bulk of crimes, ordinarily has a power of selective enforcement.

CRIMINAL PROSECUTIONS

In exercising their enormous discretionary power, prosecutors in criminal cases can make an ad hoc decision of every question, or they can in any degree confine and structure their discretionary power; they can also provide checks and procedural protections. The law seems to be that prosecutors may, if they choose, do nothing in the direction of confining or structuring or checking or providing procedural protections. The prevailing habit seems to be to do little or nothing more than the law requires. And the community seems to be largely indifferent to the uncontrolled discretion. Even so, I think major studies should be made to discover how far the uncontrolled discretion can and should be brought under control.

Because the power to bring criminal prosecutions is too multifarious to look at all of it at once, and because the problems of finding the degree of control of discretion are often difficult and often interlocked with considerations of substantive policy, the nature of some of the problems of moving from uncontrolled discretion toward controlled discretion will be suggested through a series of illustrative questions about prosecution of federal tax fraud.[10]

If an embezzler is convicted and sentenced, in what circumstances should he be prosecuted for not reporting income from his embezzlement? Should a general policy be stated as to whether and when two prosecutions will be brought for a criminal act which yields unreported income, or should each case be dealt with on an ad hoc basis? What should the prosecuting policy be for tax cheating involving less than ten dollars, less than a hundred dollars, less than a thousand dollars? Should internal rules try to keep the policy consistent? Should any of the rules be announced? Should some classes of falsity which have a large impact on the revenue, such as false dependency claims, be more frequently prosecuted than other classes of falsity, and should such prosecutions be more widely publicized? What should the policy be about settling or compromising criminal tax cases, should the policy be kept consistent through detailed guides for enforcement officers, or should decisions be made by subordinate officers on an ad hoc basis? If detailed guides are used, should they be announced? Should dismissal of felony charges be exchanged for pleas of guilty to misdemeanors, should the policy be clear and consistent, and should it be announced? Should a taxpayer's voluntary disclosure of his fraud be rewarded by less aggressive prosecution; if so, what should the reward be, and should a consistent policy be announced? Should payment of the full tax have some effect upon the prosecutors' choices; if so, what effect, and should a consistent policy be announced? Should the prosecutors follow a set of consistent policies about making recommendations to the court about sentencing, and should the poli-

cies be announced? Should promises of immunity be given in return for disclosures of information that may be valuable to the prosecutors, and should the policy about such promises be clarified and announced? What other kinds of cooperation by alleged tax evaders with enforcement officers should be rewarded, what should the rewards be, in what degree should the policies be clarified, and should they be announced? What should be the policy about prosecuting one who is critically ill and whose death may be caused or hastened by a prosecution; should the policy be clarified and announced?

As for structuring, when a position is taken on a question of policy or law in deciding whether or not to prosecute, should the facts be summarized and a reasoned opinion written? Should the accumulation of such findings and opinions be regarded as a body of precedents to guide decisions in other cases, subject to the usual processes of distinguishing or occasionally overruling? Should all the materials be open to public inspection, except when confidentiality is essential, so that the exercise of discretion by the prosecutors will reflect the potentiality of criticism?

As for procedural safeguards, should the underlying policy be to avoid serious damage to any party through either investigation or prosecution until he has had a chance to know the main charge against him and to confer with a deciding officer about it? For instance, if a practicing lawyer is likely to be adversely affected if tax officials systematically interview his clients to ascertain whether he is guilty of tax fraud, should he have opportunity for a conference about the question before the investigation is instituted? If the taxpayer's status or activity is such that institution of a prosecution, even if followed immediately by a finding of not guilty, may cause great harm, should the opportunity for an advance conference be allowed? Should procedural rules governing opportunity for such a conference be announced?

Whenever sensitivity to publicity is an especially important factor, should the court provide by procedural rule for a motion by the defendant for a closed hearing, and should such a motion be granted whenever significant harm to the defendant would remain after a finding of not guilty?

As for checking discretion, whenever investigation or prosecution may cause special harm to an individual, should subordinates' decisions to take action require approval by top officers, and when top officers are the initial actors, should they always make their decisions known to their staffs, with invitations to criticize? Should courts enlarge the area of judicial review of prosecutors' decisions for abuse of discretion?

These questions are only illustrative of the types of questions that need to be considered, just as tax fraud is only illustrative of the many kinds of prosecutions for crime. A thorough inquiry might locate ten or twenty times as many significant questions. My opinion is emphatic that such an inquiry is long overdue — that the assumptions on which prosecutors' uncontrolled discretion is founded are in need of reexamination. I am also inclined to believe — but I leave the question open — that a full study of the prosecuting power is likely to produce movement in the direction of greater control of discretion, through more confinement, more structuring, more checks, and more procedural protections. The specific answers here depend upon complex considerations that can be weighed only through studies far more extensive and intensive than the present preliminary inquiry. . . .

AN EXAMPLE OF A PROSECUTOR'S DISCRETION THAT IS FULLY STRUCTURED

One prosecutor in the United States — only one, so far as I have found — uses a system of fully structured discretion. That such a system not only exists but succeeds may be enough to prove that the idea of structuring the prosecuting power is something more than an academician's dream. The system is in full bloom not merely on the European continent but in a federal regulatory agency. The agency is the National Labor Relations Board, and the prosecutor is the Board's General Counsel. The system is very instructive.

The General Counsel's organization operates in Washington and in thirty-one regional offices. Charges are filed with regional directors, who assign them to field investigators. Most charges are of course disposed of by voluntary action — either agreement by the respondent, or withdrawal of the charge. When a charge is not disposed of by consent, the regional director and his staff either issue a complaint or refuse to do so. If a complaint is issued, the case goes to hearing and all the protections of a trial come into play. It is when a complaint is refused that the interesting and significant protections are afforded: The charging party is then entitled to (1) a statement of findings and reasons, (2) a decision which is fitted into the precedents and which itself becomes a precedent, and (3) a right to take an appeal to officers in Washington who are wholly independent of the officers in the regional office.

The disappointed charging party, as soon as he receives a written explanation for the refusal of the regional office to issue a complaint, may take his case to the Office of Appeals in the Washington office of the General Counsel. The seven supervisors and twenty attorneys in the Office of Appeals handled 1,350 cases in one recent year. An appeal goes first to an attorney who prepares a memorandum stating facts, issues, and recommendations. A supervisor works over the memorandum, and it then goes to the Appeals Committee, which makes the decision, subject to approval by the General Counsel. Unless a complaint is issued, a charging party is entitled to a reasoned opinion by the Office of Appeals. Since many problems get no further in the board's machinery than the Office of Appeals, opinions of that office are the only available precedents on some questions. They are indexed and freely used within the office, along with similar opinions given by the Advice Branch of the General Counsel's office in response to requests from regional officers for guidance on questions of law and policy. From the advice and appeal opinions, the General Counsel's office compiles a "book of digests" for the guidance of the staff on issues about which the General Counsel's decisions constitute the only relevant law. The digests that are thought especially significant, growing out of advice and appeals, are selected for publication in the General Counsel's "Quarterly Report on Case Developments." A previous practice of publishing all appeals cases through the Bureau of National Affairs was discontinued for lack of sufficient demand. Requests for inspection of unpublished opinions are so rare that the Director of the Office of Appeals remembers none, and the policy is therefore unclarified as to whether they are open to public inspection.

Although the formal rules do not so provide, either the charging party or the charged party may confer (separately) with a representative of the Office of Appeals. This opportunity for hearing is undercut, however, by availability of the full investigatory file to the Office of Appeals but not the parties.

In view of the apparently unique success of the General Counsel in structuring his discretionary power to refuse to issue complaints, should he similarly structure his discretionary power to issue complaints? The argument for his doing so is that a trial is less than a complete protection against wrongful issuance of a complaint; the argument against his doing so is that appeals to the General Counsel from decisions of a regional office to issue a complaint might simply add to the onerous procedures than an innocent respondent must pursue before he is finally found not guilty. Perhaps the answer is that such appeals are desirable only in rare cases in which the impropriety of issuing the complaint can be quickly and conclusively shown. But that is permissible now, for 29 CFR § 102.33 authorizes the General Counsel to take control of any case at any time from a regional office, and a party in an appropriate case could surely request the General Counsel to exercise that authority.

The system of the NLRB General Counsel contains the major elements of a full structuring of discretionary power — findings, reasons, precedents, checks through appeals and through internal supervision, and procedural protections. The degree of openness may be adequate, as shown by lack of requests for unpublished opinions, but the lack of requests may be based on widespread assumption of lack of availability; the doubt could be removed by an announcement of availability of such opinions.

Altogether, the system of the NLRB General Counsel is deserving of admiration. It is surely worthy of study by other prosecutors.

ADMINISTRATIVE AND JUDICIAL CHECKING

The top prosecutors of federal, state, and local governments are typically subject to little or no checking either by higher officers or by reviewing courts, no matter how seriously they have abused their powers and no matter how flagrant the injustice. This typical system may be in need of reexamination.

Especially unfortunate, in my opinion, is the complete lack of supervision of the typical city or county prosecutor. He is usually an elected official, and the theory is that he is responsible to the electorate. The reality is that nearly all his decisions to prosecute or not to prosecute, nearly all of the influences brought to bear upon such decisions, and nearly all his reasons for decisions are carefully kept secret, so that review by the electorate is nonexistent except for the occasional case that happens to be publicized. The plain fact is that more than nine-tenths of local prosecutors' decisions are supervised or reviewed by no one.

The American Bar Association's Commission on Organized Crime and Law Enforcement reported in 1952: "Apart from intervention in emergency situations the local prosecutor is usually left severely alone by the attorney general or the governor. . . . By and large throughout the country, the attorney general of the various states is not an important factor in connection with the ordinary processes of criminal justice."[11] That remark was made twenty-two years after the American Bar Association had sponsored a Model Department of Justice Act, which would centralize the prosecuting authority in the state attorney general.[12] At least seven states have adopted the idea,[13] but complete lack of supervision of local prosecutors continues in most states. Even when the state attorney general has the power of supervision, the elected subordinate usually manages to maintain a large degree of independence. I think the question is raised whether the prevailing system of electing local prosecutors is inconsistent with a sound system of discretionary justice.

When the prosecuting power is in an independent regulatory agency, no other officer of the government can review either a decision to prosecute or a decision not to prosecute. The White House has some control through the power of appointment and reappointment, but that control may be more likely to contribute to uneven enforcement than to relief from it. Congress in creating independent agencies probably lacks power to reduce the President's explicit constitutional power to "take Care that the Laws be faithfully executed," but the President normally refrains from interfering with the prosecuting power of the independent agencies. The practical fact is that that power, though enormous, is unsupervised. A check by Congress or its committees is always a possibility, and the mere potentiality of such a check may have some effect, but legislative supervision of exercise of the prosecuting power is seldom, if ever, meaningful.

Judicial review of decisions to prosecute or not to prosecute is almost totally absent.[14] The law of the federal courts is well summarized in the 1967 opinion of the Court of Appeals for the District of Columbia. The defendant and A were indicted. Negotiations between A's counsel and an assistant United States attorney led to A's being allowed to plead guilty to misdemeanors, but the U.S. attorney declined to consent to the same plea for the defendant, who argued that he and A were equally guilty and that fairness required equal treatment. The court held that it could not review to determine whether the U.S. attorney had abused his discretion. The court reviewed the authorities and declared:

Few subjects are less adapted to judicial review than the exercise by the Executive of his discretion in deciding when and whether to institute criminal proceedings, or what precise charge shall be made, or whether to dismiss a proceeding once brought. . . . Two persons may have committed what is precisely the same legal offense but the prosecutor is not compelled by law, duty or tradition to treat them the same as to charges. . . . [N]o court has any jurisdiction to inquire into or review his decision. . . . [W]hile this discretion is subject to abuse or misuse just as is judicial discretion, deviations from his duty as an agent of the Executive are to be dealt with by his superiors. . . . [I]t is not the function of the judiciary to review the exercise of executive discretion whether it be that of the President himself or those to whom he has delegated certain of his powers.[15]

Although I agree that two persons who have committed the same offense need not be equally treated, because the treatment should depend upon factors in addition to the offense committed, everything else quoted from the court's opinion seems to me deeply unsound. Instead of saying that "few subjects are less adapted to judicial review" than prosecutors' discretion, I would say that few subjects are more adapted to judicial review than a protection against abuse. Instead of saying that "it is not the function of the judiciary to review the exercise of executive discretion," I could cite a hundred Supreme Court decisions stating that it is the function of the judiciary to review the exercise of executive discretion;[16] after all, under the Administrative Procedure Act judicial review of the exercise of executive discretion is the rule and unreviewability is the exception. The court's opinion seems to me completely empty of valid reasons. Yet the authorities discussed in the opinion unquestionably support the result.

One main reason that seems to actuate federal courts in holding that discretion of prosecutors may not be reviewed to protect against abuse has been stated by the Fifth Circuit in a 1965 opinion: ". . . it is as an officer of the executive department that he [the U.S. Attorney] exercises a discretion as to whether or not there shall be a prosecution in a particular case. It follows, as an incident of the constitutional separation of powers, that the courts are not to interfere with the free exercise of the discretionary powers of the attorneys of the United States in their control over criminal prosecutions."[17] This reason is so clearly unsound as to be almost absurd. If separation of powers prevents review of discretion of executive officers, then more than a hundred Supreme Court decisions spread over a century and three-quarters will have to be found contrary to the Constitution! If courts could not interfere with abuse of discretion by executive officers, our fundamental institutions would be altogether different from what they are. If the statement just quoted from the Fifth Circuit were true, the courts would be powerless to interfere when executive officers, acting illegally, are about to execute an innocent person!

The most convincing passage I have found in support of unreviewability of prosecutor's discretion to protect against abuse of power appears in a 1949 opinion:

He [the prosecutor] must appraise the evidence on which an indictment may be demanded and the accused defendant tried, if he be indicted, and in that service must judge of its availability, competency and probative significance. He must on occasion consider the public impact of criminal proceedings, or, again, balance the admonitory value of invariable and inflexible punishment against the greater impulse of the "quality of mercy." He must determine what offenses, and whom, to prosecute. . . . Into these and many others of the problems committed to his informed discretion it would be sheer impertinence for a court to intrude. And such intrusion is contrary to the settled judicial tradition.[18]

Yes, the court is surely right that judicial intrusion into the prosecuting function is contrary to the settled judicial tradition. But why is it? Is it because the tradition became settled during the nineteenth century when courts were generally assuming that judicial intrusion into any administration would be unfortunate? Is it because the tradition became settled while the Supreme Court was actuated by its 1840 remark that "The interference of the Courts with the performance of the ordinary duties of the executive departments of the government, would be productive of nothing but mischief"?[19] Is it because the tradition became settled before the courts made the twentieth-century discovery that the courts can interfere with executive action to protect against abuses but at the same time can avoid taking over the executive function?[20] Is it because the tradition became settled before the successes of the modern system of *limited* judicial review became fully recognized?

On the basis of what the courts know today about leaving administration to administrators but at the same time providing an effective check to protect against abuses, should the courts not take a fresh look at the tradition that prevents them from reviewing the prosecuting function? Throughout the governmental system, courts have found that other administrative or executive functions are in need of a judicial check, with a limited scope of review.[21] The reasons for a judicial check of prosecutors' discretion are stronger than for such a check of other administrative discretion that is now traditionally reviewable. Important interests are at stake. Abuses are common. The questions involved are appropriate for judicial determi-

nation. And much injustice could be corrected.

The usual assumption that the prosecuting power is inherently unsuitable for judicial review is contradicted by the experience in West Germany, and it is contradicted by a slight amount of American experience. We do have a bit of review of prosecutors' discretion around the edges. For more than a century Michigan has had a statute providing that when a prosecuting attorney investigates a case and decides not to prosecute he shall file with the court a written statement "containing his reasons in fact and in law" and that if the court is not satisfied with the statement it may direct that the case be prosecuted.[22] The Michigan system seems well designed to protect against discriminatory prosecuting policies and against abuses stemming from political influence. The Michigan idea seems worthy of full consideration elsewhere.

A federal court can review a decision to prosecute when the defendant shows an abuse of discretion in failing to prosecute his competitors. The Supreme Court declared in the key case: "If the [Federal Trade] Commission has decided the question [whether cease and desist orders should be withheld until respondents' competitors are proceeded against], its discretionary determination should not be overturned in the absence of a patent abuse of discretion."[23] The statement clearly implies that the discretionary determination can be overturned upon a showing of a patent abuse of discretion. The Seventh Circuit has specifically so held, in a case in which it found that the commission had "selected one whose share of the market is less than 6%, although the practice complained of is common to the industry."[24] The Supreme Court approved the view expressed by the Seventh Circuit by declaring that the commission "does not have unbridled power to institute proceedings which will arbitrarily destroy one of many law violators in an industry," but the Supreme Court found "no basis for a conclusion that the practice held illegal by the Commission was prevalent throughout the plumbing industry."[25]

If an abuse by the Federal Trade Commission in exercising its prosecuting power is thus judicially reviewable, why should not any abuse by any prosecuting officer or officers be likewise judicially reviewable? If some courts may review a prosecutor's nolle prosequi,[26] why not all? If some courts may review deals made through plea bargaining and thereby correct some injustice[27] why not all? If some courts review intentional discrimination by a prosecutor,[28] why not all? If some courts can compel prosecutors to take affirmative action,[29] despite the anachronistic theory that separation of powers forbids the judicial branch of the government to correct abuses by officers of the executive branch,[30] why not all? In general, if some abuses of some prosecutors are reviewable in some courts, why should not all abuses of all prosecutors be reviewable by some court?

Perhaps the law of the long-term future can be glimpsed in a dissenting opinion in the Supreme Court. A tax evader was prosecuted under a statute with a greater penalty, even though he could have been prosecuted under a statute with a lesser penalty. The trial judge refused to charge the jury that it could find him guilty of violating the statute with the lesser penalty, and the Supreme Court affirmed. The dissenters objected to what they found to be "unreviewable discretion of one individual" — the prosecutor. They asserted that such unreviewable discretion seemed to them "wholly incompatible with our system of justice."[31] I agree, except that I think our system of justice has been drifting too far toward unreviewable discretion of prosecutors. The attitude of the dissenters may be the harbinger of tomorrow's law. I think it should be.

The entire large problem of judicial check of prosecutors' discretion is in need of a full study — a study which will be free from the false assumptions that now dominate American thinking about the discretion of prosecutors.

NOTES*

1. 24 *J. Amer. Jud. Soc.* 18–19 (1940).
2. Perhaps nine-tenths of the abuses of the prosecuting power involve failure to prosecute, and courts normally have no occasion to review such cases. Even when an abuse is affirmative, a court is unlikely to review the exercise of the prosecutor's discretionary power.
3. Alexander Pekelis, *Law and Social Action* (1950), 81–83.
4. Ibid., p. 80. Although some major features of the prosecuting systems of the continental countries stand in contrast with those of the English speaking nations, still some differences from one continental country to another are significant. For instance, prosecutors in Denmark and Norway have a very wide discretion to waive prosecution, but such waivers are generally limited to less serious offenses and are exceptional for serious crimes. In Sweden and Finland, the "principle of legality" means that prosecutors have a legal duty to prosecute if they find guilt sufficiently established; the main exceptions relate to young offenders. See Andenaes, *The Legal Framework*, 9, 10.

The contrast between England and the continent is brought out by a British writer, Glanville Williams, "Discretion in Prosecuting," [1956] *Crim. L. Rev.* 222: "It is completely wrong to suppose (as is sometimes done) that the institution of prosecution is an automatic or mechanical matter. This is, indeed, the theory in some Continental countries, such as Germany, where the rule is that the public prosecutor must take proceedings for all crimes that come to his notice for which there is sufficient evidence, unless they fall within an exception for petty offences, in respect of which he is given discretion. In England, however, there is discretion in prosecuting in respect of all crimes."
5. Professor Max Rheinstein of the University of Chicago.
6. Dr. Ernst K. Pakuscher.
7. Professor Fritz Scharpf of the University of Constance, who was visiting professor at the Yale Law School 1964–66 and at the University of Chicago during 1966.
8. Associate Professor Gerhard Casper and Assistant Professor Peter Schlechtriem, both currently teaching at the University of Chicago Law School.
9. With respect to certain small misdemeanors, including traffic offenses, both the police and the prosecutors in Germany have a substantial power of selective enforcement. This exception is explicitly recognized in the statutes.
10. See Charles S. Lyon, "The Crime of Income Tax Fraud," 53 *Col. L. Rev.* 476 (1953), which has inspired most of the questions here stated about income tax fraud.
11. Report (1952), 244.
12. 59 A.B.A.R. 124 (1934).
13. California, Iowa, Nebraska, New Mexico, North Carolina, Oregon, and Pennsylvania.
14. A judicial trial is an acceptance of a prosecutor's decision to prosecute, not a review of it. Even a quick finding of not guilty may leave un-

*Footnotes have been abridged, edited, and renumbered.

touched the harms that flow from the prosecution. Of course, the big power which can be discriminatorily exercised is the power not to prosecute. Of one thousand decisions not to prosecute, the usual number totally unknown to judges is probably one thousand.

15. Newman v. United States, 382 F.2d 479 (D.C. Cir., 1967).

16. The case law is fully presented in Chap. 28 of my *Administrative Law Treatise*.

17. United States v. Cox, 342 F.2d 167, 171 (5th Cir.), certiorari denied 381 U.S. 935 (1965).

18. Howell v. Brown, 85 F. Supp. 537, 540 (D. Neb. 1949).

19. Decatur v. Paulding, 39 U.S. (14 Pet.) 497, 516 (1840).

20. The turning point may have come in American School of Magnetic Healing v. McAnnulty, 187 U.S. 94 (1902). The action of the Postmaster General could be reviewed because: "Otherwise, the individual is left to the absolutely uncontrolled and arbitrary action of a public and administrative officer." 187 U.S. at 110.

21. The general federal rule, which has exceptions, is embodied in the Administrative Procedure Act, 5 U.S.C. § 701–706.

22. Mich. Stat. § 28.981, dating from 1859 provides: "It shall be the duty of the prosecuting attorney of the proper county to inquire into and make full examination of all the facts and circumstances connected with any case of preliminary examination as provided by law, touching the commission of any offense whereon the offender shall be committed to jail . . . and if the prosecuting attorney shall determine in any case that an information ought not to be filed, he shall . . . file with the clerk of the court a statement, in writing, containing his reason in fact and in law, for not filing an information . . . such court may examine said statement, together with the evidence filed in the case and if, upon such examination, the court shall not be satisfied with said statement, the prosecuting attorney shall be directed by the court to file the proper information and bring the case to trial."

23. Moog Industries v. FTC, 355 U.S. 411, 414 (1958).

24. Universal-Rundle Corp. v. FTC, 352 F.2d 831 (7th Cir., 1965).

25. FTC v. Universal-Rundle Corp., 387 U.S. 244, 250, 251 (1967).

26. E.g., State v. Ashby, 43 N.J. 273, 204 A.2d 1 (1964).

27. *The Crime Commission's Task Force Report on The Courts* said at page 9: "Although the participants and frequently the judge know that nego-tiation has taken place, the prosecutor and defendant must ordinarily go through a courtroom ritual in which they deny that the guilty plea is the result of any threat or promise. As a result there is no judicial review of the propriety of the bargain — no check on the amount of pressure put on the defendant to plead guilty. The judge, the public, and sometimes the defendant himself cannot know for certain who got what from whom in exchange for what."

28. E.g., People v. Utica Daws Drug Co., 16 App. Div.2d 12, 225 N.Y.S2d 128 (4th Dept. 1962).

29. See the Michigan statute at note 22.

30. See the 4-3 division of the court in four opinions in United States v. Cox, 342 F.2d 167, 171 (5th Cir.), certiorari denied 381 U.S. 935 (1965).

31. Berra v. United States, 351 U.S. 131, 139, 140 (1956). The dissenters said: ". . . We should construe these sections so as not to place control over the liberty of citizens in the unreviewable discretion of one individual — a result which seems to me wholly incompatible with our system of justice. . . . Of course it is true that under our system Congress may vest the judge and jury with broad power to say how much punishment shall be imposed for a particular offense. But it is quite different to vest such powers in a prosecuting attorney. A judge and jury act under procedural rules carefully prescribed to protect the liberty of the individual. . . . No such protections are thrown around decisions by a prosecuting attorney. Substitution of the prosecutor's caprice for the adjudicatory process is an action I am not willing to attribute to Congress in the absence of clear command."

See also Bazelon, J., dissenting, in Henderson v. United States, 349 F.2d 712, 713–714 (D.C. Cir., 1965): "At oral argument I asked Government counsel why this appellant, a non-addict found with large quantities of narcotics, was treated so much better than addicts accidentally found in possession of $40 worth of drugs, or persuaded into making a $10 sale to a police undercover agent or informer. Government counsel offered this explanation: the United States Attorney may have reason to think that such addicts are substantial operators, but may have no way to prove it. Such reasoning is at the heart of the tyranny in the invisible prosecutorial choice he is permitted to make. I am dismayed at the proposition that a prosecutor may sentence offenders to jail terms longer than appears to be warranted by the transaction with which they are charged, because he *thinks* they are involved in bigger stuff — and that this choice may never be reviewed."

IV. Courts and Judges

11. EXERCISING DISCRETION ON THE BENCH: THE TRIAL JUDGE'S PERSPECTIVE

LENORE ALPERT

■ Trial judges exercise an enormous amount of discretion. In this original essay, Professor Alpert examines some of the reasons why this discretion exists and suggests how it is exercised in child custody and criminal sentencing decisions. The important contribution which this essay makes to our understanding of discretion rests upon how it emphasizes the fluidity of the judicial role; that is, much discretion exists because most judges are able to define their roles in reference to how they perceive the scope of court authority and how they, as individuals, wish to utilize that power. There is a remarkable lack of formal decision-making structure for most trial judges. Moreover, important differences exist in how discretion is exercised in civil and criminal cases. ■

THE WORLD OF TRIAL judges is one filled with discretion, a quality that flows from the unstructured nature of the judicial role. Not only are judges given wide flexibility in defining their tasks, so that backgrounds and personalities play an important part in molding the judicial role, they are also virtually unlimited in the performance of their tasks on the bench. While they are supposed to follow precedent in making their decisions, as a practical matter there are few cases that are successfully appealed and reversed. Consequently, what trial judges do and how they interpret the law as it applies to the specific factual situations they hear is determined by individual judgments of trial judges, with very few constraints.

This fluidity associated with what trial judges should or should not do was recognized several decades ago by Jerome Frank, who commented on one aspect of the independence of judicial decision-making and the lack of supervision imposed upon the judicial office:

And now I come to a major matter, one which most non-lawyers do not understand, and one which puts the trial courts at the heart of our judicial system: An upper court can seldom do anything to correct a trial court's mistaken belief about the facts. Where, as happens in most cases, the testimony at the trial was oral, the upper court usually feels obliged to adopt the trial court's determination of the facts. Why? Because in such a case the trial court heard and saw the witnesses as they testified, but the upper court did not. The upper court has only a type-written or printed record of the testimony. The trial court alone is in a position to interpret the demeanor-clues, this 'language without words.' (Frank, 1930, 23)

Not only are trial judges relatively free from review and formal rules in carrying out their tasks, they also have the considerable power and authority inherent in the office and this makes discretion inevitable. Judges translate abstract legal concepts into particular decisions, thus determining how local courts respond to the mores and values of their communities. Judge Charles Wyzanski captured the essence of this role of trial judges:

Let us not suppose that because our [trial judge's] jurisdiction is limited, because so much of our work goes unreported, because we are immersed in the detail of fact, [that] we trial judges are clothed with small responsibility in relating law to justice. It is we who make the law a living teacher as we transmit it from the legislature and the appellate court to the citizen who stands before us. It is we who watch the impact of the formal rule, explain its purpose to laymen, and seek to make its application conform to the durable and reasonable expectations of our communities. It is we who determine whether the process of common-law growth shall decay or flower with a new vigor. (Wyzanski, 1952, 60)

This chapter will focus upon how trial judges evaluate the discretion inherent in their office, how they conceptualize judicial authority and power as it relates to their role definition, and how they translate this role into behavior as they exercise discretion on the bench. The underlying theme is that trial judges are relatively free to shape their roles on the bench in any direction they choose; they can mold their tasks to become whatever kind of judges they wish. By exploring how judges define their judicial role, we can discover how they structure the broad discretion of their office.[1]

In examining the trial judge's discretion and role perceptions, we shall focus upon two substantive areas, both of which involve a considerable amount of discretionary decision-making, but each of which is quite different in terms of how this discretion is utilized. Both raise competing policy issues that tend to extend judicial discretion, in part because they are subject to few statutory restrictions limiting choices among alternative decisions. Instead, both types of cases — criminal sentencing and child custody cases — provide opportunities for broad discretion on the bench by trial judges.

With regard to the lack of statutory restrictions, criminal sentencing in Florida is limited by only minimum and maximum sentences for each offense. Judges have flexibility in selecting the specific type and length of sentence, with the exception of mandatory minimums required for robbery offenders using a firearm and of legislative guidelines for sentencing in capital cases. Thus criminal statutes impose few constraints upon judges' choices of sentence, since the legislature provides few guidelines for sentencing, affording opportunity for judges' injecting their own values into this decision process. While judges may order a pre-sentence report by a probation officer, they are in no way bound by this sentencing recommendation. Further, few criminal sentences are ever successfully appealed, insuring that judges' decisions will be virtually unreviewed.

Likewise, in child custody cases, the legislature has left it up to individual trial judges to determine placement in the best interests of the child; they alone must hear evidence and determine which parent can best fulfill the child's emotional and physical needs. While social service officers may conduct investigations and recommend custody to a particular parent, the judge hears the evidence and testimony and makes the custody decision. Again, few cases are ever successfully appealed, thus escaping review from other judges and insuring the autonomy of trial court decisions in this area.

With regard to policy issues in the two types of cases, trial judges have a wide range of choices. Whether they are harsh or lenient, their decision can be easily justified. In criminal sentencing, they can argue that they are protecting society if they choose a harsh punishment or that they are rehabilitating offenders if they choose a lenient punishment. In custody cases, equally compelling grounds often exist to grant custody to one parent or the other, who may be similarly qualified.

Thus parallels exist in both areas of the law that suggest an analogous decision process, although substantive differences between the two types of cases suggest that different considerations must be taken into account by trial judges. Both areas of law are marked by an absence of legislative guidelines for making decisions which, coupled with lack of judicial review by higher courts, provide opportunities for unfettered discretion in the decision process. This is not to say that trial judges necessarily abuse their discretion or are unfair. Rather, they respond to the lack of restrictions structuring their decisions, filling the legislative vacuum with their own determination about what factors to consider in the final decision.

The interviews suggest two themes that illuminate the issue of discretion. Broadly speaking, the way trial judges handle power on the bench and define their judicial roles helps structure their exercise of discretion. The latter is the vehicle by which trial judges adapt to the power of the office and structure their authority. For example, judges who perceive power narrowly are likely to inject fewer personal values into the decision process than those who perceive power broadly. Secondly, the factors that enter into the decision process provide insights into how judges fill this vacuum created by lack of legislative or judicial guidelines. While these interviews by no means include all of the factors that might be important in criminal sentencing or in custody cases, they do reflect the potential role of personal values in this process, illustrating how varied judicial responses can still remain within the bounds of the law.

HANDLING THE POWER AND AUTHORITY OF TRIAL JUDGING

In discussing the judicial role, judges describe their attitudes toward the power and authority of the office as well as the behaviors that result from those attitudes. These attitudes shape behaviors as judges respond to their environment on the bench and fashion their judicial role. Accepting the power of the office is the first step in developing the judicial role:

I'm well aware of the fact that there's awesome power in my pen. There are many times where for some reason, it's not really that kind of a case, but I've seen this while signing an order, and all of a sudden it dawns on me — This order does many things. It takes away property, gives property, makes somebody pay money, somebody gets money, puts somebody in jail, lets somebody get out of jail. It's a pretty big signature. . . . I think people should be aware of the fact that they have a tremendous amount of authority and that they ought to be aware of their responsibilities regarding that authority. They ought to understand and know and be able to feel what that means to someone else. . . . You should know what the job is, what it means, and your responsibilities toward it. . . . Judges should know that, yes, they do have power, but it doesn't make them God. They shouldn't abuse it. Unfortunately, like everything else, there are abusers in the judiciary, there are abusers in medicine, there are abusers in all walks of life.

Another judge echoed this need to accept the authority of the judicial office as a means to behave responsibly on the bench. Like other jobs, trial judging requires that individuals becomes sensitive to the expectations of the position and fulfill those demands. In the case of judging, unless authority is exercised, the work of the courts cannot proceed, as this judge experienced:

I had found that the use of authority is an absolutely necessary thing. You simply must decide unequivocably . . . I was simply the guy who had to make the decisions in order for the day to proceed. . . . I found out that I was the guy who was responsible for getting the show on the road, for getting it on the stage, and getting the performance over with and going on with the next one.

. . . I found out very quickly that my style of operating had a great deal of influence over everybody, that I was the principal figure in the whole show and that I was the lead character, and the director of the play. . . . I found out that I really was director of the show and that I had to control it.

The exercise of discretion on the trial bench flows from the considerable power that trial judges wield over litigants that come before them. It is a crucial learning problem for newcomers to the bench, as well as for some veterans, for handling this authority structures not only relationships with attorneys, litigants, and court staff, but also with the community at large. It is often a disconcerting experience, as illustrated by one newcomer's initial adjustment to this authority:

I am aware that very significant changes took place during my first year. When I started, when I first sat on the bench, I was very uneasy, I suppose was the feeling, I was very uncomfortable. Sitting in a position of authority does not come easily to me; I don't like that kind of role as a personality. I am more of a reflective person . . . so I found it very uncomfortable to exercise the role of authority. . . . I grew with time to be more comfortable with the authority that I had. . . . I felt I was being reasonable but I grew more and more confident with the position and the power that I had which at first I was pretty uncomfortable with. I was very shocked at the impact of everything I said had on people, not only on the individuals who were there for the litigation — the parties — but on the lawyers, on the court personnel, and others. I was not accustomed to that being an individual practitioner for the past 8 years — that people would hang on every word I said. But I grew more and more accustomed to that.

In describing the interaction between power and authority in trial judging, judges recognize the power of self in office as a means to constructively structure that authority. Reconciling self with office — or power with authority — may be linked to a judge's self-concept and his own personal fulfillment, suggesting intricate psychological interaction in resolving this key socialization dilemma. The general norm seems to be that "the more authority you have, the less you have need to use it," as illustrated in the reflections of one trial judge:

I think it's an interesting phenomenon — power and authority — how they interact — whether or not there's almost a dependence that develops in us . . . [on] that authority, in order to build our pseudo-power, our security . . . our self-confidence, our self-concept . . . The authority is there . . . a tremendously uplifting kind of thing . . . the same thing I would . . . say [about] a minister or priest. . . . Judges must be measured in the area of power and their ability to cope with their own power. I believe that the less power that a person perceives himself deep inside having, if they are fortunate to ascend to a position of judge, the worst judge they are . . . because they tend to fill in that authority that they have in the position . . . and you see things that are very abusive by judges. . . . On the other hand, my theory is that the person who is more self-fulfilled and has a strong sense of power and can use the power, knows how to use it, knows how to own it . . . knows that they're using it and why they're using it, that they would tend to be better judges because they would not rely upon the authority of their position. In fact they would use their power much less as a judge. They would need to use it less because the authority is cloaked over them and it's not necessary. I find that I rarely have to really use power in order to achieve anything in the judiciary. . . . The question is "How much of my power as an individual is tied into my authority and how much of my power as an individual is owned by me?"

Structuring authority may require developing flexibility on the bench, maintaining respect for the position while at the same time permitting litigants and lawyers to express themselves fully in the courtroom. For some judges, this posture may pose problems in that some expression must be curtailed, but for other judges such a flexible stance permits closer rapport with those in their courtroom, an important part of the judicial role:

I was aware of the awesomeness of the job. I am an extremely sensitive individual, and I am sensitive about the use of politics. And I did not seek the office for the reason that I was hopeful of being able to play God; that was not in my mind . . . I believe that the court can keep its demeanor without iron-clad rulings . . . and that kind of thing. . . . So, I am perhaps a lot different about the authority. I believe that where necessary, the power that is utilized should be used quietly. I don't think that you have to throw your weight around in order to get anything done. I think the mere fact that you are a judge allows that most people are still respectful of the

institution of the judiciary or of the judiciary as an institution, and I think that when you are respectful to other people, even to the point sometimes when you let them go a step further than they should, they will be committed to say the things that they really should — want — to say. I find that when they get it off their chests, that you are a great guy if you just let them say it. I've held my power back to let people be aggressive in their pursuits in the court. Not to the extent of harrangues or that kind of thing. I didn't feel that a halo came around my head and that I had infinite wisdom because I became a judge. So I have tried to act that way, and I set myself apart from the people and the lawyers, and at the very same time, I am among them. I don't think that good leadership at the level of the judiciary or anything else allows that one can be standoffish and I don't intend to be.

In using their power, judges must develop humility on the bench. In order to fulfill expectations of the judicial role, they need to curtail their power. This implies that they are behaving in a neutral, objective manner, part of the demands of the judicial office. One judge described his efforts to minimize his power on the bench:

I hope I'm humble about the whole thing because I don't ever try to be overbearing or anything. The best use of power is never to use it. Once you throw your weight around and use a lot of power, then you're in trouble. So the best use of power is never to use it. Therefore I try to be humble and hold back. I try to let the lawyers do their thing. It's their case; I try to let them handle it in their way and not jump on them or criticize them or move them this way or that way. . . . Lots of times you have to sort of "grit your teeth" and let the lawyer do what he wants.

In shaping the judicial role, it may be a question of limiting flexibility. In contrast to the judge above, another judge sees danger in not establishing tight constraints on behavior in his courtroom, which he feels threaten the authority of the bench. Clearly this judge would run a "tighter ship" in his interactions with those in his courtroom, delineating clearly the parameters dividing bench from bar. His perception of his judicial role is one of greater exercise of authority than that described above:

Everything has to be in a formal atmosphere. You have to be sort of a stuffed shirt. You can't turn the courtroom into "Saturday Night Live." . . . The robe must have respect. I don't particularly desire much in my personality to be a judge on the outside [off the bench], but in the courtroom you have to have it because that's the authority of the court. You can't let anyone run roughshod over the authority of the court. Outside, I don't particularly care how people deal with me as long as they don't carry it into the courtroom and try to take advantage, not knowing liberty from license.

Handling the authority of trial judging is subject to the particular personality traits of individual judges. How judges perceive their appropriate roles and behavior is shaped by inner needs they have. In this context, while organizational demands are important, the fluidity of trial judging leaves much room for flexibility. Because there are few formal rules governing behavior, trial judges are free to fashion their roles and behave accordingly, filling in the vacuum with personal preferences. This may lead to abuses on the bench among those judges whose personalities cannot handle this power:

Sometimes when a guy puts on a robe he thinks it's supposed to have a big red "S" and he's Superman. Or he says, "Shazam," and he's immune to everything. You've got prima donnas everywhere, whether they be doctors, lawyers, dentists, housewives, or whatever. We have good judges, bad judges, indifferent judges. It's just a personality thing — some guys got it, some guys don't.

Other judges label this phenomenon "judgitis," and warn against its pitfalls on the bench. "Judgitis" raises the negative aspects of wielding the authority of judging and the potential for abuses of power:

We have to be careful of that psychic development — getting 'judgitis.' That's the fellow that sooner or later feels that he's not appointed, he's annointed, that [he] can do no wrong . . . You have to practice humility at all times . . . I think you have to seek out some things to involve yourself [in] other than strictly judging, to grow, or to stay effective really. . . . Now I personally feel that they should be court-related or judge-related. . . . There is kind of a fine line in how far to go.

To avoid judgitis requires that judges keep their perspective and remember their position is separate from themselves. Judges are often warned about getting judgitis before they reach the bench:

One of the attorneys who sat on the judicial nominating commission said to me before I took office: "Look, don't get judgitis once you're over there." So I've sworn not to get judgitis. I think judgitis is when all of a sudden you walk away and you forget what it's like to be on the other side. You think because of the black robe and because your bench is up higher than everybody else's that automatically that makes you some kind of super-hero, or know-it-all, or whatever. It really doesn't.

Expressing this idea in more graphic language, one judge cautioned about maintaining a proper perspective about oneself in office:

I think the most important thing is that you shouldn't get infatuated with yourself. I think some judges do. They get the idea that their robes make them tremendously different. The purpose is to listen to people, give them a fair shake, and interpret the law as best you understand it.

Part of this perspective involves empathizing with the other person's position and making decisions on the bench accordingly. Or, as one judge expressed it, remembering that you are a public servant first and foremost:

I feel like the courts really belong to the people. The courts are there to serve the people. One of the . . . "Ten Commandments" for a new judge . . . is "Remember that you're the servant of the people, not the master of the people." And that's one thing I've tried to keep in mind. I've tried to be human and understand the people — real human people. In a way, I'm in a position, if I want to, to toy with their lives because I'm the one who makes the decision. . . . I've tried to be sensitive and live up to what they would expect out of a court. How would I feel if I were in court? What would I want the judge to act like? How would I want my case handled?

But most importantly, judges must realize where the image ends and the person begins. They must not forget that they too have feet of clay and are subject to human frailties. It is often too easy to believe that they have become the image of judge in office rather than minimizing that image of self in office. According to one judge, it is one of the most serious problems judges must learn to cope with on the bench:

I would think that the one quality that is important in government, especially if you have authority, i.e. the exercise of power, and that is an attribute that judges need to exercise some discipline [on] because the feeling is generated by everyone around you that everything you do is damn wise, damn good and unless you necessarily believe that as a fact, it becomes a part of your environment and judges tend to resist any suggestion that they may not be all knowing and I think that sometimes you have to go to even to the point of recognizing and tolerating outspoken dissent that may even be beyond the four corners of courtroom discipline. It is easy to rely on the fact that you're protecting the court, when it is not yourself, but sometimes I think it is very easy to let some expressions come in when I'm exercising kinds of discipline we have. . . . I think that the judges have enough power so that they can afford to wield it lightly. I think that is something they have to be careful of and they have to be careful that they don't pontificate too much. I think that there is a real tendency to really get to believe the image of yourself and using all the trappings that are supposed to minimize the individual and only maximize the image, but what we tend to do sometimes is to maximize the individual. We're supposed to represent the state. We wear those robes, but we're not supposed to believe that that is really us, that it is somebody else. . . . I think it is a problem, a serious problem among judges.

As these examples illustrate, trial judges manage the authority of the office in a multitude of ways, with as much variation in carrying out judicial roles as there are types of individuals. It is largely a matter of accommodating oneself to a situation while at the same time making adjustments in the situation. Thus trial judges not only adapt to the office but also shape that office to meet their needs as individuals. As one judge reflected:

How he handles matters, a lot has to do with the judge's background, his experiences he's calling on, his legal training — his personality has a lot to do with how he handles certain cases, his temperament, whatever it might be.

DEFINING THE JUDICIAL ROLE

In meeting individual needs and shaping the office accordingly, judges devise different methods for carrying out their judicial role. In developing styles of judging, it is clearly a matter of wide latitude, limited only by trial judges' own perceptions of their appropriate role on the bench. One judge described the individualist nature of the judicial role, attributing it to underlying personalities:

Judges tend to be highly individualistic. I won't say that their egos make them that way, but there's something about it that we're sort of on our own. When we're sitting on that courtroom or on our own . . . we're sitting there on our own. . . . I know there are all different kinds of judges. We all have different personalities. Personality has got to enter into it, no matter what you say. I have a somewhat retiring personality, rather than aggressive and that too makes a difference. . . . When I was a lawyer and for many years after becoming a judge, it was considered and I still consider it that . . . a judge was not to be aggressive. I believe they use the word activist nowadays. There are activist judges and there are judges who are not activists. In general, I am not an activist judge, and yet occasionally I have grasped something and moved forward without waiting for one side or the other to bring it to my attention. I will do it when it seems very necessary in the interest of justice . . . [if] I feel it's not being done by the adversary system.

Many judges believe their decision process is influenced by their own attitudes as much as it is by prevailing precedent and legal considerations. In highlighting this point, one judge referred to his past experiences:

Any decider of fact, provided he is a product of hiw own value system — his set of values, his past experiences determine how he holds. Now, how I react to a particular argument about a particular state of things, to say that it's something you hear in a vacuum is wrong — that's deluding yourself. You react to it as the sum total of your past experiences.

Injecting values into the decision process requires balancing precepts of justice about a particular case with relevant precedent. Yet many judges don't perceive these rules as serious limitations on their discretion in making decisions. One judge summed it up well as he talked about problem-solving on the bench:

Your method of dealing with the problem is almost within the bounds of rules, of the rules that we have. Almost unfettered. If you see an injustice being done, you have the force of the state, you have the opportunity to summon witnesses on your own behalf. You have the opportunity to spend as much time as you feel is necessary on it. You have the world where you can draw from in terms of solving that particular problem or righting that wrong.

Other judges feel that precedent must be followed even where it conflicts with personal notions of justice. To these judges, there is no choice about following precedent where the law is clear:

I have ruled against my view of justice in a case because of clear and directly relevant precedent. Where I have a choice, then my view of justice plays a part. Where the law is clear, I don't have a choice.

While not a prevailing view, some judges argue that a higher allegiance to justice and conscience requires overruling precedent:

Yes, I do what's right sometimes — in spite of it [precedent], although I know I'm doing wrong. But I still have to sleep with myself. . . . The only way to change the law or innovate is to rule the way you know is right or feel is sincerely right and give your reasons therefore.

Between these two extremes lies a more moderate approach to precedent — that part of the trial judge's function is to make the law make sense in the context of achieving justice, particularly when precedent is not clearly applicable. This situation occurs in many cases judges hear, where precedent is cited by opposing attorneys to support legal arguments on both sides of an issue. Neither set of precedent may have exactly the same facts as the case the judge is deciding — i.e., the case is not "on all fours" — thereby allowing the judge to use his discretion to construe the law. This approach permits exercise of discretion but within the confines of existing precedent:

I think that we have a feeling of the case, but we also have a sense of justice, a sense of what is right, what is wrong, what is fair, what is unfair . . . one of the functions of a judge is to try and make the law make sense, and if we are going to construe it in a way that doesn't make sense, then we must be wrong.

Oftentimes this common sense approach to the law requires reconciling the relevant law with the equities of the case. By injecting their notions of common sense into the decision process, judges reveal the values underlying specific decisions:

Common sense is really the quality that you need more than anything in law. Nine out of ten decisions are common sense decisions when you get right down to it. After all, that's all the law is anyway. Law is a common sense way of working out relations between people. So if you feel you've got good common sense and you listen to both sides, it's not all that hard — it's easy.

For some judges, this common sense aspect of judging is a relative factor that is closely related to personal views of justice:

You've got to try to perceive the case in relation to all the factors concerned in coming to a decision. I try to keep it in perspective like that. It is my view of justice in the case — what's right. . . . For instance, I can't get as upset with a homicide that happens in a bar where people are drunk or as a result of a fight-type situation between two individuals fighting over money, or a girl, or a man, or whatever it is as opposed to other types of homicides. For instance, a premediated or a felony murder, or even a manslaughter which involves a person drunk at the wheel killing innocent people — these things really bother me as opposed to a bar fight.

This common sense approach to decision-making has been called a "gut reaction" or "a feeling of an innate sense of justice." It's been described by judges as the soundest basis for doing justice in any particular case:

If there's any doubt, the first thing you should satisfy is your inner feelings if you can do so, and if you satisfy your inner feelings, you're generally going to be pretty close to being right about the justice . . . of course [my view of] the precedent and the facts [is important], but my view of justice does I think become a higher criterion than the others the longer you're on [the bench].

Sometimes injecting common sense into decisions becomes an intuitive process. It is a subtle means by which personal feelings can influence behavior on the bench. One judge linked this intuition to attitudes and life experiences:

Probably everybody thinks he has a intuitive process and I'm sure that it affects everyone to some extent. It's the same sort of thing that probably is affected by all of your prior experiences in life and your attitudes towards life as to right and wrong — the importance of what may be before you. This doesn't mean the importance of any particular case, but you do have a feeling about what is right or wrong after the case — sometimes before the case is very far along. . . . Even if you are not the trier of fact, even if it's a jury trial, you have a feeling about this. To say that this doesn't influence you I'm sure is incorrect. It probably influences everyone subconsciously. When you're the trier of fact, your feelings should really be limited to what the facts are, but again this gets to be subjective where there is conflict and where most of it is their oral testimony or is in documentary form that is not crystal clear. Everyone likes to urge his interpretation both on testimony and on written documents as well if there is any chance for moving it around.

Some judges feel this intuition is unreliable and caution against it, suggesting a negative aspect to decisions that rely on a judge's intuition. By deciding on the basis of intuition, the process becomes too subjective and value-laden, according to this viewpoint. In contrast to the approach expressed above, judges who perceive their role as ignoring intuition may be more concerned with following precedent, although it is debatable to what extent their decisions are truly value-free. As one judge expressed it, personal value judgments are inappropriate in judicial decision-making:

There might be an element of intuition involved in that decision, fact-finding process. And I do think judges work backwards sometimes. I do think intuition is a part of that then. It is intuitive in the sense that they might feel that this little old lady was injured and somehow, somewhere, some defendant ought to pay her some money. . . . I think we should fight intuition, or at least recognize when decisions are intuitive because they're unreliable, essentially unreliable. And anytime we can quantify decision-making, then I think that's a good idea. . . . And I think the effort should be made in the judiciary that the same facts, the same circumstances basically should be decided the same way by any of the judges. The more intuitive it becomes, the more decisions depend on the outlook of the judge. We have one judge, for example, who views himself as a very religious, devoutly religious man. He doesn't gamble, he thinks it's a sin. He doesn't drink, he doesn't think other people should drink. He doesn't smoke, he doesn't think other people should smoke. He's kind of an intolerant fellow. And I can imagine him in a custody matter, for

example, if the testimony is that one of the parties smoked and drank and the other one didn't. I think *that* alone — he would decide the case. And he would say, "well" — intuitively say — "Well, the child should go to the nonsmoking, non-drinking parent." Those are only factors. In other words, if you remove your intuition from it and try to look at it objectively, those are value judgments. And I don't think they should be determinative in and of themselves. That's why you know they are important — common sense is important and justice is important.

These contrasting views of the judical role with regard to intuition highlight the flexibility of the decision process. It is a process unfettered by rules and almost entirely dependent upon a judge's interpretation of what is appropriate behavior on the bench. Judges are relatively free to formulate their own ideas of how decisions should be made and to inject individual values into these decisions, if they so desire.

Because so much of what trial judges do is unstructured, adaptation to the judicial role is remarkably flexible. In this context it is easy to see how individual personal values may structure on-bench behavior. The acceptance and use of the power of the office may surface in many areas of a trial judge's work, as one judge summarized:

I appreciate very deeply and recognize the awesome responsibility and power that a circuit judge has. When he can sentence a man to be put to death, and he can sentence a woman, to forfeit their freedom for the rest of their lives, he can divide up children and families, say this parent or that parent gets the child, order a home sold or foreclosed, and [make] unlimited judgments against people, it's an awesome power, something that a man cannot take lightly — Not if he's going to be the kind of judge that he ought to be. I feel very keenly on that point. I try to exercise it.

DECIDING CHILD CUSTODY CASES

Judges are not immune to personal influences on their decision-making powers, particularly in the areas of criminal sentencing and child custody matters, where their discretion surfaces most dramatically. It may be that the human element of judging is more visible in these areas of the law, that one judge suggests makes the decision more difficult:

I think that there are agonizing decisions to make in every area of the law. There are some areas where the decisions are relatively simple, compared to others; domestic relations, for example, is not that great a legal decision. The law is set if you keep up with the advance sheets. But where you get into the areas where you're not talking law, but human relations — child custody problems, which parent should receive custody, that is agonizing at times. From a legal standpoint, domestic relations is easier than condominium law or fancy no-fault insurance problems. From the standpoint of human relations, it's tougher than those others.

Other judges reinforce this notion that custody cases raise difficult human relations issues that in turn make decisions so agonizing. Here there are no black and white or right and wrong, but rather degrees of right and wrong that must be addressed. It is this ambiguity in the legal issues that makes such decisions so burdensome, not to mention the awesome power of the judge in changing a child's life. According to one judge, who was most troubled by custody cases, accepting responsibility for these cases is no easy matter:

The only cases I've ever taken home were custody cases. . . . When you sit there and have to take a child away from a parent, and you try to sugarcoat the pill as much as you can, you put the child in both their custodies and you do all those kind of things, but still you know that you're telling his father that the child's going with his mother or this mother that the child's going with his father, and that can be tough. The toughest part is when they're both good parents. . . . That's tougher than when they're both pain in the necks.

Another judge focused upon the emotional issues in these cases, that tend to differentiate them from other types of cases. For him, the range of emotions raised in domestic cases makes them especially anguishing to decide:

On the civil bench, the hardest are child custody cases because there you have parents that are equally good or equally bad. In divorces, people don't come in [with] one wearing a black hat and one wearing a white hat. Even though they each think the other person is the one that's all wrong, it never is that way. It's usually 50-50.

Every judge, I would think, would tell you that the hardest part of judging are child custody cases and that can be very anguishing because you tear children away from one parent and give them to another. It's very, very emotional. So those cases, with all of that emotion, are the worst. Cases where you have businessmen arguing over a contract and money, it's just money and then you go on to the next deal and so forth; it's not emotional. It's just a matter of dollars and cents. But when you get into the emotional cases, they are the hardest ones of all.

SENTENCING CRIMINAL OFFENDERS

Sentencing on the criminal side of judging also raises human relations issues. Like custody cases, these criminal cases are subject to immense discretion as judges strive to make their sentencing fit the offender and the offense. Many judges defend disparity in sentencing as necessary if justice is to be achieved:

I think if you had ten judges that had looked at a pre-sentence investigation and sentenced the same individual on the same set of facts, with the same background, I don't think the disparity would be great because you're talking about the same man and the same background and the same crime, but I think you'd find little differences between each one. And again that comes back to the fact that you have ten different individuals with ten backgrounds and ten points of reference — at least ten points of reference. So I think until you have a computer that decides what the sentences are, you're going to have disparity. I think even with the computer you're going to have disparity. The prison people say that I've got five men that are charged with breaking into a house and they've got five different sentences and there's ill-will and ill-feeling with the system because of the fact. But from my point of view, you've got five different individuals, with five crimes, and they've got five backgrounds, and on top of that you probably have five different judges that sentenced them. So if you have any two that are the same, it's probably going to be a chance situation. I don't think it is good that we have disparity, and certainly I'd like to move away from it, but . . . I haven't found a workable alternative at this point.

Other judges extend this argument by criticizing uniformity of sentencing as unrealistic and unfair. In their mind, not only is disparity necessary, it is also desirable:

Disparity is a liberal, uninformed criticism of the sentencing processes. I don't think that you can have any uniform sentence that would be fair. I think there must be disparity in sentences just like there is disparity in personality, people, background, what have you. I think each case ought to be considered on its own individual basis, the facts of the case, the background of the person, the criminal record of the person, future prospects of the person, any psychiatric or other professional information you can have, and each one weighted on its own merits. If you do that, which is the only proper way to do it, then you're going to have disparity. Now I've been a mean scalawag in my life and you've been a sweet angel; we both get picked up drinking while intoxicated. Would you like to be lumped in an 18 month mandatory jail sentence? That is an example.

In justifying disparity in criminal sentencing, some judges focus upon the offender rather than the offense. As judges are quick to point out, different offenders deserve different punishments:

I like to think you sentence the man rather than the crime, although the cry this day is that sentences are so disparate. The same crime committed by two ought to get about the same sentence. I'm still finishing up sentencing . . . where one man, just a kid, joins another man that had been in prison two or three times and the kid's never had any problems with the law. They both join together to commit the same crime. People don't understand how bad it is for one man to get twenty years and another man to get three or four years when they're committing the same crime. In given cases, that diversity of sentencing, disparity as they call it, is entirely justified in my judgment.

While criminal cases can be appealed, as a practical matter the appellate courts influence rulings on procedure more than those on substantive legal issues. Thus in the area of substance, trial judges are left with broad discretion in which to make their rulings. Again, as in other areas of decision-making, personal values fill in the vacuum created by the absence of rules:

I think [trial courts] are influenced by what they feel is right as well as by what some other appeals court rules. I think mostly the appeals court rulings influences the judges on procedure rather than on substance. I think if they have a rule that says, "In 30 days you have to do such and such," and this was done on the 31st day, the judge will say, "Well, I have no choice in this." But if they have a rule that says, "If you search somebody, find marijuana, then it's a question of probable cause," a lot of it will depend on how the judge feels about the case and how he feels about the offender . . . He'll say, "To hell with the appeals court, I'm going to rule the way I want to; if they want to reverse me, let them do it." So I think in substantive matters that the justice of the issue will prevail but not in [procedural matters].

Some judges speak candidly about how their personal values influence their sentencing behavior, suggesting the potential for exercising discretion on the bench. But for these judges, it is appropriate to fashion their judicial role to include these individual attitudes:

I really believe in Micah 6:8, "He hath showed thee, O man, what is good; and what doth the Lord require of thee, but to do justly, and to love mercy, and to walk humbly with thy God?" I tell you when I get to heaven, the last thing I want is justice — I want mercy. And I don't figure I can obtain it if I don't show it. So I give nearly everybody a second chance, unless it is a crime of violence, like armed robbery or something of that nature. . . . I have never sent anyone to prison for possession of marijuana — never — never will. If a kid uses it, or he has less than a pound or something like that, I ain't going to send them — To hell with it. But I read him the Riot Act.

Judicial attitudes surface in decisions in both of these areas of the law. In both custody cases and criminal sentencing, trial judges exercise largely unfettered discretion, giving full vent to personal values and biases. They are almost entirely unchecked with regard to formal rules governing their decision-making behavior. Thus to understand the decision process, it is necessary to explore the discretion underlying it and the ways in which trial judges define their judicial roles. In defining their roles, judges structure their discretion and behavior on the bench. Discretion becomes the key to understanding how and why judges act as they do. Placing limitations upon discretion is a matter of values — specifically, whose values are offended or aided by the exercise of discretion. Because someone always wins and someone always loses, discretion is a zero sum game that is not easily resolved. Balancing the flexibility of discretion with the rigidity of uniformity involves controversial choices. And as the judges interviewed here suggest, limiting discretion is not only difficult but also undesirable if substantive justice is to be achieved. From the judges' perspective, discretion is a necessary and essential element for delivering justice on the trial bench, inherent in the role of trial judges.

NOTE

1. This research is part of a larger study of on-bench socialization among Florida trial judges sitting on the bench in 1979–1980. That work included both interviews and surveys of these state court judges, as well as ratings by attorneys in four sites in Florida evaluating judges' behavior. The research reported here focuses upon 61 interviews conducted in 1978, 1979, and 1980 in four areas of Florida (Miami, Ft. Lauderdale, Orlando, and northern rural Florida). Most interviews were taped, averaging 60 minutes in length and ranging from 30 minutes to two hours. The distribution of judges interviewed is fairly evenly divided among tenure groups and geographic areas. About 80% of those interviewed completed the surveys. All judges in each site who would consent to an interview were seen. Interviews focused upon on-bench socialization — the kind of learning, role sources, approaches to judging, and experiences on the bench.

REFERENCES

Frank, Jerome. *Law and the Modern Mind*. Princeton: Princeton Univ. Press, 1930.
Wyzanski, Charles. "A Trial Judge's Freedom and Responsibility," *Atlantic Monthly*, 190 (1952), 55–60.

ACKNOWLEDGMENT

Research support for this project was received from the Graduate School at Northwestern University under a doctoral dissertation grant and from the National Institute of Justice in the U.S. Department of Justice under grant #80-IJ-CX-0005. This research could not have been undertaken without their support, which I greatly appreciate. The views expressed are those of the author alone and do not reflect opinions of the National Institute of Justice nor the Graduate School of Northwestern University.

Special thanks are due the circuit judges in Florida who participated in this study and so graciously permitted interviews and observations, as well as completed the surveys.

12. CRIMINAL SENTENCES; LAW WITHOUT ORDER

MARVIN E. FRANKEL

■ Sentencing criminal defendants represents one of the important aspects of trial judge's decision-making. While legislation has been passed in many states curtailing sentencing discretion, the fact remains that many judges still exercise enormous discretion over whether or not a defendant will receive a prison sentence and for the formal length of time that the sentence will run. Marvin Frankel, a federal judge, suggests many of the problems associated with sentencing discretion. Among the important problems he identifies is that many trial judges have never received formal instruction in the sentencing process. ■

I

LAW WITHOUT ORDER
OR LIMIT

WE BOAST THAT ours is a "government of laws, not of men." We do not mean by the quoted principle that men make no difference in the administration of law. Among the basic things we do mean is that all of us, governors and governed alike, are or ought to be bound by laws of general and equal application. We mean, too, that in a just legal order, the laws should be knowable and intelligible so that, to the fullest extent possible, a person meaning to obey the law may know his obligations and predict within decent limits the legal consequences of his conduct.

The broad principle applies with special point to the criminal law, where one of its expressions is in the hoary solemnity of an ancient Latin canon, *Nullum crimen, nulla poena, sine lege* — meaning there can be no crime, *and no punishment*, except as a law prescribes it. Again, the premise embodies the idea of a law reasonably precise and specific. The point was made with characteristic vigor by Mr. Justice Hugo L. Black. Though the quoted words were written in the course of a dissent, they are not matters for debate among us:

Experience, and wisdom flowing out of that experience, long ago led to the belief that agents of government should not be vested with power and discretion to define and punish as criminal past conduct which had not been clearly defined as a crime in advance. To this end, at least in part, written laws came into being, marking the boundaries of conduct for which public agents could thereafter impose punishment upon people. In contrast, bad governments either wrote no general rules of conduct at all, leaving that highly important task to the unbridled discretion of government agents at the moment of trial, or sometimes, history tells us, wrote their laws in an unknown tongue so that people could not understand them or else placed their written laws at such inaccessible spots that people could not read them.[1]

The agreed principles the Justice invoked would not be served, obviously, by a "law" proclaiming that "Anything deemed wrong by the Supreme Potentate (or a judge or a jury or anyone) shall be suitably punishable by imprisonment or death." If that quoted hypothetical seems too absurdly extreme to notice, or if the Latin aphorism sounds too utterly trite, it may pay to recall now and then how much blood and sacrifice have been spent for the seeming banality. It is worth remembering that through much of recorded history, men have lived under the tyranny of "laws" scarcely less arbitrary and unpredictable than my imaginary provision for the unfettered will of the Supreme Potentate. And before the reference to "history" leads to an excess of contemporary smugness, let me hasten to the present point of this discussion: that the principle of *nulla poena sine lege* is largely ignored by the penalty provisions of our criminal laws.

Our system does tolerably well in following part of the Latin maxim — the part that says *nullum crimen* (no crime) except under law. With some exceptions — not necessarily insignificant ones, but still fairly called exceptions — we follow the precept that conduct may not be branded criminal unless it has been proscribed by a reasonably intelligible law in advance of its occurrence. We strive, with a decent measure of success, to follow this famous pronouncement of our Supreme Court in a decision of early 1926: "a statute which either forbids or requires the doing of an act in terms so vague that men of common intelligence must necessarily guess at its meaning and differ as to its application, violates the first essential of due process of law."[2] But while that standard is generally implemented with respect to the laws' definitions of crimes, it is generally ignored in the portions of the same laws prescribing the range of permissible punishments. As to the penalty that may be imposed, our laws characteristically leave to the sentencing judge a range of choice that should be unthinkable in a "government of laws, not of men."

To underscore it by repetition, my first basic point is this: the almost wholly unchecked and sweeping powers we give to judges in the fashioning of sentences are terrifying and intolerable for a society that professes devotion to the rule of law.

For examples of such unbounded "discretion" (as it is called), it might suffice to consult the common experience of almost anyone even slightly acquainted with the criminal law. Let me recall only a few from the federal criminal code, with which I work. An assault upon a federal officer may be punishable by a fine and imprisonment for "not more than" ten years. The federal kidnapping law authorizes "imprisonment for any term of years or for life." Rape, which (believe it or not) may be a federal offense, leads to "death, or imprisonment for any term of years or for life."[3] To take some of our most common federal crimes — driving a stolen car across state lines may result in a term of "not more than five years," robbing a federally insured bank "not more than twenty-five years," and a postal employee's theft of a letter "not more than five years." The key phrase is, of course, the "not more than." It proclaims that federal trial judges, answerable only to their varieties of consciences, may

and do send people to prison for terms that may vary in any given case from none at all up to five, ten, thirty, or more years. This means in the great majority of federal criminal cases that a defendant who comes up for sentencing has no way of knowing or reliably predicting whether he will walk out of the courtroom on probation, or be locked up for a term of years that may consume the rest of his life, or something in between.

I would not wish to exaggerate; the reality is horrid enough without that. Defendants and their lawyers are able to anticipate within broad ranges in a fair number of cases. It is unlikely that the convicted murderer will be freed on the spot — though he may be. There are cases (depending upon the judge) in which probation is a good bet, though not a sure thing. But the law as it is written, and as it operates upon hapless defendants, is not significantly more knowable or predictable than the unregulated sentencing provisions indicate on their face. It is even an illicit form of qualification to insert a parenthetical "depending upon the judge," as I did a couple of sentences ago. For that goes, after all, to the very core of the evil our principles denounce. We claim, remember, to have a government of laws, not men. That promise to the ear is broken to the hope[4] when a sentence may range from zero up to thirty or more years in the unfettered discretion of miscellaneous judges.

The result, to be dwelt upon a little in the next chapter, is a wild array of sentencing judgments without any semblance of the consistency demanded by the ideal of equal justice. And it could not be otherwise under our non-system of so-called laws prescribing penalties.

The broad statutory ranges might approach a degree of ordered rationality if there were prescribed any standards for locating a particular case within any range. But neither our federal law nor that of any state I know contains meaningful criteria for this purpose. Our Congress and state legislatures have failed even to study and resolve the most basic of the questions affecting criminal penalties, the questions of justification and purpose. Why do we impose punishment? Or is it properly to be named "punishment"? Is our purpose retributive? Is it to deter the defendant himself or others in the community from committing crimes? Is it for reform? rehabilitation? incapacitation of dangerous people? Questions like these have engaged philosophers and students of the criminal law for centuries. There are no easy — probably no single, simple — answers. But perhaps differing from concerns about angels and pins, these problems as to the purposes of criminal sanctions are, or should be, at the bedrock of any rational structure of criminal law. It makes all the difference in the world, for instance, whether we think, as it is fashionable nowadays to say, that only rehabilitation of the offender can justify confinement. It is impossible on that premise to order a week in jail for the elderly official finally caught after years of graft, now turned out of office and disgraced, and neither in need of nor susceptible to any extant kinds of rehabilitation. Leaving this subject for the time being, I make the point that our legislators have not done the most rudimentary job of enacting meaningful sentencing "laws" when they have neglected even to sketch democratically determined statements of basic purpose. Left at large, wandering in deserts of uncharted discretion, the judges suit their own value systems insofar as they think about the problem at all.

It may be supposed by many that the broad discretion of the sentencing judge is actually limited by the discipline of the profession, including a body of criteria for placing a given case within the statutory range of up to "not more than" life in prison. The supposition would, unfortunately, be without substantial basis. There are, to be sure, some vague species of curbstone notions — gravity of the particular offense, defendant's prior record, age, background, etc. — that are thought to serve as guides in the particular case. But there is no agreement at all among the sentencers as to what the relevant criteria are or what their relative importance may be. Again, the point is made in all its stark horror by the compelling evidence that widely unequal sentences are imposed every day in great numbers for crimes and criminals not essentially distinguishable from each other.

The sentencing powers of the judges are,

in short, so far unconfined that, except for frequently monstrous maximum limits, they are effectively subject to no law at all. Everyone with the least training in law would be prompt to denounce a statute that merely said the penalty for crimes "shall be any term the judge sees fit to impose." A regime of such arbitrary fiat would be intolerable in a supposedly free society, to say nothing of being invalid under our due-process clause. But the fact is that we have accepted unthinkingly a criminal code creating in effect precisely that degree of unbridled power.

Beyond their failure to impose meaningful limits upon the judges, our criminal codes have displayed bizarre qualities of illogic and incongruity. Studies in the recent past revealed such things as these: a Colorado statute providing a ten-year maximum for stealing a dog, while another Colorado statute prescribed six months and a $500 fine for killing a dog; in Iowa, burning an empty building could lead to as much as a twenty-year sentence, but burning a church or school carried a maximum of ten; breaking into a car to steal from its glove compartment could result in up to fifteen years in California, while stealing the entire car carried a maximum of ten. Examples like these could be multiplied. The specific ones I cite may have been repaired in recent revisions. Their essentially illustrative character remains a fair reflection of the haphazard, disorderly qualities of our criminal penalty provisions. And while this motley look is disturbing, it is, of course, less fundamentally atrocious than the characteristic allowance of unfettered discretion to the sentencing judge selecting a term anywhere up to the high maximum.

Both qualities — the crazy-quilt statutory patterns and the blank-check powers of judges — reflect a number of important, if not uniformly pleasant, things about our society. In one of his many quotable insights — though it was not by any means exclusively his — Winston Churchill said:

The mood and temper of the public with regard to the treatment of crime and criminals is one of the most unfailing tests of the civilization of any country.

The "mood and temper" reflected in our

laws assigning punishments include a kind of simpleminded puritanism in which it is premised that conduct we dislike will end or sharply decrease if we pass a criminal law, with harsh sanctions, against it. Many of our criminal laws are enacted in an access of righteous indignation, with legislators fervidly out-shouting each other, with little thought or attention given to the large numbers of years inserted as maximum penalties. Written at the random, accidental times when particular evils come to be perceived, the statutes are not harmonized or coordinated with each other. The resulting jumbles of harsh anomalies are practically inevitable.

The more profound problem of excessive judicial power reflects a congeries of causes, advertent and accidental. To look only at the most important and positive of these, the prevalent thesis of the last hundred years or so has been that the treatment of criminals must be "individualized." The Mikado's boast, we have proudly thought, was silly; the punishment in a civilized society must fit the unique criminal, not the crime. The "crime," after all, may describe with a single, mechanical label kinds of misconduct and, more importantly, kinds of individual offenders displaying no similarities of any substantial sort. To assign rigidly a prescribed penalty for each crime (the so-called "tariff" system) is Procrustean. Sentiments like these carried the day long ago; it is scarcely imaginable that they could be questioned today.

Yet is is high time to question and confine them. Like all good ideas allowed to bloom without pruning or other attention, the notion of individualized sentencing has gotten quite out of hand. Reverting to elementary principles for a bit, we ought to recall that individualized justice is prima facie at war with such concepts, at least as fundamental, as equality, objectivity, and consistency in the law. It is not self-evident that the flesh-and-blood judge coming (say) from among the white middle classes will inevitably achieve admirable results when he individualizes the narcotics sentences of the suburban college youth and the streetwise young ghetto hustler. More importantly and more generally, is it perfectly clear that we want our judges to have such

power? In most matters of the civil law, while our success is variable, the quest is steadily for certainty, predictability, objectivity. The businessman wants to know what the tax will be on the deal, what the possible "exposure" may be from one risk or another. His lawyer may predict more or less successfully. But what no businessman wants (if he is honest) is a system of "individualized" taxes and exposures, depending upon who the judge or other official may turn out to be and how that decision-maker may assess the case and the individual before him.

This does not mean, of course, that everybody pays the same tax or is held to the same standards of liability. It does mean that the variations are made to turn upon objective, and objectively ascertainable, criteria — impersonal in the sense of the maxim that the law "is no respecter of persons" — and, above all, not left for determination in the wide-open, uncharted, standardless discretion of the judge administering "individualized" justice. The law's detachment is thought to be one of our triumphs. There is dignity and security in the assurance that each of us — plain or beautiful, rich or poor, black, white, tall, curly, whatever — is promised treatment as a bland, fungible "equal" before the law.

Is "individualized" sentencing consistent with that promise? Certainly not under the broad grants of subjective discretion we give to our judges under most American criminal codes today. The ideal of individualized justice is by no means an unmitigated evil, but it must be an ideal of justice *according to law*. This means we must reject individual distinctions — discriminations, that is — unless they can be justified by relevant tests capable of formulation and application with sufficient objectivity to ensure that the results will be more than the idiosyncratic ukases of particular officials, judges or others. I think an approach to such a standard is possible. I shall attempt to sketch it later on. In the meantime, however, if we had to choose between our status quo and a system of narrow "tariffs" for each category of crime, only my prejudiced belief that many judges are humane would make me pause in preferring the latter.

Having said that, let me flee from the appearance of undue complacency about the judges. The judges simply are not good enough — nobody could be — to redress the fundamental absurdities of the system. Some thoughts about the character and limits of the sentencers are the business of the next chapter.

II

INDIVIDUALIZED JUDGES

The absurdities of our sentencing laws would remain aesthetically repulsive, but might be otherwise tolerable, if our judges were uniformly brilliant, sensitive, and humane. Though I yield only to numerous judges in my admiration for those on the bench, I must acknowledge that we do not, in fact, approach any such state of affairs. Judges, I think, tend to be like people, perhaps even some cuts above the mine run but, unfortunately, less than gods or angels. And how, after all, could we dream it might be otherwise? Consider whence we acquire our judges, how we select them, how they are trained before and after they don robes.

To start near the beginning, most of our judges have been trained as lawyers. (There is a disappearing breed of petty magistrates for whom this is not necessarily true, and the picture is more bleak with respect to them.) Substantially nothing in the law curriculum is relevant to problems of sentencing. Indeed, until the last decade or so, the entire field of criminal law, being neither lucrative nor prestigious, occupied only a small and disfavored corner of our law schools' attention. While that state of neglect has undergone extensive repairs, these have scarcely grazed the area of interest here. Law students learn something about the rules of the criminal law, about the trial of cases, and, increasingly, about the rights of defendants before and during trial. They receive almost no instruction pertinent to sentencing. They may hear some fleeting references to the purposes of criminal penalties — some generalities about retribution, deterrence, etc. But so far as any intentional consequences of their legal education are concerned, they are taught by people

and exposed to curricula barren of even food for thought about sentencing.[5]

From among the total supply of law graduates who have not studied sentencing, there emerges in twenty or thirty years the narrower group from which we select the bulk of our judges. The most notable thing about this group for present purposes is that its members have mostly remained unencumbered by any exposure to, or learning about, the problems of sentencing. Characterized by their dominant attributes, our judges are men (mostly) of no longer tender years who have not associated much with criminal defendants, who have not seemed shrilly unorthodox, who have not lived recently in poverty, who have been modestly or more successful in their profession. They are likely to have had more than an average lawyer's amount of experience in the courtroom, though it is a little remarkable how large a percentage of those who go on the bench lack this credential.[6] They are unlikely to have defended more than a couple of criminal cases, if that many. They are more likely to have done a stint as prosecutors, usually as a brief chapter in the years shortly after law school. However much or little they have been exposed to the criminal trial process, most people ascending (as we say) the bench have paid only the most fleeting and superficial attention to matters affecting the sentences of convicted defendants. In this respect, the pattern set in the law school is carried forward and reenforced. The professional show ends with the verdict or the plea. The histrionics later on at the sentencing proceeding may be moving or embarrassing, even effective on occasion, but are no part of the skills the average lawyer prizes and polishes as special tools of his trade.

Whatever few things may be said for them, our procedures for selecting judges do not improve the prospects of sensitive, knowledgeable sentencing. It may happen sometimes, but I do not recall ever hearing anything relevant to that subject in discussions of the qualifications of prospective judges. I put to one side for this purpose the disgraceful process, widely used, of political nominations, where the candidates are too often selected without concern for any of the qualities supposedly wanted in suitable judges. Even where relevant questions are asked, the professional criteria, reflecting the training and the profession at work, simply do not include meaningful inquiries as to whether the prospective judge is fit to wield the awesome sentencing power. Apart from elementary, and usually superficial, glances at vague qualities of "temperament," we would not know really where to look or what to ask on a subject destined to loom so large among the prospective judge's impacts upon his fellow citizens.

The judges fetched up in the process are a mixed bag, without many surprises. Some grow to be concerned and spend substantial time brooding about their sentencing responsibilities. Most, I think, are not so preoccupied. Judges are commonly heard to say that sentencing is the grimmest and most solemnly absorbing of their tasks. This is not exactly hypocrisy. It is, however, among the less meaningful things judges report about their work. Measured by the time devoted to it, by the amount of deliberation and study before each decision, and by the attention to the subject as a field of intellectual concern in general, the judges' effective expenditures of themselves in worries over sentencing do not reflect a profound sense of mission. Judges don't talk much, to each other or to anyone, about the issues and difficulties in sentencing. They don't read or write about such things. Because strictly "legal" problems are rare in this area, and appeals are normally not allowed to attack the sentence, the reading pile rarely contains anything pertinent. The judge is likely to read thick briefs, hear oral argument, and then take days or weeks to decide who breached a contract for delivery of onions. The same judge will read a pre-sentence report, perhaps talk to a probation officer, hear a few minutes of pleas for mercy — invest, in sum, less than an hour in all — before imposing a sentence of ten years in prison.

Some judges, confronting the enormities of what they do and how they do it, are visted with occasional onsets of horror or, at least, self-doubt. Learned Hand — to some, the greatest of our judges; to all,

among a small handful of the greatest — reflected such sentiments. Never accounted soft towards criminals among any who knew his work, he said of his role in sentencing: "Here I am an old man in a long nightgown making muffled noises at people who may be no worse than I am." A distinguished committee of federal judges, with Hand among its members, acknowledged "the incompetency of certain types of judges to impose sentence." It spoke of judges "not temperamentally equipped" to learn this task acceptably, of judges who compensate for their own inadequacies by "the practice of imposing severe sentences," of judges "who crusade against certain crimes which they feel disposed to stamp out by drastic sentences."[7] Other judges have expressed similar misgivings — about their own and (perhaps more strongly) about their colleagues' handling of powers so huge and so undefined over the lives of their fellow men.

Self-criticism, uncertainty, and a resultant disposition toward restraint are useful qualities in judges — for sentencing and for other aspects of the job. They are not, however, in oversupply. The kinds of people who make their way onto the bench are not by and large given to humility. If there are seeds of meekness to begin with, the trial bench is not the most fertile place for their cultivation. The trial judge may be reversed with regularity; he may be the butt of lawyers' jokes and an object lesson in the law schools; but the incidents of his daily life — the rituals of deference, the high bench, the visible evidences of power asserted directly and face-to-face — are not designed to shrink his self-image. It should be said in all fairness that the Hamlets of this world are not suited to the business of presiding over trial courts. Scores of things must be decided every day. It is often more important, as Brandeis taught, that the decisions be made than that they be correct. Both the volume and the nature of the enterprise — the regulation of the flow of evidence, the predictable eruption of emergencies, the endless stream of cloudy questions demanding swift answers — generate pressures for decisive action. And so the trial judge, who starts his career well along the course of a life in which self-effacement has not been the key thing, is encouraged to follow his assertive ways.

Conditioned in the direction of authoritarianism by his daily life in court, long habituated as a lawyer to the stance of the aggressive contestant, and exercising sentencing powers frequently without practical limits, the trial judge is not discouraged from venting any tendencies toward righteous arrogance. The books and the reliable folklore are filled with the resulting horror stories — of fierce sentences and orgies of denunciatory attacks upon defendants. One need not be a revolutionist or an enemy of the judiciary to predict that untrained, untested, unsupervised men armed with great power will perpetrate abuses. The horrible cases may result from moral or intellectual or physical deficiencies — or from all together. But we can be sure there will be some substantial number of such cases.

Everyone connected with this grim business has his own favorite atrocity stories. James V. Bennett, the enlightened former Director of the Federal Bureau of Prisons, wrote this often-quoted passage, which appears in a 1964 Senate Document:

That some judges are arbitrary and even sadistic in their sentencing practices is notoriously a matter of record. By reason of senility or a virtually pathological emotional complex some judges summarily impose the maximum on defendants convicted of certain types of crimes or all types of crimes. One judge's disposition along this line was a major factor in bringing about a sitdown strike at Connecticut's Wethersfield Prison in 1956. There is one judge who, as a matter of routine, always gives the maximum sentence and who of course is avoided by every defense lawyer. If they have the misfortune of having their case arise before him they lay the ground for appeals since experience has indicated the appeals court is sympathetic and will, if possible, overturn the sentencing court. I know of one judge who continued to sit on the bench and sentence defendants to prison while he was undergoing shock treatments for a mental illness.[8]

Forgoing the temptation to parade more lurid instances, I think a couple of mild, substantially colorless cases within my own ken give some sense of the unchained sentencing power in operation. One story concerns a casual anecdote over cocktails in a rare conversation among judges touching the subject of sentencing. Judge X, to designate him in a lawyerlike way, told of a defendant for whom the judge, after reading the presentence report, had decided tentatively upon a sentence of four years' imprisonment. At the sentencing hearing in the courtroom, after hearing counsel, Judge X invited the defendant to exercise his right to address the court in his own behalf. The defendant took a sheaf of papers from his pocket and proceeded to read from them, excoriating the judge, the "kangaroo court" in which he'd been tried, and the legal establishment in general. Completing the story, Judge X said, "I listened without interrupting. Finally, when he said he was through, I simply gave the son of a bitch five years instead of four." None of the three judges listening to that (including me) tendered a whisper of dissent, let alone a scream of outrage. But think about it. Not the relatively harmless, if revealing, reference to the defendant as a son of a bitch. But a year in prison for speaking disrespectfully to a judge.[9] Was that, perhaps, based on upon a rapid, subtle judgment that a defendant behaving this way in the courtroom showed insufficient evidence of remorse and prospects of reform? I confidently think not. Should defendants be warned that exercise of their "right" to address the court may be this costly? They are not.[10] Would we tolerate an act of Congress penalizing such an outburst by a year in prison? The question, however rhetorical, misses one truly exquisite note of agony: that the wretch sentenced by Judge X never knew, because he was never told, how the fifth year of his term came to be added.

That short story epitomizes much that prompts me to be writing this: the large and unregulated character of the sentencing power, the resulting arbitrariness permitted in its exercise, the frightening chanciness of judicial tempers and reactions. Whatever our platonic vision of the judge may be, this subject, like others, must be considered in the setting of a real world of real, mixed, fallible judicial types.

Let me turn here to my second, somewhat more appalling, anecdote. I happened a few years ago to preside at a widely publicized trial of a government official charged with corrupt behavior and perjury, convicted finally on a perjury count. While the conviction was for perjury only, the aura of corruption tended to overhang the case. In the weeks between the verdict and the sentence, as sometimes happens, I received some unsolicited mail, often vindictive in tone, not infrequently anonymous. One letter was from a more august source. A state trial judge, from Florida, wrote as follows:

Dear Judge Frankel:

I have read with interest the proceedings in the case involving above Defendant and his influence peddling, perjury, etc. . . . .

One of the more serious problems confronting Judges in the State Courts, such as the one in which I preside, is the leniency extended by the Federal Judiciary and the pampering of prisoners and parolees by the Federal Penal and Parole Systems. It is difficult for me to justify giving an individual 10, 15, 20 years or life for armed robberies involving a few dollars when persons in the Federal Judicial System are usually given much smaller sentences and are paroled after having served a few months or years of their sentences, and then are proceeded to be loosely supervised by an overly compassionate and headturning parole system.

Accordingly, as an individual, as a Judge in the State Court, as a father of a young man serving upon the High Seas of the country as an enlisted man, and as the step-father of a drafted Army Private on Asiatic soil, and as an individual who has served honorably for five years in the service of the United States Navy in wartime, let me strongly urge upon you that you impose the maximum sentence as provided by law upon the above Defendant, and upon any other individuals who would tend to destroy and demoralize our nation's government from within.

The author of that letter was deeply in earnest. What he wrote was not intended as a caricature. I am sure he did not mean to document the enormities we invite when we empower untested and unqualified officials to spew wholesale sentences of "10, 15, 20 years or life for armed robberies involving a few dollars. . . ." He was not applying for the analyst's couch when he tendered up

his generations of patriotism, his cruelty, and his confident ownership of ultimate truths. He was not — I assume, regretfully, he still is not — slowed for a second by any shibboleth about "individualized treatment" when he offered advice on sentencing to a fellow judge based upon newspaper intelligence, without even seeing the defendant or reading a presentence report.

What that Florida colleague did was merely to dramatize the macabre point that sweeping penalty statutes allow sentences to be "individualized" not so much in terms of defendants but mainly in terms of the wide spectrums of character, bias, neurosis, and daily vagary encountered among occupants of the trial bench. It is no wonder that wherever supposed professionals in the field — criminologists, penologists, probation officers, and, yes, lawyers and judges — discuss sentencing, the talk inevitably dwells upon the problem of "disparity." Some writers have quibbled about the definitiveness of the evidence showing disparity. It is among the least substantial of quibbles. The evidence is conclusive that judges of widely varying attitudes on sentencing, administering statutes that confer huge measures of discretion, mete out widely divergent sentences where the divergences are explainable only by the variations among the judges, not by material differences in the defendants or their crimes. Even in our age of science and skepticism, the conclusion would seem to be among those still acceptable as self-evident. What would require proof of weighty kind, and something astonishing in the way of theoretical explanation, would be the suggestion that assorted judges, subject to little more than their own unfettered wills, could be expected to impose consistent sentences. In any event, if proof were needed that sentences vary simply because judges vary, there is plenty of it. The evidence grows every time judges gather to discuss specific cases and compare notes on the sentences they would impose upon given defendants. The disparities, if they are no longer astonishing, remain horrible.

The broad experience of former Prison Director Bennett merits another quotation here from the 1964 Senate Document mentioned earlier:

Take, for instance, the cases of two men we received last spring. The first man had been convicted of cashing a check for $58.40. He was out of work at the time of his offense, and when his wife become ill and he needed money for rent, food, and doctor bills, he became the victim of temptation. He had no prior criminal record. The other man cashed a check for $35.20. He was also out of work and his wife had left him for another man. His prior record consisted of a drunk charge and a nonsupport charge. Our examination of these two cases indicated no significant differences for sentencing purposes. But they appeared before different judges and the first man received 15 years in prison and the second man 30 days.

These are not cases picked out of thin air. In January the President of the United States commuted to time served the sentence of a first offender, a former Army lieutenant, and a veteran of over 500 days in combat, who had been given 18 years for forging six small checks.

In one of our institutions a middle-aged credit union treasurer is serving 117 days for embezzling $24,000 in order to cover his gambling debts. On the other hand, another middle-aged embezzler with a fine past record and a fine family is serving 20 years, with 5 years probation to follow. At the same institution is a war veteran, a 39-year-old attorney who has never been in trouble before, serving 11 years for illegally importing parrots into this country. Another who is destined for the same institution is a middle-aged tax accountant who on tax fraud charges received 31 years and 31 days in consecutive sentences. In stark contrast, at the same institution last year an unstable young man served out his 98-day sentence for armed bank robbery.[11]

Protesting more than enough, let me say again that the tragic state of disorder in our sentencing practices is not attributable to any unique endowments of sadism or bestiality among judges as a species. Without claiming absolute detachment, I am prepared to hypothesize that judges in general, if only because of occupational conditioning, may be somewhat calmer, more dispassionate, and more humane than the average of people across the board. But nobody has the experience of being sentenced by "judges in general." The particular defendant on some existential day confronts a specific judge. The occupant of the bench on that day may be punitive, patriotic, self-righteous, guilt-ridden, and more than customarily dyspeptic. The vice in our system is that all such qualities have free rein as well as potentially fatal impact upon the defendant's finite life.

Such individual, personal powers are not evil only, or mainly, because evil people may come to hold positions of authority. The more pervasive wrong is that a regime of substantially limitless discretion is by definition arbitrary, capricious, and antithetical to the rule of law. Some judges I know believe (and act on the belief) that all draft resisters should receive the maximum sentence, five years; this iron view rests variously upon calculations concerning time off for good behavior, how long those in uniform serve, how contemptible it is to refuse military service, etc. Other judges I know have thought, at least lately, that persons opposing service on grounds of moral or other principle, even if technically guilty of a felony, should be subjected to token terms in prison, or none at all. It is not directly pertinent here whether either category of judge is right, or whether both have failed to exercise, case by case, the discretion with which the law entrusts them. The simple point at the moment is the contrast between such individual, personal, conflicting criteria and the ideal of the rule of law.

Beyond the random spreads of judicial attitudes, there is broad latitude in our sentencing laws for kinds of class bias that are commonly known, never explicitly acknowledged, and at war with the superficial neutrality of the statute as literally written. Judges are on the whole more likely to have known personally tax evaders, or people just like tax evaders, than car thieves or dope pushers. Dichotomies of a similar kind are obvious beyond the need to multiply examples. Can such items of personal experience fail to have effects upon sentencing? I do not stop at simpleminded observations about the substantial numbers of judges who simply do not impose prison sentences for tax evasion though the federal law, for example, provides a maximum of five years per count (and tax-evasion prosecutions frequently involve several tax years, with each a separate count). There are more things at stake than judicial "bias" when tax evaders average relatively rare and brief prison terms, while more frequent and much longer average terms (under a statute carrying the same five-year maximum) are imposed for interstate transport of stolen motor vehicles.[12] Whatever other factors may be operating, however, it is not possible to avoid the impression that the judges' private senses of good and evil are playing significant parts no matter what the law on the books may define as the relative gravity of the several crimes. And, although it anticipates a later subject, this is certainly the focus of the familiar jailhouse complaint that "the more you steal, the less of a sentence you get." I believe the complaint has a basis in the fundamental realities and in the way justice is seen to be dispensed. The latter aspect is important in itself: among our sounder aphorisms is the one teaching that justice must not only be done, but must appear to be done. Both objectives are missed by a system leaving to individual preferences and value judgments the kind of discretion our judges have over sentencing.

I have touched upon individual traits of temperament and variations of an ideological, political, or social character. The sentencing power is so far unregulated that even matters of a relatively technical, seemingly "legal" nature are left for the individual judge, and thus for whimsical handling, at least in the sense that no two judges need be the same. Should a defendant be deemed to deserve some leniency if he has pled guilty rather than going to trial? Many judges say yes; many, perhaps a minority, say no; all do as they please. Should a prior criminal record enhance punishment? Most judges seem to think so. Some take the view that having "paid the price" for prior offenses, the defendant should not pay again now. Again, dealer's choice. Many judges believe it a mitigating factor if defendant yields to the pressure, moral or other, to pay back what he has taken. Others condemn this view as an illicit use of criminal sanctions for private redress. Once more, no rule of law enforces either of these contradictory judgments. There are other illustrations — relating, for example, to family conditions, defendant's behavior at trial, the consideration, if any, for turning state's evidence — all subject to the varying and unregulated views of judges. The point is, I hope, sufficiently made that our sentencing judgments splay wildly as results of unpredictable and numerous variables embodied in the numerous and variegated inhabitants of our trial benches.

Among the articles of wisdom for which we honor those who wrote the American Constitution was the keen concern to test all powers by the possibility of having wicked or otherwise unsound men in office. In this realistic light, it was deemed vital to confine power as much as possible and to hedge it about with checking and balancing powers. Like everything, such precautions can be overdone. But we have lost sight of them almost entirely, and without justification, in our sweeping grants of sentencing authority.

NOTES*

1. *Ginzburg v. United States.* 383 U.S. 463, 477 (1966).
2. *Connally v. General Construction Co.*, 269 U.S. 385, 391 (1926).
3. "Whoever, within the special maritime and territorial jurisdiction of the United States [ships, federal land, buildings, etc.], commits rape shall suffer death, or imprisonment for any term of years or for life." U.S. Code, Title 18, section 2031.
4. "And be these juggling fiends no more believ'd,
   That palter with us in a double sense;
   That keep the word of promise to our ear,

And break it to our hope." *Macbeth*, v. 7. 48–51.
5. Everything in law, as in life, has exceptions. So I should acknowledge that there are here and there in the law schools some meaningful offerings on the subject. Professor Leonard Orland of the University of Connecticut Law School has lately been giving a well-stocked course on postconviction matters, including significant and provocative ideas about sentencing. My thoughtful and energetic colleague on the Federal District Court for the Southern District of New York, Judge Harold R. Tyler, Jr., has been finding time in recent years to offer enlightenment on similar

*Footnotes have been abridged, edited, and renumbered.

subjects at the New York University School of Law. I am certain there are other things of the sort in progress elsewhere. The general point I have made remains basically accurate even today and was sound without noticeable qualification when people now judging went to law school.

6. I am not myself in a position for exuberant stone-throwing. Before I became a trial judge in 1965, I had spent many years working mainly as an appellate lawyer. I had tried some cases and done a fair amount of trial lawyer's work, but had managed somehow never to face a jury. I had argued criminal appeals, but had never been on either side of a criminal trial. In defense of myself and the bar-association committees that found me acceptable, if not the answer to their prayers, I think it fair to add that the mechanics and economics of big-city law practice lead the members of large, respectable law firms to settle most of their clients' disputes short of actual trial.

7. Judicial conference of Senior Circuit Judges, *Report of the Committee on Punishment for Crime*, pp. 26, 27 (1942).

8. "The Sentence — Its Relation to Crime and Rehabilitation," in *Of Prisons and Justice*. S. Doc. No. 70, 88th Cong., 2d sess., p. 311 (1964).

9. Only the prissiness of a lawyer's training would require a footnote here to acknowledge that I have neglected the calculation of probable time off for good behavior.

10. Dr. Willard Gaylin, in his work *In the Service of their Country — War Resisters in Prison* (New York, Viking Press, 1970), p. 283, reports an episode identical with mine about Judge X. There is other evidence — including, I fear, some results of my own introspection — that the defendant's rare outburst may carry a monstrous price.

11. "Countdown for Judicial Sentencing" in *Of Prisons and Justice*. S. Doc. No. 70, 88th Cong., 2d sess., p. 331 (1964).

12. It may serve only to confirm a priori hunches, but consider these illustrative figures for federal sentences in the fiscal year 1969. Of 502 defendants convicted for income tax fraud, 95, or 19 percent, received prison terms, the average term being three months. Of 3,791 defendants sentenced for auto theft, 2,373, or 63 percent, went to prison, the average term being 7.6 months. From the Administrative Office of the U.S. Courts' publication, *Federal Offenders in the United States District Courts*, 1969, pp. 146–7 (1971).

13. PHILADELPHIA REVISITED: AN EXAMINATION OF BAIL AND DETENTION TWO DECADES AFTER FOOTE

JOHN S. GOLDKAMP

Reprinted, with permission of the National Council on Crime and Delinquency, from John S. Goldkamp, "Philadelphia Revisited: An Examination of Bail and Detention Two Decades after Foote," *Crime & Delinquency*, April 1980, pp. 179–92.

■ Bail decisions by judges are administered for the purpose of assurance that defendants will be present at court proceedings. Quite often the administration of the bail process by the judiciary is made for reasons other than the assurance of court appearance.

This practice leads to the use of discretionary abuse on the part of judges and according to Goldkamp, "judges are still free to arrive at their decisions impressionistically, idiosyncratically, or conscientiously according to existing guidelines." This selection focuses on Caleb Foote's landmark study of bail in Philadelphia in 1954 and contrasts its findings with a 1977 study conducted in the same city. This second study by Goldkamp was not intended to be a replication of Foote's research, but rather to offer an opportunity to measure the progress of reform in the bail process over a twenty-year period. ■

AS A RESULT OF the publication of Professor Caleb Foote's study of bail and detention in Philadelphia in 1954,[1] Philadelphia became a symbol of all that was "wrong" with the American bail system. Although Foote was certainly not the first to criticize the American way of bail,[2] he was the first to undertake a comprehensive examination of bail practices, pretrial detention, and their implications for criminally charged defendants. The Philadelphia Bail Study, as his study was called, was significant not only because it documented many inequities and raised questions concerning the constitutionality of bail and detention practices, but also because it served as a major catalyst for bail reform efforts that began in New York in early 1960s. Many years after publication of the study — and partly as a result of it — Philadelphia came to be viewed as an en-

tirely different kind of bellwether: as a model of bail reform and exemplary pretrial services that other cities sought eagerly to emulate. From the point of view of bail practices, Philadelphia had been transformed from a "traditional" to a "reform" jurisdiction.[3]

The aim of this paper is to explore some of the changes that have occurred in bail practices in Philadelphia since the time of Foote's study and to consider their implications. This will be achieved by using Philadelphia as a unique case study of the recent concern about the administration of bail. More specifically, the major findings set forth in Foote's 1954 study of bail in Philadelphia will be contrasted with a more recent study of bail decision making in the same city[4] to assess the extent to which the major difficulties pointed out by Foote have or have not been addressed and resolved after more than twenty years.[5] The second study of bail in Philadelphia, it should be noted, was not designed as a replication of the first; thus, comparision of specific findings is not appropriate. However, comparison of the general findings of both studies using the issues set forth by Foote may provide a gauge for evaluating the present state of affairs in bail, bail reform, and pretrial detention.

THE PHILADELPHIA BAIL STUDY

It is difficult to discover an issue that was addressed by the bail reform movement of the 1960s that was not first discussed by Foote in his 1954 study. Because of the comprehensive treatment of bail and detention in that study, it may be helpful to organize the issues raised by Foote according to the following perspectives for the purposes of this discussion: the unstructured exercise of discretion in bail matters, the procedural impediments to the fair administration of bail, the presumption of guilt and pretrial punishment, the inequitable treatment of defendants at bail, and questions about the effectiveness of bail practices.[6]

PROBLEMS WITH DISCRETION IN BAIL
DETERMINATIONS

Foote argued persuasively in the Philadelphia Study and in subsequent discussions[7] that bail was administered for only one legitimate purpose: to assure the presence of defendants at required court proceedings.[8] In his examination of Philadelphia bail practices, Foote sought evidence to support a finding that bail decisions had that specific objective. After many observations of court bail proceedings and analysis of data collected from the courts and the prosecutor's office, he was unable to conclude that bail judges in Philadelphia were transacting their business on the basis of standards reflecting that concern. Instead, bail appeared to be decided accordingly to only one criterion, the criminal charge:

Custom has established a standard related to the nature of the crime charged, a standard which is sufficiently flexible to permit in any crime an amount sufficient to have the practical effect of holding most defendants in prison. The individual is subordinated to the class into which he is placed according to the type of crime with which he is charged, although what relationship to the risk of non-appearance this may have is unknown.[9]

Foote explained that the bail judges' reliance on the charge criterion was a product of "the administrative problems created by a large volume of cases" that necessitated "the creation of a standard which can be easily and rapidly applied." He acknowledged also the logic behind use of such a standard: "As the severity of the crime and possible punishment increases, the defendant, having more to fear, becomes more likely to jump bail."[10] However, doubting the validity of such a rationale, Foote perceived the popularity of the charge criterion as reflecting the judges' preference for an all-purpose standard that could be easily manipulated to accomplish a variety of aims.

Foote encountered evidence of some highly discretionary and highly questionable uses of bail. Most notable among these — and most objectionable according to Foote's view — were the manipulation of cash bail by judges intent on detaining defendants they deemed particularly dangerous (preventive detention) and the use of cash bail (and detention) for punitive purposes. In short, bail determinations in Philadelphia were seen as easily prone to abuses of discretion and as based on a standard that was so broad that it could be used for any purpose.

The role of the bondsman in the bail system in Philadelphia at that time was criticized as another source of potential abuse of discretion. In 1954, when nearly all bail decisions were framed in terms of cash amounts, bondsmen brokered the prospects of pretrial release for a great share of defendants. Whether or not a defendant was able to gain release may have depended frequently on the bondsmen's discretionary selection of their clientele. That is, certain defendants may not have been viewed favorably as "good business" by bondsmen — and thereby been prevented from raising the cash needed for their release — because they did not meet the bondsmen's selection criteria based on business concerns. Often these criteria had little to do with risk of flight; conceivably, poor defendants with low bails may have been turned down merely because the fees to be earned by the bondsmen would have been considered too small. (Bondsmen may also have considered persons charged with petty offenses as much more likely to abscond and thus as not worth the trouble or the financial risk.)

PROCEDURAL IMPEDIMENTS TO
THE FAIR ADMINISTRATION OF BAIL

Foote portrayed the bail decision-making machinery in Philadelphia as characterized by "divided responsibility," with the result that many defendants experienced considerable delays awaiting bail setting or had bail denied altogether because of procedural inefficiencies. Persons charged with minor offenses stood the best chance of having bail set relatively quickly, because this was done by magistrates in the lowest court. But defendants charged with more serious crimes (felonies and capital cases) had bail denied in the lowest court at their first appearances pending application to a higher court through the district attorney's office. According to Foote, it was often not clear to defendants who had bail refused in the original bail court that they had the right to have bail set upon application to the higher court. Even those represented by counsel (who submitted the request automatically) were detained a week or more while waiting for the second hearing. Thus, the defendants charged with more serious crimes were not only likely to have higher bails set (because of the unwritten law that fixed bail according to the seriousness of the charge), but, in addition, had to submit to procedural delays and denials simply because of the nature of their charges. Foote concluded that "the division of responsibility, which makes possible such infringements of the right to prompt bail, is an anachronism which has no practical utility."[11]

FOOTE'S RECOMMENDATIONS
FOR IMPROVING BAIL PRACTICES

Based on this thorough evaluation, Foote offered several recommendations for improving the bail system. Failure to appear at court should be made, he suggested, into a criminal offense. The use of cash bail should be substantially reduced in favor of other nonfinancial conditions (such as personal recognizance). In what must certainly have been received as a "radical" statement at that time, he argued that "the ultimate abolition of the bail system is the only solution for the prejudice to jail defendants which results from their low economic status."[12] Furthermore, short of abolishing cash bail for poor defendants, bail amounts ought to be substantially reduced to render release affordable to more defendants. (Foote had noted that many

poor defendants facing nonserious charges were being detained on relatively small amounts of bail.) The preventive detention use of bail decision making ought to be curbed, for bail was not the appropriate means for addressing the danger question: "If it is feared that defendants will commit further crimes if released, the remedy is not preventive detention but a prompt trial."[13] Finally, Foote recommended that the damage to the presumption of innocence of detained defendants be tempered by minimizing the punitive features of pretrial confinement.

CURRENT BAIL PRACTICES
IN PHILADELPHIA

As part of a broader investigation of bail decision making and the role of pretrial detention in American criminal justice, bail practices in Philadelphia were again studied in 1977. Cases of a large number of defendants who had bail decided in the fall of 1975 were studied after their final resolutions by 1977.[14] Between 1954 and the more recent inquiry, the major occurrence of relevance was the bail reform movement — in which Foote's work played an important seminal role. Logically, the most noticeable changes in Philadelphia's bail practices can be explained principally as a result of bail reform. The most striking difference in Philadelphia "before" and "after," consequently, is the radical alteration of the structure of the early phases of its criminal justice system that deal with bail and pretrial release. These structural changes are capsuled here.

Perhaps the most striking departure from the Philadelphia of 1954 in present bail matters is the fact that the bail function is transacted in a centrally organized fashion. All defendants (except homicide defendants) have bail decided no more than twelve hours after their arrest, at a court held in one location and then only after they have been thoroughly interviewed for information on community ties, employment, income, health problems, and prior record. All of the municipal court judges whose responsibility it is to decide bail have available to them reports from the Pretrial Services Division providing the alternative kinds of data that Foote and his predecessors considered necessary for "individualized" bail decisions. Gone is the "divided responsibility"; and entire division of the Philadelphia court system is now responsible for pretrial services, which includes supervising defendants on release (notifying them of court dates, etc.) and providing thorough background information on defendants going to their first appearances before a judge. Notably, "individualization" has occurred in Philadelphia without the delays foreseen by Foote. Not only do lower court judges have additional defendant data to consider as alternatives to the charge standard criticized by Foote, but, in addition, all non-law-trained lower court judges have been replaced by lawyer judges.

The Foote of more than two decades ago would be further astonished to discover that, according to the more recent study, the use of cash bail as a decision option has considerably diminished. Nearly half of all defendants in the 1977 study were granted release on personal recognizance. Compared with the 75 percent detention rate reported by Foote in 1954, only 25 percent of Philadelphia defendants experienced pretrial detention beyond a twenty-four-hour period in 1975; half of these — only 12 percent of all defendants — remained confined during the entire preadjudicatory interval. In addition, defendants in 1975 who were not released immediately after first appearance still had a further recourse: They were considered for conditional release, a form of release that is conditioned by participation in certain programs or supervision. There is evidence also that defendants who were detained in Philadelphia in 1975 were confined for considerably shorter periods than previously. Where possible, they were given an accelerated court calendar. (Philadelphia, like the rest of Pennsylvania, has been operating in accordance with a "speedy trial" provision.) Moreover, special sessions of court were held at the jail to expedite the processing of minor cases (usually misdemeanors) that might otherwise have been unnecessarily delayed.

In addition to centrally organized bail and pretrial release functions and the appearance of "individualized" bail decision making, a further major alteration in the Philadelphia way of bail can now be observed: the disappearance of the bondsman. In a major reform, Philadelphia's courts have replaced bondsmen with a Ten Percent program which allows defendants to deposit 10 percent of the amount of their cash bail with the court. The deposit is refundable (minus a service charge) as soon as it has been ascertained that the defendant has appeared in court. In the event that defendants cannot affort the 10 percent amount themselves, the use of third-party bail is strongly favored as a way of inducing relatives or friends to have a stake in assuring that a defendant will not face the necessity of resorting to a bondsman. Apparently, many of Foote's criticisms concerning the use of cash bail in Philadelphia were addressed by the time of the 1977 study.

HAVE THE MAJOR ISSUES BEEN RESOLVED?

Clearly, major reforms have been implemented in Philadelphia since the time of Foote's study. Philadelphia has been transformed from a jurisdiction symbolizing the disorder and abuses characteristic of the American bail system in the 1950s to a model bail reform jurisdiction. But have the major issues raised by Foote in 1954 been fully resolved? Perhaps not.

DISCRETION

On the surface, at least, it would appear that the discretion which under the former system was so vulnerable to abuse has not been solidly structured. Judges are presently instructed in the *Pennsylvania Rules of Court*[15] to weigh as many as sixteen items of information about defendants in deciding bail. (Among these are not only the nature of the charge and the prior record, but also a variety of other kinds of data, such as defendants' community ties, employment, and financial resources.) The Pretrial Services Division was created to make possible this information-gathering and digesting function. Although implementation of this reform appears to be the very embodiment of the "individualization" ideal that evolved from Beeley[16] and the Wickersham Commission[17] through Foote, it is interesting to note that the 1977 study found that the nature of the criminal charge still played the dominant role in bail determinations.[18] The "standard," criminal charge, that was so criticized by Foote appears to survive undaunted — despite the existence of newer decision-making guidelines and an ROR (personal recognizance release) program to help operationalize them.

The fact that the alternative kinds of defendant data (e.g., community ties) diligently collected by the ROR program staff in Philadelphia did not play an influential role in either bail determinations or the determination of relase or detention in the recent study suggests two hypotheses: (1) Either judges remain convinced that criminal charge is the most reliable predictor of risk of flight, or (2) they remain steadfast in adhering to a flexibile, all-purpose standard that, as Foote explained, has the "practical effect of holding" any defendants who for various reasons may have impressed bail judges unfavorably. In short, not only is judicial consideration of standards governing bail decision making still highly discretionary, but so are the uses to which the bail function may presently be put. Because judges are not required to communicate the reasoning behind their bail decisions, there can be no guarantee that decision goals may not shift freely from appearance concerns to preventive detention bases on defendant dangerousness, as well as punitive, political, or other discretionary purposes.[19]

INEQUITABLE TREATMENT OF DEFENDANTS IN BAIL PRACTICES

The inequities inherent in procedural delay and in the role of bondsmen in the former Philadelphia practices have been virtually eliminated, as noted above, but the problem of disparity in bail decisions has not. The 1977 study did not address the issue of judge-to-judge inconsistency, but there is no reason to assume that such variation has been noticeably affected by bail reform practices. (This statement is supported by the 1977 finding noted above that judges were not influenced by the availability of data on community ties provided as a

result of bail reform.) More than that, however, a major finding of the 1977 study was that, after acknowledging the influential role of the criminal charge, and two or three other less influential items, a great amount of the variation in bail decisions could not be explained by any recorded defendant data.[20] (At least fifty items of information pertaining to legal, demographic, and other defendant characteristics were considered in the empirical analysis in that study.) The implication of this finding is that other factors that are difficult to measure — such as the personal judicial philosophies of those setting bail and their perceptions of defendants — may have accounted for a large amount of variation in bail decisions. To the extent that bail decisions were not explainable empirically by observable patterns, irregularity or disparity remained one of their principal features. It is difficult to feel confident that, even today, similar defendants in Philadelphia are likely to receive similar outcomes at bail. Clearly, serious questions of the fairness of bail decisions remain.

In repone to the issue of economic discrimination inherent in a system of cash bail raised by Foote in 1954, it must be said that reforms in Philadelphia have made substantial inroads. To begin with, ROR in 1975 was used in nearly half of all cases — compared with a negligible percentage of cases in 1954. For that half of defendants, then, economic discrimination is no longer a relevant concern.[21] For the other half, it is certain that the economic impact of cash bail has been lessened through the Ten Percent program. If it cannot be stated for certain that the "price" of cash bail has gone down under the program (and some have suggested that judges have simply adjusted the amount of bail upward to compensate), it can at least be stated that defendants now regain the amounts that previously would have been lost to the bondsman's fee. Nevertheless, because even low bail may be unaffordable to poor defendants, any bail system relying on cash bail will always be discriminatory to a certain extent, by defintion.

The third equity issue raised by Foote concerning the possible disadvantage suffered by detained defendants in the subsequent processing of their cases was specifically examined in the 1977 study. The question here was whether pretrial custody in itself had an influence on later outcomes of defendants' cases. After detailed empirical analysis of the relationship as it pertained to dismissal, diversion, conviction, and sentencing, it was found that the relationship survived the exercise of controls only when sentencing outcomes were considered.[22] In short, it appeared that the relationship between pretrial custody and later outcomes was nonexistent (for the decisions regarding dismissal/continuation and acquittal/conviction) or spurious (for the decision about diversion/nondiversion) except at sentencing when sentences were dichotomized as nonincarcerative/in carcerative. Specifically, detained defendants whose cases later progressed through the criminal process all the way to sentencing were substantially more likely to receive sentences to incarceration than their counterparts who had been released before the adjudication of their cases. Though the applicability of the "effects of detention" issue has been narrowed by the analysis conducted in the 1977 study from the more general statement made in 1954, it still presents a serious equal protection dilemma.

CONCLUSION

Apparently, the assessment of bail practices in Philadelphia published by Professor Foote in 1954 has served as a blueprint of issues and change for the years of reform that succeeded his study. Two decades after his landmark study, bail reform has wrought substantial changes in the administration of bail in Philadelphia, and many of the issues raised by Foote have been addressed with fairer and more efficient procedures. Many of his recommendations appear to have been either prophetic or to have contributed directly to changes that were later institutionalized as part of the routine of the contemporary Philadelphia court system. In the 1970s, Philadelphia has become as much a symbol of enlightened criminal justice reform in the pretrial area as it has in the 1950s gained notoriety as a symbol of all that was ignominious about American bail practices. The usefulness of comparing the two Philadelphias as a case study extends beyond that city's special experience, for many other cities have been involved in similar reform struggles during roughly the same interval.

On a more troublesome side, this exercise has served to point out areas where major bail and detention issues have not been resolved. Apparently, the bail decision still lends itself to highly discretionary uses and individualistic procedures for evaluating defendants at bail — this despite all the trappings of a modern court bail reform agency. Judges are still free to arrive at their decisions impressionistically, idiosyncratically, or conscientiously according to existing guidelines, or not — as fate might have it. Bail reform has offered bail judges new resources to aid their decision-making process (recall that Foote reported judges in 1954 had little more than a description of the offense on which to base their decisions), but the 1977 study has shown that these resources may be ignored or used to reinforce the very decision-making practices that were the targets of the reform measures.

Serious questions about disparity in bail decisions that had been reaised by the Foote study were not resolved in the 1977 study; rather, they were increased. Because of the uncertainty over the purpose of the bail decision (is it oriented toward appearance or dangerousness?) and the confusion over the means to be used in arriving at the decision, it is quite probable that similar defendants would in contemporary Philadelphia be treated in very different fashions by different bail judges. Furthermore, criticisms concerning economic bias in bail practices will not be overcome as long as cash bail continues to be a major bail option and as long as many defendants continue to be economically disadvantaged. (Yet, it should be noticed that economic bias will be minimized in a system like Philadelphia's where ROR is used in half of all cases and the bondsman has been replaced by a Ten Percent program.) The final issue that has not disappeared in two decades is the question concerning the effect of detention on the final outcomes of defendants' cases. It now appears that this relationship may apply only to defendants reaching the sentencing stage, and there those who have been detained are considerably more likely than those released to receive severe incarcerative sentences. Clearly, this is an issue that needs to be investigated further.

NOTES*

1. Caleb Foote, "Compelling Appearance in Court: Administration of Bail in Philadelphia," *University of Pennsylvania Law Review*, June 1954, pp. 1031–79.

2. See Roscoe Pound and Felix Frankfurter, *Criminal Justice in Cleveland* (1922; rep. ed., Montclair, N.J.: Patterson Smith, 1968); Arthur Beeley, *The Bail System in Chicago* (Chicago: University of Chicago Press, 1927); and Wayne Morse and Ronald Beattie, "Survey of the Administration of Criminal Justice in Oregon," *Oregon Law Review*, 1932 (rep. ed., New York: Arno Press, 1974).

3. Paul Wice, *Freedom for Sale* (Lexington, Mass.: D. C. Heath, 1974).

4. John S. Goldkamp, "Bail Decisionmaking and the Role of Pretrial Detention in American Justice" (Ph.D. diss., School of Criminal Justice, State University of New York at Albany, Albany, N.Y., 1977).

5. As part of a broader investigation of bail decision making and the role of pretrial detention in American justice, bail decision making in Philadelphia was examined as a case study in 1977. In this study the cases of a cohort of defendants (weighted *n* = 8,300) arriving for initial appearance between August 1 and November 2, 1975, were followed until completion — in many cases until 1977. The specifics of the 1977 study differend in many ways from the earlier Foote study, but many issues can be seen to overlap in both. The 1977 study is reported in different parts and formats in the following documents: Ibid.; John S. Goldkamp, "Bail Decisionmaking in Philadelphia," Working Paper 11 (Albany, N.Y.: Criminal Justice Research Center, 1978); and John S. Goldkamp, "Release or Detention before Trial in Philadelphia," Working Paper 12 (Albany, N.Y.: Criminal Justice Research Center, 1978). It also constitutes a portion of John Goldkamp, *Two Classes of Accused: A Study of Bail and Detention in American Justice* (Cambridge, Mass.: Ballinger, 1979).

6. This conceptualization of the issues raised by Foote in his 1954 study is the author's own; it is hoped that this interpretation fairly describes the substance of that study as it is relevant to the present analysis.

7. Caleb Foote, "The Coming Constitutional Crisis in Bail: I," *University of Pennsylvania Law Review*, vol. 113 (1965), p. 959; and Caleb Foote, "The Coming Constitutional Crisis in Bail: II," *University of Pennsylvania Law Review*, vol. 113 (1965), p. 1125.

8. There are clearly other views of the bail function, for instance to protect the community from dangerous defendants — just the view to which Foote has objected. A recent analysis of sources of legal policy in the area of bail has shown that both the appearance view and the dangerousness view may be supported, though such guidelines are quite vague in many respects. See Goldkamp, *Two Classes of Accused*.

9. Foote, "Compelling Appearance in Court: Administration of Bail in Philadelphia," p. 1043.

10. Ibid., p. 1035.

11. Ibid., p. 1046.

12. Ibid., p. 1073.

13. Ibid, p. 1077.

14. The study was conducted in 1977, but the sample consisted of cases entering the early states of criminal processing at initial appearance in Philadelphia during the fall of 1975. Because the later outcomes of these cases were also important to the study, it was necessary to allow a sufficient period of time for their resolution. By early 1977 all cases had been completed.

15. *Pennsylvania Rules of Court* (1976).

16. Beeley, *The Bail System in Chicago*.

17. Wickersham Commission, *National Commission on Law Observance and Enforcement*.

18. Goldkamp, *Two Classes of Accused*.

19. This conclusion in the 1977 study is based on interviews with Philadelphia bail judges, observations of first appearances, and empirical analysis of bail decisions for an estimated 8,300 Philadelphia defendants.

20. Goldkamp, "Bail Decisionmaking in Philadelphia."

21. Study to date has not demonstrated, however, whether defendants granted ROR are those who most need relief from cash bail or individuals who would be able to pay for their release under a cash bail system.

22. The 1977 study had consideration of this relationship as a special focus. That analysis was carefully constructed to employ the appropriate sample for each judicial decision examined. See John S. Goldkamp, "The Effects of Detention on Judicial Decisions: A Closer Look," *Justice System Journal*, Winter/Spring 1980.

*Footnotes have been abridged, edited, and renumbered.

14. DISCRETION AND THE DETERMINATE SENTENCE: ITS DISTRIBUTION, CONTROL, AND EFFECT ON TIME SERVED

TODD R. CLEAR, JOHN D. HEWITT, AND ROBERT M. REGOLI

Reprinted, with permission of the National Council on Crime and Delinquency, from Todd R. Clear, John D. Hewitt, and Robert M. Regoli, "Discretion and the Determinate Sentence: Its Distribution, Control, and Effect on Time Served," *Crime & Delinquency*, October 1978, pp. 428–45.

■ There are a variety of reasons why proposals for sentencing reform have become commonplace today. Some are motivated by policy goals seeking to enhance the deterrent effect of sanctioning criminal offenders. Others are premised upon a desire to enhance the equitable distribution of punishment by reducing the disparity in the sentences handed down by trial court judges. A common concern of many of these proposals is eliminating, or at least reducing, the sentencing discretion of trial judges. Indiana's sentencing reform law, in operation since 1977, illustrates the philosophy and problems associated with sentencing reform. Among the observations made by Clear, Hewitt, and Regoli about the Indiana law is that discrepencies typically exist between the political rhetoric of sentencing reform and the political realities of determinant sentencing. The fact of the matter is that rather than reducing or eliminating sentencing discretion, reform laws frequently simply redistribute discretion among different actors in the criminal justice system, especially prosecutors and parole officers. ■

TODAY, NO OTHER single criminal justice reform measure is receiving more widespread support and optimistic legislative consideration than is determinate sentencing. Several states have adopted determinate sentencing codes,[1] and legislatures in at least another dozen are debating proposals for some type of fixed sentencing. Those states that have not considered fixed sentencing reform will soon be the exception. Given the fact that criminal justice legislation usually proceeds at a snail's pace and decades pass before innovations come to be disseminated widely, this warm response by our usually stodgy state legislators is exceptional indeed.

In advocating fixed sentences, the reformers define their goal as threefold. First, they aim to achieve a "post-conviction process that is humane, visible and just"[2]: "The elimination of most discretion to shift many practices such as sentencing . . . out of the hands of administrative agencies and into the realm . . . of due process and equal protection of the law."[3] Second, the intention is to create a system that is "more effective in terms of reducing crime than the one currently in operation."[4] They propose to control the sentencing decision, reducing discrepancies in sentencing, so as to create "relative uniformity of sentences for persons of equivalent criminal records convicted of the same offense. . . . [The] sentence should be relatively predictable before the offense is committed."[5] Third, the reformers hope to redistribute time served from the *less serious* to the *more serious* felons without significantly increasing the *total* man years served and hence the associated incarceration costs."[6]

THE NEW INDIANA PENAL CODE

The Indiana Penal Code represents more than mere sentencing reform: It is a comprehensive restructuring of the substantive Indiana criminal law. Among other changes, the previous set of over 5,000 stated Indiana crimes (with the last major revision in 1905) was consolidated into approximately 200 "new" offenses, with a number of modifications in the elements of the various offenses. Some sentencing reformers have argued that fixed sentence reforms should be seen as only one aspect of a larger penal code reform effort.[7] The Indiana Code cer-

SENTENCING DISCRETION IN INDIANA

Generally, sentencing reform has two objectives: first, to place limits on the availability of discretion, and second, to give *more* discretion to the judge and less to correctional administrators. Examining the Indiana Code critically, we conclude that the reformers failed to achieve the first objec-

Table 1. The Sentencing Structure of the Indiana Penal Code

Class of Offense	Terms of Imprisonment	Enhancement for Aggravation	Reduction for Mitigation
Murder	40 years (or death)	1–20 years	1–10 years
Class A felony	30 years	1–20 years	1–10 years
Class B felony	10 years	1–10 years	1–4 years
Class C felony	5 years	1–3 years	1–3 years
Class D felony	2 years	1–2 years	NA
Class A misdemeanor	0–1 year	NA	NA
Class B misdemeanor	0–6 months	NA	NA

tainly meets this requirement, for it is an attempt at wholesale criminal code reform.

Table 1 presents the major sentencing provisions of the Indiana penal code and includes five classes of felonies and two categories of misdemeanors. Most offenses span two or three felony classes: Serious injury, use or threat of deadly force, age of the victim, and so on, may make an otherwise class C or B offense a class A felony.

Furthermore, upon presenting a written justification for the departure from sentencing guidelines, a judge may either enhance penalties because of aggravating circumstances related to the offense or, alternatively, reduce the penalty in light of "mitigating factors."[8] Probation (suspended sentence) is available only to first-time offenders not convicted of certain types of felonies (generally, those which involve use of a weapon, result in bodily injury, or are committed against a child). The code adopts a bifurcated sentencing procedure, whereby a judge determines the sentence by means of a hearing that follows, but is separate from, the trial.[9] At the sentencing hearing, the prosecutor may present evidence of aggravation or mitigation and recommend appropriate modification of the sentence.[10] A defendant who has two prior unrelated felony convictions may be found to be a "habitual offender" and have thirty years added to the sentence.[11]

tive and were only partially successful in achieving the second.

One of the reasons for this is the reformers' apparent failure to consider what Franklin Zimring has labeled "multiple discretion." One of the recurrent myths in the popular perception of criminal justice is that judges "do" sentencing. In fact, "there are four separate institutions that have the power to determine criminal sentences — the legislature, the prosecutor, the judge, and the parole board or its equivalent."[12] A reduction in the discretion available to one participant in the process generally results in an increase in the discretionary powers available to the others. The legislature, in writing substantive law and establishing penalties, sets the broad limits on sentencing power; the other parties act to specify further the sentence potential until it becomes the "time served." Looking at the limits set by the Indiana legislature, if we include the interpretation of aggravating and mitigating factors, these limits appear quite broad. Each of the parties to the sentencing process — the prosecution, the judge, and correction — retains substantial discretionary power.

Prosecutorial Discretion.

The Indiana Code has been described by many insiders as a "prosecutor's law," for it serves to extend greatly prosecutorial discretion. An important instance of this involves offenses for which suspended sentences are prohibited by law. The new penal code provides that any "nonsuspendable" offense may also be charged as an "attempted" offense, which (except murder[13]) carries an identical penalty except that it is also suspendable. The new clause has the dual effect of giving the prosecutor flexibility to bargain while silently exerting pressure on the defendant to cooperate, since the elements of proof surrounding an "attempted" offense are much less rigorous than the regular criminal statutes.

Beyond the general pressure on first offenders to plead guilty for probation, the prosecutor has a useful set of overlapping charges with which to confront a defendant. Even in the case of a person who is destined to serve at least some time in prison, the prosecutor can use the offender's natural desire to minimize the potential penalty[14] by presenting a virtual shopping list of lesser related offenses. A typical example is the "robbery" statute:

Sec. 1. A person who knowingly or intentionally takes property from another person or from the presence of another person; or
(1) by using or threatening the use of force on any person; or
(2) by putting any person in fear; commits robbery, a Class C felony. However, the offense is a Class B felony if it is committed while armed with a deadly weapon, and a Class A felony if it results in either bodily injury or serious bodily injury to another person.[15]

On the other hand, if a prosecutor believes a lesser penalty is appropriate for a person who committed a robbery, he may charge the person with theft, which is a Class "D" felony (the least severe felony sentencing class).

For second offenders, who are technically not allowed suspended sentences, the pressure to bargain will be even greater. Particularly when the second offense is not extremely serious, or when the prosecutor has a weak case,[16] the defendant may be permitted to plead guilty to a misdemeanor charge in order to receive a suspended sentence. And the heavy penalties provided by the law create similar pressures on three-time losers, who will be fighting to avoid habitual criminal *state* sentence enhancements.

In addition to bargaining for reduced charges, the prosecutor will be able to affect the defendant's options at the sentencing hearing. While the law specifies the aggravating and mitigating factors that may be considered, the prosecutor can agree to ignore some aggravating circumstance or stress a mitigating factor in exchange for a guilty plea. These are alternatives in addition to the prosecutor's ordinary power to make a recommendation or even stand silent regarding sentence — two traditional guilty plea inducements.[17]

The broader issue, whether justice is enhanced by this investment of vast and enriched discretion in the hands of the prosecutor, will be debated, of course. Prosecutors certainly seem to think so. But the criminals — who may feel more pressure to plead guilty, or who see a second offender offered a misdemeanant charge and probation when the best arrangement a first offender can make is a class D felony with probation, or who plead guilty in the face of heavy penalties even when the prosecutor has a weak case — may not be impressed by the improvement.

Judicial Discretion

Ordinarily, one would think that a determinate sentencing law would substantially reduce judicial discretion. However, the lawmakers recognized that discretion must be placed in the hands of the judiciary in order to guard against inflexible penalties being inappropriately applied in individual cases. In fact, under the new code, judges may actually have more effective discretion than was available to them under the former indeterminate system — though the scope of the discretion in any given case is constrained, in part, by the prosecutor's bargaining power.

As was true before, judges will have discretion with first offenders to suspend execution of sentence and place the offender on probation.[18] The most extensive formal discretion pertains to the interpretation of aggravating and mitigating factors, which will influence both the decision to suspend sentences (where applicable) and the selection of fixed penalties.

It is difficult to foresee precisely how the judges will use the discretion to interpret aggravation and mitigation. While some of the available factors stated in the law are quite specific, other, more ambiguous aspects of the offense may be interpreted differently by different judges. For example, there is not yet a reliable method for establishing when the offender ''is in need of correctional or rehabilitative treatment that can best be provided by his commitment to a penal facility.''[19]

One probable outcome is that interpretation of aggravation or mitigation will often be a product of group discretionary decisions made by the judge, the prosecutor, and the defense attorney working together. This may be particularly true when the prosecutor is unable or unwilling to offer a charging bargain that is acceptable to the defendant, and therefore some negotiation concerning the sentence is necessary. In any event, judges certainly retain the power to sentence offenders convicted of the same offense to widely disparate penalties. The fact that there is substantial discretionary overlap in potential penalties for class B, C, and D felonies (for example, an aggravated class C offense could result in an eight-year term, but a defendant convicted of a mitigated class B offense could receive six years) may have the effect of reducing the experienced offender's confidence in charge bargaining, thus forcing judicial involvement in granting sentencing consideration in order to generate guilty pleas.

Correctional Administrator Discretion

Termination of parole-release decisions under the new law would seem to eliminate correctional participation in the sentencing decision. However, Indiana legislators recognized that correction officials may need a powerful tool to maintain discipline among prison inmates; therefore, the state has activated and simplified its credit time system.

Inmates are placed into one of three classes for purposes of receiving credit time. Class I is a 50 percent sentence reduction where the inmate earns one day for each day of imprisonment; class II is a 33 percent reduction, where one day is earned for each two; class III earns no credit time.[20] All incarcerated offenders are initially assigned to the class I category. Reassignment to class II or III may occur because of the inmate's violation of a department of correction rule or regulation, but only after a hearing before a disciplinary committee comprised of correctional staff appointed by the commissioner of correction. The inmate's ''rights'' at this hearing are limited to the right to notice, the right to present testimony, and, unless the committee finds ''good cause'' for denying it, the right to confront and cross-examine witnesses.[21]

Under the law, credit time no longer vests: '' A person may be deprived of any part of the credit time he has earned if he violates a rule or regulation of the department.''[22] This decision is made by the disciplinary committee, after a hearing in which, in addition to the rights at reclassification hearings, the inmate is entitled to the assistance of a ''lay advocate,'' a written statement of finding, and ''administrative review.''[23] The comissioner has sole authority for upward reclassification or restoration of credit.[24]

All of this represents the allocation of substantial discretion to correctional officials. Advocates of the system argue that credit time places the control over time served more directly in the hands of the inmate, based on his institutional behavior.

Although previous law in Indiana provided for credit time — a fact often cited by advocates of the system — with the use of parole release as a disciplinary sanction, adjustments in credit time occurred infrequently and only in the most extreme cases. There is every indication that the elimination of the parole decision as a means of control will increase the importance of credit time. Indeed, the correctional department already reports wider use of credit time decisions, and there appears to be a preparation for greater reliance on credit time for maintaining discipline. In his speech at the Governor's Conference on the Indiana Penal Code, the commissioner of correction stated that he disagreed'' . . .

philosophically with the concept of permitting all inmates to enter the system in a maximum time earning class."[25] While the commissioner praised the current model, he pointed to a need to evaluate offenders more frequently than the current "semi-annual basis to determine the overall performance of the inmate"[26] and intimated that he would prefer that an inmate "earn" the right to a class I adjustment of sentence.

Clearly, the commissioner looks forward to a liberal exercise of sentencing discretion under the code's credit time provisions. Thus, the discretion available to the correctional administrators is, at least technically, extensive: The department controls up to fifteen years for most class A offenses, five for class B, up to two and one-half years for class C, and up to one year for D felonies. This probably reflects discretionary power over about as much prison time as was formerly affected by parole decisions. Ironically, the proponents of reform often argued that one problem of parole was its tendency to be too responsive to the needs of correctional administrators. Now the parole boards that were responsible only to the governor have been replaced by correctional department staff appointed by the commissioner.

CONTROL OVER SENTENCING PRACTICES IN INDIANA

In the redistribution of sentencing discretion through fixed sentencing, there are two primary intended beneficiaries. The first is the legislature, which gains increased influence over the eventual penalty. The second is the inmate, who theoretically benefits by the ability to control credit time through institutional behavior, thereby reducing the uncertainty of the eventual release date. In practice, these parties may not have the additional control over the sentence that they might expect.

Legislature Control

The focus of the legislature's new control is on suspended sentences; specifically, the legislature made certain felonies non-suspendable and, in a most controversial provision, made *all* second felonies non-suspendable.[27] However, the availability of "attempt" charges effectively gives the prosecutor the ability to bypass these requirements. And, as described earlier, the legislature has provided judges with substantial discretion in the selection of penalties. A special provision for class D felonies may give judges the opportunity to avoid mandatory incarceration for second offenders. The law provides that, upon a conviction for a "class D felony, the court may enter judgment of conviction of a class A misdemeanor and sentence accordingly."[28] While opinion remains divided on the practical implications of this section of the law, many practitioners believe that this allows a suspended sentence with probation, a sentence uniformly available to class A misdemeanants, regardless of the presence of one or more previous felony convictions.

In addition to these formal options that reduce legislative control over sentencing, the prosecutor may fail to call attention to prior felonies at the sentencing hearing, thus avoiding the law's habitual criminal and mandatory sentencing requirements.

Inmate Control

To assume that inmates might ever easily exert control over the time served in a system organized to keep them locked away from the world is simply naive. One of the best tools for keeping an inmate population quiescent is firm control over the length of sentences and a willingness to use this control.

About one-half of an inmate's sentence is subject to his behavior in relation to the rules and regulations contained in the *Adult Authority Disciplinary Policy* by the Indiana Department of Correction. Seventy-one different offenses are listed, including such infractions as "failing to perform work as instructed by a supervisor," "tattooing or self-mutilation," and the catch-all offense of "disturbing the peace and quiet or orderly running of the institution or other area in which the inmate is located."[29] By committing one of these and or the countless other infractions, an inmate may be reclassified or even lose credit time.

The full meaning of this administrative control over inmates can be understood in the light of the general disciplinary procedure. The process begins with the written accusation by a correctional officer of a transgression by an inmate. This is followed by a hearing before the Conduct Adjust Board (CAB), a group of institutional staff members appointed by the institution adminstrator and representing a cross-section of the prison personnel (i.e., officers, counselors, and custodial staff). If the CAB finds the inmate guilty, that inmate may lose privileges or be isolated in solitary confinement. Further, the CAB may recommend to the central disciplinary committee that the inmate's credit time classification be changed or even that he be deprived of credit time.

Thus, a great deal of effective control over the inmate's sentence has been placed directly in the hands of the correctional officer who watches over him. In fact, that control has been formalized by the new law, and, even assuming the best intentions on the part of all concerned, the result may be a more repressive atmosphere for inmates.

It is not discretion alone that results in unwanted disparities. Rather, it is the combination of discretion and the lack of effective control over its situational use. Unfortunately, the new Indiana code may be creating substantial potential for discretion without effective constraints. Comparable defendants are still apt to serve widely different prison terms.

TIME SERVED UNDER INDIANA CODE

Projecting patterns of time served under the new codes, particularly those which contain as much discretion and are as broad as the Indiana Code, is a treacherous business. While proponents of fixed sentencing have tended to argue in favor of stablized or even reduced prison populations, others have predicted that the new system will lead to increased prison populations.[30] A comparative reading of the old and new Indiana codes gives the impression that penalties have been enhanced, but it is not clear how much.

To estimate better the potential effects of the new code on patterns of time served for felonies, a study was conducted using a sample of all felony admissions to the Indiana Department of Correction between January 1, 1976, and June 30, 1976, as the basis for comparison. Of that sample, only first-time felons (54.9 percent of all admissions during that period) in eight selected offense categories (covering 87.4 percent of all admissions during that period) were included in the analysis.[31] This accounted for a total of 234 cases, or 47.6 percent of all admissions during this period.

To compare time served under the two codes, we estimated the actual penalties that would be served by these offenders. These calculations project that this group of offenders would have served 47.4 percent more prison time if they had been sentenced under the new code. This finding is even more striking when one realizes that the sample includes *first offenders only* and that we assumed that they would earn all the potentially available credit time.

It is also interesting to note the fluctuations between offense categories. One of the arguments of those advocating fixed sentencing has been that their reforms would result in a redistribution of punishments, with violent offenders receiving heavier penalties and the nonviolent more lenient sanctions. This argument is only partially supported by the data in this table. It is true that murder (+70 percent), armed robbery (+33 percent), and rape (+115 percent) all carry increased punishments, while theft (−37 percent) and forgery (−90 percent) are reduced; however, negligent homicide, certainly a violent offense, carries a reduced penalty (−19 percent), and burglary and unarmed robbery, both predominantly nonviolent offenses, have *increased* penalties (123 percent and 16 percent, respectively).

The results seem to indicate that the reform in Indiana is more sporadic than systematic. Certainly, the more than doubling of burglary penalties coupled with a reduction of theft penalties by more than one-third may reflect some abstract understanding of "justice" in the 1970s. Yet we would be hard-pressed if asked to explain such a change.

The results may also create problems for the Indiana Department of Correction, which will apparently bear the weight of this increased demand for services. In fact, the findings have already led several professionals to predict a rapidly approaching need for additional space. On the other hand, though, it is equally likely that Indiana judges, prosecutors, and defense attorneys will engage in unobtrusive negotiations to control prison populations. We suggest that there may be some increase in populations under the code, but it is unlikely that the increase will be as overwhelming as this table projects.

CONCLUSION

Our closing comments may well be summarized as a question: Why did they bother with it?

The new Indiana Penal Code provides such wide discretion, coupled with untenably heavy penalties, that a most likely result will be the creation and solidification of a formal system of decisions and rules that barely conceals a low-visibility, busy, and pragmatic system of informal decisions regulating the actual sentence, largely in the control of prosecutors, judges, and correctional officials. The new sentencing scheme may come to bear a strange resemblance to what reformers hoped to eliminate.

The true disparity in sentencing will be further hidden by the informal manipulation of prosecutorial charges and the evaluation of inmate behavior through the allocation of credit time. Experienced felons will still know how to play the justice game better than first offenders, and the actual sentence will still be based on the appearance of remorse and change in behavior. The public will still be mollified by what it believes to be a harsh, new set of laws, and the system will still be able to accommodate its own crudely determined estimation of commensurate penalties. All this will be done in the name of openness, procedural regularity, and predictability. And, most significant of all, the new law may well allow the legisla-

ture to ignore criminal justice in Indiana for another ten years. Norval Morris understood the significance of all this when he gave the after-dinner speech at the recent statewide Governor's Conference on the Indiana Penal Code. Focusing on the nonsuspendable provisions of the code, he produced both red faces and a smattering of applause when he said, "Of course, no one expects these provisions to be enforced in the way they're written — they are simply for public relations."[32]

However, in the recognition of the law's weaknesses lies the potential for creating its greatest strengths. Whatever its shortcomings, the code is a first attempt at a rational plan for justice in Indiana, a "new tool for fighting crime."[33] There appears to be some acceptance — on the part of both the public and the code's initiators — of the need to identify areas for change. To the degree that the changes can be based on "sound research and rational planning," discretion may be structured around potentially beneficial aspects of the code. Particularly if harsh penalties are reduced, Indiana citizens may find themselves with a more equitable, predictable, and understandable criminal code and procedure.

Whether a future version of this code or other fixed sentencing codes will realize the lofty goals toward which they are aimed will depend on several key factors. Foremost is a willingness on the part of lawmakers to adopt reasonable penalty schemes, not plans designed for public relations. Second, reformers must recognize that discretion is not only warranted, it is also inevitable. Reforms that attempt to eliminate discretion through substantive law simply serve to force it into less visible patterns. Finally, if justice is really to be achieved, reformers must act to expunge utilitarian goals from fixed sentencing models. When determinate sentences are combined with incapacitative and deterrent goals, the results may be harsh sentences that are never regularly enforced and hidden discretionary powers that are regularly abused.

NOTES*

1. The first was Maine, on May 1, 1976.
2. George Cole, "Will Definite Sentences Make a Difference?" *Judicature*, August 1977, p. 63.
3. Friends, *Struggle for Justice*, p. 144.
4. Twentieth Century Fund, *Fair and Certain Punishment*, p. 9.
5. Ibid., p. 32.
6. David Fogel, *"We Are the Living Proof . . .": The Justice Model for Corrections* (Cincinnati: W. H. Anderson, 1975), p. 310.
7. Andrew von Hirsch, "Is Rehabilitation a Realistic Correctional Strategy?" (Presentation to the Academy of Criminal Justice Sciences, San Mateo, California, Mar. 15, 1976).
8. Aggravating factors extend but are not limited to cases in which —

   1. The person has recently violated the condition of any probation, parole, or pardon granted him.

   2. The person has a history of criminal activity.

   3. The person is in need of correctional or rehabilitative treatment that can best be provided by his commitment to a penal facility.

   4. Imposition of a reduced sentence or suspension of the sentence and imposition of probation would depreciate the seriousness of the crime.

   5. The victim of the crime was sixty-five years of age or older.

   6. The victim of the crime was mentally or physically infirm.

Mitigating factors include but are not limited to cases in which —

   1. The crime neither caused nor threatened serious harm to persons or property, or the person did not contemplate that it would do so.

   2. The crime was a result of circumstances unlikely to recur.

   3. The victim of the crime induced or facilitated the offense.

   4. There are substantial grounds tending to excuse or justify the crime, though failing to establish a defense.

   5. The person acted under strong provocation.

   6. The person has no history of delinquency or criminal activity, or he has led a law-abiding life for a substantial period before commission of the crime.

   7. The person is likely to respond affirmatively to probation or short-term imprisonment.

   8. The character and attitudes of the person indicate that he is not likely to commit another crime.

   9. The person has made or will make restitution to the victim of this crime for the injury, damage, or loss sustained.

   10. Imprisonment of the person will result in undue hardships for himself or his dependents.

See *IC*, sec. 35-41-4-7.
9. Juries are involved in sentencing only in the case of murder, where they may recommend to the judge that he demand the death penalty. However, the judge is not required to follow the jury's recommendation. Ibid., sec. 35-50-2-9.
10. Ibid., sec. 35-4.1-4-3.
11. Ibid., sec. 35-50-2-8.
12. Franklin Zimring, "Making the Punishment Fit the Crime: A Consumer Guide to Sentencing Reform" (Paper presented to the Illinois Academy of Criminology, November 1976).
13. *IC*, sec. 35-41-5-1.
14. Lloyd E. Ohlin and Frank J. Remington, "Sentencing Structure: Its Effect upon Systems for the Administration of Criminal Justice," *Law and Contemporary Problems*, Summer 1958, pp. 495–507.
15. *IC*, sec. 35-42-5-1.
16. Dominick R. Vetri, "Plea Bargaining: Compromises by Prosecutors to Secure Guilty Pleas," *University of Pennsylvania Law Review*, April 1964, p. 865–908.
17. Donald J. Newman, "Pleading Guilty for Considerations: A Study of Bargain Justice," *Journal of Criminal Law, Criminology and Police Science*, March–April 1956, pp. 788–90.
18. *IC*, sec. 30-50-2-2.
19. Ibid., sec. 35-4.1-4-7-(c)-(3).
20. Ibid., sec. 35-50-6-3.
21. Ibid., sec. 35-50-6-4.
22. Ibid., sec. 35-50-6-5-(a).
23. Ibid., sec. 35-50-6-5-(1), (2), (3).
24. Ibid., sec. 35-50-6-5-(c).
25. Gordon H. Falkner, "Code and Corrections:

*Footnotes have been abridged, edited, and renumbered.

The Challenge of Change'' (Presentation to the Governor's Conference on the Indiana Penal Code, Indianapolis, Sept. 2, 1977, p. 6).

26. Ibid., pp. 6–7.

27. *IC.*, sec. 35-50-2-2.

28. Ibid., sec. 35-50-2-7.

29. Indiana Department of Correction, *Adult Authority Disciplinary Policy* (Indianapolis: Indiana Department of Correction, 1976), pp. 65–67, 69.

30. See "Governor Walker's Proposed Justice Model: An Analysis of Its Impact," mimeographed (John Harvard Association, 1975).

31. Repeat offenders were excluded because of the difficulty of providing, with any degree of validity, the provisions of the new code related to the suspension of sentence. The offense categories were selected because of the availability of data in the *Uniform Parole Reports.*

32. Norval Morris, "In the Wake of the Penal Code" (Address to the Governor's Conference on the Indiana Penal Code, Indianapolis, Sept. 1, 1977).

33. Untitled news release for the Governor's Conference on the Indiana Penal Code, Indianapolis, Aug. 31, 1977, p. 1.

V. Corrections

15. DECISION-MAKING IN A PRISON COMMUNITY

STEVEN GIFIS

WISCONSIN LAW REVIEW, © 1974. Reprinted by permission.

■ The administration of criminal justice does not terminate with the disposition of a defendant's case by the courts. Rather, those defendants who have been found guilty enter the next stage of the system (often euphemistically referred to as "corrections") in which an additional series of discretionary circumstances arise. The articles in this section identify some of the sources of discretionary justice found in prison disciplinary actions, explain the decision-making process of parole officials, and suggest ways in which abuses of official discretion may be curtailed. Defining the boundaries between prisoners' rights and custodial discretion is a difficult responsibility that the courts are now facing. The following research study focuses on the procedures and substance of day-to-day regulations of inmate life and the decision-making process of custodians. Gifis describes how sanctions are imposed upon prisoners and what standards appear to guide these decisions. ■

INTRODUCTION

THE TYPICAL LAW school instruction in criminal law adequately surveys most problems of definition, values, and purposes in the criminal area. The rights of the accused are a matter of intense examination. Curiously, however, the law school basic curriculum ends its intense study when direct and collateral attacks on a conviction have been exhausted.[1] The actual criminal sanction — except for the usual discussion of the wisdom and utility of capital punishment — is rarely explored.[2]

Apart from the seldom exercised death penalty, the most serious sanction the criminal law imposes is incarceration. In an era when all inmates in penal institutions were treated alike, the law student might justifiably have little interest in the prison's operation.[3] The inmates were fed, clothed, stored, and sometimes put to work. Under the so-called silence system they were not allowed to interact with other inmates and were ex-

pected to spend their time in reflective penitence.[4] In such a system the law insisted only on minimum standards of health and sanitation for the prisoners. The notion that a convicted man might possess enforceable legal rights was alien; it was his good fortune that humanitarian reform had spared him his life:

[The prisoner] has, as a consequence of his crime, not only forfeited his liberty but all his personal rights except those which the law in its humanity accords to him. He is for the time being the slave of the State.[5]

Today the penitentiary has been replaced with the "correctional institution." The sanction of incarceration is viewed primarily as an opportunity to rehabilitate the offender and prepare him for a useful life in society.[6] Judges exercise wide discretion in selecting the proper sentence for a particular offender.[7] Use of indeterminate sentences is expanding. When a man arrives at the correctional institution, a diversified program is established in an effort to meet his needs.[8] In the more progressive systems the options for correctional officials are very broad.[9] Types of security vary and with them the nature of imprisonment itself. Recently adopted work-release programs allow an inmate to spend his day working in the community while he reports back each night for nighttime custody either in the institution or in a special rooming house complex.

The differential treatment now given to convicted criminals has lodged enormous discretion in the hands of their keepers.[10] The familiar and long-standing reluctance of the courts to intervene in prison administration seems finally to be succumbing to the reality that important human rights may be affected by the decisions of prison administrators. The eroding of the judicial "hands off" doctrine has prompted a growing onslaught of inmate petitions challenging various aspects of their incarceration. More frequently today the custodian must justify his practices in much the same way as any other government official must defend coercive measures taken against a citizen. Today, it can be said with some confidence that the convicted man brings with him to the institution all of his personal rights except those which the nature of his incarceration requires that he temporarily forfeit.

Marking the boundaries between the inmate's rights and the custodian's discretion is a difficult task which the courts are just beginning to undertake. There has been an enormous amount of literature written within the past three years in the prisoners' rights area.[11] This article does not attempt to duplicate any of this effort, nor to analyze the scope of prisoners' rights. Rather, it will focus more directly on the inmate's daily life and hopefully shed some light on the decision-making process of the custodians. The article will examine the procedure and substance of day-to-day regulation of the inmate and suggest some answers to the following questions: How is the program for the inmate developed? Who decides whether the inmate will be placed in a minimum security dormitory or a maximum security cell? How are work-release inmates selected? How are the daily rules of conduct adopted, and what notice do the inmates have of them? When violations occur, who decides what sanction to impose and on what basis? In all of these decisions what role does the inmate play? What role should he play in a sound correctional system? What right does our constitutional framework of government require that he have in this decision-making process? Finally, how should the extensive discretion of the keepers be directed and controlled?

These are difficult questions; their answers must be suggested at least in part by persons trained in the law. Yet, the law has traditionally ignored the field of corrections. Before we too quickly assume that due process models, which were developed for use in other contexts, can be applied to these kinds of questions, we must gain some appreciation for the unique characteristics of decisions made in a "total institution"[12] such as a prison. Data is scarce. To remedy this in part and to provide a factual background for my thoughts, I have studied in

detail a single prison community's structure of decision-making. After explaining the research design and its limitations, this article will describe the structure which was observed. Equipped with this background the reader can evaluate the merits of the tentative statements found at the conclusion of this article which attempt to develop a rationale for decision-making in the prison community.

THE DISCIPLINARY PROCESS

This section will be a comprehensive examination of certain aspects of the "disciplinary process." The disciplinary process of a prison is in effect its method of governance. A prisoner's sleep, play, and work are not subject to separate spheres of regulation as they are in society at large. Rather, nearly every aspect of his existence is controlled by one central authority; scheduling is rigid and opportunities for self-determination very limited. Yet, despite the appearance of total control, violence, fraud, theft, and aberrant sexual behavior are commonplace occurrences within a prison community. As in the outside society, the number of less serious rule violations which are met with formal detection and sanction represents only a small fraction of the total number of prohibited acts. There is a stated preference of prison administrators for informal disposition — "chewing inmates out" — for minor offenses. The new officer is told that a good officer only rarely resorts to official sanctions. It is assumed that the prison could not function any other way. Strict formal enforcement is attempted only for more serious offenses such as assaults, stealing, insolence, and refusals to work.

All members of the prison community participate in the disciplinary process if it is conceived as a system of rule enforcement. The correctional officers and shop supervisors play the primary role in initiating the formal enforcement process. The other staff members issue informal directives and only occasionally file disciplinary reports. The interest of the inmate members of the community in the maintenance of order should not be overlooked. The inmate's concern for the security of his person and property is very real. This concern is subverted, however, by the inmate code that prohibits "ratting" at almost any cost. Thus, an inmate who is assaulted must be either strong enough to respond himself or hope for official intervention without much cooperation on his part. And, this same code of conduct creates its own norms for behavior and methods of internal enforcement.

The research design did not permit an examination of informal rule enforcement either by staff or inmates. There is apparently very little official direction in the exercise of rule enforcement authority by the staff except for the preference for informal handling of minor disciplinary problems. Younger staff members seem to resort more frequently to official sanctions than do the more experienced officers. A meaningful view of this kind of activity, however, would require one to work or live at the prison for some period of time. Thus, the following material will focus on the violations that did result in formal action and the procedures used to apply official sanctions.

Notice and Content of Rules

The official position of the prison staff is that for two reasons no formal notice of prison rules need be given to inmates: First, because the informal informational network of the prison rendered impossible the prospect of an uninformed inmate, and second, because most activities proscribed within the prison were also illegal on the outside. The first reason seems inadequate. It is unlikely that the informal network can guarantee that all inmates know instantly all rules that are adopted from time to time by the prison administration. The second reason is simply false. It is true that if an inmate steals something from another, assaults him, destroys state property, or makes an indecent sexual advance, he is committing a statutory crime. But consider how many citizens would expect to be arrested for any of the following violations: failure to wear shirt tucked into the trousers, smoking at the dining table, carrying money, wearing suede shoes, having a beard, being out of place, wearing a pendant, circulating a petition, or refusing to work. The question of notice cannot be dispensed with by saying these prison rules are substantially similar to the laws of the general society. The prison rules surely include such laws, but they also include formal regulation of nearly every act of choice.

Although prison officials believed that formal notice of the rules was unnecessary, notice of the prison rules was given by the booklet distributed to new inmates, by posted notices, by officer or supervisor directives, by the inmate's social worker, and through the remarks made at the classification or other hearings. Some informal notice is no doubt also given by fellow inmates and by observed patterns of enforcement.

The rules of the institution are designed to achieve "peace and quiet." Whatever position one might take on the debate between custodial and treatment philosophies, the goal of peace and quiet is nearly universally accepted. It is a very restrictive end since it tends to prohibit that minimum of commotion, aggravation, aggression, and tension which marks any group of different persons pursuing self-defined goals. Peace and quiet is thought attainable only if individual differences in dress, behavior, and possessions are kept to an absolute minimum. Thus, the dress code prohibits jewelry, fancy or suede shoes, long hair, beards, or privately-owned outside clothing. Undergarments can be distinctive because presumably they are not a visible mark of distinction.

The principle of equality of treatment for similar persons in similar circumstances is central to the prison structure. In the prison community the most minute amount of injustice in terms of unequal treatment is perceived, commented upon, and magnified. Frequent or gross deviations from this standard would greatly endanger the peace and quiet of the community.

A new inmate guide, which was under preparation, was to contain a thorough and elaborate description of the rules of conduct. Yet, it is impossible to write a definitive listing. In a total institution where every act of choice is controlled, every resource rationed, and every moment of the inmate's life subject to direction, a common law code of conduct must prevail. A draft copy of the new "Inmate Guide" makes this very explicit when it states:

Obedience to orders given by any employee shall be carried out in a prompt, cooperative, and polite manner. Refusal to obey and disobedience are reasons for disciplinary action.[13]

The message is very clear: *all* orders must be obeyed. The command is not qualified to apply only to *lawful* or *proper* orders.

Sanctions for Misconduct

Prior to 1955 the deputy superintendent of Concord had complete authority over the imposition of sanctions for disciplinary violations. In 1955 in accordance with the recommendations of a legislative study, Concord created a disciplinary board with exclusive jurisdiction to impose sanctions.[14] Such "courts" are now common in correctional institutions and follow the standards set by the American Correctional Association. In the federal system the "court" is called the adjustment committee; reliance on terms other than "court" avoids confusing the disciplinary agency with a judicial body.

The disciplinary board is a three-man panel generally composed of the deputy superintendent (chairman), the head social worker, and an assistant deputy superintendent. The membership is not constant; the superintendent replaces the deputy superintendent in his absence; another social worker often replaces the head social worker; and there are five assistant deputy superintendents who may fill the third position on the board.

The sanctions available to the D board (as it is called) include the following:

1. Warning and reprimand
2. Loss of privileges (radio earphones, yard, TV, movies, commissary, visiting, mail, etc.)
3. Isolation (maximum of 15 days for each offense)
4. Change of job, security, or residence
5. Suspension of any of the foregoing, usually for 30 days
6. Referral to the psychiatrist
7. Recommend transfer to another institution

The D board may combine some of these sanctions or may take no action at all. In the latter case the charge might be erased (and the report destroyed), or more often a notation of "not proved"[15] will be made. A suspended sentence must be served if the inmate during the period of suspension receives any other formal sanction, including in most cases a warning. The institutional transfer may be to Walpole, to Bridgewater for observation and a finding of mental responsibility, or in very rare cases to a special segregation unit at Walpole reserved for serious troublemakers. Recommended transfers by the D board are exceptional.

The most common dispositions are the warning and a number of days in isolation. An inmate automatically loses three days of good time credits for each day in isolation. This policy of automatic forfeiture is set by the Department of Corrections. Good time credits at Concord serve to reduce the maximum sentence. Since most men are serving indeterminate sentences and are paroled well before the maximum period, the usual effect of good time credits is a reduction in the period of parole supervision. For the majority of inmates, therefore, the loss of these credits would not seem to be a substantial sanction. A more severe collateral consequence of isolation or any D board appearance, however, is its effect on parole consideration. All members of the prison community assume that this effect is very great; the actual effect was not measured but the consensus is probably correct. In any event, it is this collateral consequence that would seem to make the official sanctions effective.

The isolation cells are referred to generally as the "hole" or more commonly at Concord as the "boards." In prior times the inmate's diet was restricted to bread and water. Today they are entitled to one meal, lunch, and in practice are permitted to save a portion of that for other times of the day. Most of the isolation cells have toilets; they are lighted during the day; officers visit every hour; only bible reading is allowed. While the "hole" is not a pleasant experience, it does not appear to be a dreaded one either; for some inmates a day in the "hole" is said to improve their reputation and status among the other inmates.

The Disciplinary Report

The resort to official sanctions is initiated

by filing in duplicate a "disciplinary report." When an officer decides that an official sanction for misconduct is required, he will place the inmate under arrest.[16] Other officers will be called, and the inmate will be taken to a special wing in the New Line building for persons awaiting action (AA). This is called a "lockup." The practice of segregating all rule violators while they await action by the disciplinary authority is not common in prisons. Ordinarily just the dangerous or unruly inmate is locked up in the larger prisons. The justification for the Concord practice is not clear. The relatively small size of the prison population makes possible this sort of segregation; it operates as an independent punishment, though the prison insists that placing persons in AA is not punishment — they are not made to work and are entitled to visitation, but not mail privileges.[17] When asked for an explanation of the practice of prehearing detention, the response was that the system always has worked that way and no harm has been done by it. Further questioning produced more substantial reasons. If an inmate was insolent or refused to work, merely informing him that a disciplinary report would be filed, officials believed, would seem an ineffective way of changing his current behavior. And, even in the case where contraband was found in an inmate's room, it was felt that a failure to lock up the inmate might subject him to abuse from the possible owners of the contraband or from possible conspirators.[18]

The harshness of preliminary detention is in theory mitigated by a bail system. The deputy superintendent or any assistant deputy superintendent can authorize the release of an inmate pending a hearing by the disciplinary board. The deputy strongly frowns on this practice feeling that a man who has been locked up requires a "cooling-off" period. He might consider bailing if the charge is minor and the detention cells are overcrowded. Some of the assistants, however, are more inclined to grant bail for minor offenses when the hearing date is not the next day. The D board itself may order bailing of an inmate if it must postpone final action after an initial hearing. Granting bail would seem to be the exceptional practice.

The complaining officer ordering the lockup files the disciplinary report that charges the inmate with an offense and names the confederates and witnesses, if any. Then space is provided for a detailed account of the offense and the surrounding circumstances. Generally this account will be fairly brief, although some officers write several pages. Then the officer signs his name and states his title.

The inmate is not given a copy of the disciplinary report. When he is placed under arrest, the officer will usually inform him of the charge to be made. Sometimes, however, the inmate will be informed by the officer only that he is being locked up for doing X, but he will not be told the precise charge. An example of a typical report is the following case.

CASE 1

Charge: Lying, insolence to an officer
Confederates: None
Witnesses: None
Detailed Account:
Starting at about 1:45 after R and K were locked up, X started to pester me to call Father M, whom I did call and he said that he would see him when he could. I told X, but that was not good enough for him. He then wanted me to call Mr. Y and Mr. Z in that order. I told him that I wouldn't make any more phone calls for him. He kept pestering me. Finally at 3:30 he started yelling at me and telling me to call Father M, because his mother was dying of cancer and had been dying for two days now. He was yelling like a fool.

The disposition in this case was one day in isolation. It was apparent from the discussion of facts at the hearing that no lying or insolence occurred; rather, this was a case of creating a disturbance. The officer's formal characterization of the offense, however, is never changed to fit the facts as developed at the hearing, and this may have important consequences for the inmate. For example, the board is not likely to issue a separate charge against the inmate even if the hearing discloses an additional or different offense. Conversely, however, an inmate charged with two offenses such as refusal to work and insolence to an officer, but only found guilty of one, is likely to receive a penalty more severe than if he were only charged with refusal to work.

After the lockup the inmate's person and room will be searched as a matter of routine. Since unexpected room shakedowns occur at regular intervals, the reason for the room shakedown following an arrest is not apparent. One reason might be that if the inmate is going to be before the disciplinary board, any other charges that could be made should be made at that time. Only rarely, however, do the shakedowns result in separate violations. The next case is an example of such an instance.

CASE 2

Charge: Possession of coffee and heat element

Detailed Account:

After a lockup, I was told to shake K's room down. I did this and found articles of contraband. They were one stinger and one 6-ounce jar of instant coffee. Evidence submitted.

The lockup was for an "out-of-place" charge. The inmate had received a two day isolation suspended sentence. The light sentence was due primarily to a recommendation of a member of the disciplinary board who was pleased with the inmate's good record in the kitchen. The additional charge of possessing contraband resulted in an additional one day isolation suspended sentence. When more serious contraband such as prohibited drugs are found following a lockup, a separate and substantial sanction is likely.

Hearing Procedures

a. Meetings

The disciplinary board meets regularly on Monday, Wednesday, and Friday of each week. The meeting is called by the deputy superintendent or in his absence by the superintendent. The assistant deputy superintendent on duty and a social worker (usually the head social worker) are notified. If the session extends beyond a shift of duty for one of the assistant deputies, the man coming on duty will replace the man leaving after the completion of a case then pending.

b. Prior investigation

Two copies of the disciplinary report are attached to the inmate's violations card which is given to the chairman when he arrives at the detention area. The report generally has not been read before this time by any member of the D board. No formal investigation is conducted before the hearing. If the charge is very serious or an officer has been injured, some preliminary questioning of staff witnesses may be undertaken. Also, on some occasions the officer filing the report will offer his views to the deputy or another board member before the hearing.

c. Reading the disciplinary report

When the board is ready to hear the inmate's case, it will call him into a conference room in the detention area. He is not permitted counsel or representation of any kind;[19] the presence of a social worker is deemed sufficient. The inmate sits facing the three members of the board across from a long table. There are no phones in this room, and although a member may be called out to receive a message, this is unusual. In sharp contrast to the atmosphere surrounding the job transfer board hearings, the atmosphere of the discipinary hearing is quite serious. Nevertheless, the chairman usually attempts to ease the inmate's uncomfortableness by friendly and polite gestures. Several inmates appeared very nervous during the hearings while others seemed more accustomed to the process.

The disciplinary report is generally read to the inmate in full even if lengthy. It is the inmate's first exposure to it. Portions are not read, however, if the board is interested in hearing the inmate's version of the events first. This is the practice, for example, when the inmate has been accused of lying.

d. Inmate's opportunity to be heard

After hearing the report the inmate is asked to give his "story." Alternatively, the chairman might directly ask the inmate: "Why did you do this?" The inmate's opportunity to be heard is confined to making a statement rather than giving trial testimony. He is generally presumed to be guilty, and the board is only seeking information to guide it in its choice of sanctions.

The presumption of guilt stems from the board's attitude that unsworn statements in the disciplinary report are statements of fact rather than testimony to be evaluated. Even the charge is made in terms of "assault" rather than "suspicion of assault." Despite this presumption, the inmate may still prevail. Occasionally, substantial ambiguities in the report will prompt detailed questioning of the inmate. Sometimes the inmate's version of events will be substantiated by a call to the necessary staff member. Neither witnesses nor the complaining officer, however, ever appeared before the board. Thus, the inmate had no opportunity to cross-examine or confront his accuser. More often it is the inmate who prompts the board to call an officer on the phone or examine particular physical evidence. An inmate's offer to produce other inmates as witnesses, however, will be ignored. The explanation by prison administrators for this is that experience has proved that the value of such witnesses is near zero; it is universally believed that they will always testify for the inmate and against the administration.

e. The factfinding process: case illustrations

The best way to convey an overall sense of the factfinding process and the hearing procedures is to discuss specific cases that were observed. Throughout this section and the descriptions to follow, the reader is cautioned that the "Hawthorne effect" may have been operative. That is, the behavior of the board members may have departed from usual practice not necessarily out of a conscious effort to please or persuade but because of the inevitable subconscious psychological effect said to attend any knowingly observed human behavior. The procedures remained fairly constant, however, and what was observed in all likelihood bears a close resemblance to actual practice.

CASE 3

Inmate *T* was charged with lying to an officer, disobedience of orders, and illegal possession of another inmate's clothing. *T* worked in the laundry, and the possession of another inmate's clothing was thought to be due to a "special pressing" job that *T* had either promised his friend or sold to a customer. This has been a recent problem at Concord, and the staff was determined to crack down on it. The report was read and *T* denied his guilt. The report stated that *T* was found in possession of unmarked pajama bottoms and a

sweat shirt belonging to *P*. When questioned about this, the officer reported that *T* said that *P* gave him the sweat shirt. It was seized as evidence. *P* was questioned by the officer and said that he had not given a sweat shirt to anyone. [It is against the rules to transfer personal clothing without permission and without a change in laundry marking.]

T insisted that the pajamas were his and that he did not mark them because he could clean them himself in the laundry. He offered to show a matching pajama top in his cell. As for the sweat shirt, *T* insisted that he did receive them from an inmate but that the sweat shirt was owned by *R* and not *P* and was clearly so marked. The board members could not believe that the officer would incorrectly identify the marked ownership of the sweat shirt, but it was brought in and in very large letters bore the name of *R* and not *P*. The board was inclined immediately to acquit, but I suggested that *R* now be asked if he gave the sweat shirt to *T*. [This intervention was something that was avoided, but at times the temptation was too great.] *R* was asked by a wing officer and reported that he did give *T* the sweat shirt. *T* was exonerated of all charges.

Several features of this case are worth noting. First, the factual error was probably due to a misunderstanding of what *T* told the officer locking him up that could very easily have been prevented by a casual examination of the sweat shirt. Second, after this error no effort was made to check out the inmate's story as to his pajamas. The feeling was that since the inmate knew that it could easily be checked out, he would not lie on this point to the board. The impression given was that with the gross error in the report, the board was anxious to release the inmate and forget the whole incident. Third, when the inmate left the session, one member of the board expressed his view that the defense was manufactured; that by prior agreement *R* had been told to say that he gave *T* the sweat shirt should *T* get caught giving it the "special press." This feeling may have been the reason for the board's apparent reluctance to bother to check out *T*'s story after the error was found in the report. Finally, note that an illegal transfer had nonetheless occurred between *T* and *R*. However, even when I raised this issue, the board refused to reconstruct the report. The inmate was not charged with an illegal transfer of clothing but with possessing another inmate's clothes. He was not to be tried on a charge not made in the report even when the facts clearly demonstrated a violation.

CASE 4

Inmate *H* was charged with intention to assault with a club. A short time before, he had been playing basketball and was punched in the mouth by another player, inmate *E*. *H* was injured badly enough to require stitches in his lip. He went back to his dormitory room and later was seen with a club, the handle for a wash barrel. The officer assumed that he intended to use the club for revenge on inmate *E*. The officer tried to take it away from him. The report stated that *H* could be subdued only with a "struggle." Several officers were needed to effect the lockup. While the report did not indicate it, the assistant deputy informed the other board members that in the scuffle an officer had broken a rib and that *H* had been described to him as a "madman" during the incident.

H forcefully asserted that he did not intend to assault *E* and that he could have assaulted *E* if he wanted to but that he was anxious to keep a good record until his parole hearing date only two months off. He emphasized how much an assault would cost him in terms of his parole chances if found guilty. He insisted that this was the reason he walked away from the game after being assaulted by *E*. He stated that he was holding the barrel handle in order to take it up to his room and use it in cleaning some blood on the floor from his lip.

The board did not believe inmate *H*'s story. They reasoned that a man with a cut bad enough to require four stitches would not want to clean up his room; he had "struggled" with the officers — the specific word indicating that there must have been substantial resistance to giving up the club. The assistant deputy told *H* that he had broken an officer's rib and that he had been described by the officers present as a "madman" during the incident. *H* responded that the officers were choking him and that no one had asked him to give up the handle; rather, he had just been attacked by the officer, and he had responded in self-defense.[20] No effort was made to question further the officers involved, or check out *H*'s story. He was given five days of isolation. After he left the session, the assistant deputy noted that *E* was white and *H* was black and that the officers up at the farm had been concerned that the incident might de-velop into a black versus white confrontation.

CASE 5

Apparently after the lockup of inmate *H* in Case 4, inmate *E* who had first punched *H* on the basketball court was locked up. Part of the reason for this decision to lock up *E* seemed to be to cool the tensions that were developing between black and white inmates over the lockup of inmate *H*. The charge against *E* was fighting or assault against another inmate. The disciplinary report said little more than that *E* punched *H* in the mouth while playing basketball.

E was asked to explain why he hit *H*. He stated that he thought *H* had poked him in the eye intentionally and that he lost his temper and punched him. He emphasized that it was a single punch only, that immediately after he did it he brought himself under control, and that had *H* hit him back he would have deserved it and would not have fought back. He said that he regretted doing it, that he had apologized to *H* already, and that his actions were foolish and would not be repeated.

Since Cases 4 and 5 were related, the board heard the facts of each before pronouncing sentence in either. After it had given *H* five days isolation, the board felt it must give *E* the same punishment. He also received five days of isolation, a common penalty for a fight or assault in an uncrowded place. Had *H* not exploded later back in the dormitory, *E* would probably have never been locked up for the single punch. Instead he received an identical punishment in the interests of equality of treatment despite his apology, admission of guilt, and previous seven months of good behavior. The board emphasized that *E*'s loss of temper had cost an officer a broken rib.

f. Choice of sanctions

Even without a presumption of guilt, the vast majority of the disciplinary violations would be based on undisputed facts. An inmate who is found with contraband in his room, for example, does not ordinarily dispute the presence of contraband. He is asked where he obtained it, and the stock answer is that an inmate who had recently left Concord gave it to him. In one case the board in a friendly way pressed the inmate for a better answer. Finally, the inmate said that he could not be expected to rat on another guy and that this was not a serious enough matter for the board to try to make him do so. The matter was dismissed, and the inmate's candor was rewarded with a suspended sentence.

In some cases inmates appeared quite bitter and charged the complaining officer with malice and animosity towards the inmate; the inmate was depicted as the victim of an officer with a "bug" about something. This attitude did not improve the inmate's chances before the board, and if the inmate was persistent, it probably resulted in a more severe sanction. There were instances, however, where the board was in apparent sympathy with the inmate's characterization of the officer. Inmates who were apologetic and indicated they would try to refrain from similar violations in the future made a more favorable impression on the board and usually received suspended sentences. An exception to this would occur when the principle of equality intervened to require a punishment equal to that given another inmate as in Case 5 above.

Inmates were exonerated or the charge otherwise disposed of without any sanction in about 10 percent of the observed cases. This compares favorably with the percentage of acquittals in the outside criminal courts of most jurisdictions for the cases actually going to trial. But in the criminal courts, prosecutorial discretion has weeded out the week and inappropriate cases. In the prison setting only the officer makes the judgment whether or not to file a report, and only if it appears clearly superfluous to another pending report, will it be destroyed. If the report is destroyed, it will be eliminated from all prison records. Generally though even the "not proven" charges have an important effect on the inmate. In one job transfer session, for example, an inmate was asked how many lockups he had on his record. He responded with a number, and the social worker replied that he had many more reports in his file. The inmate replied that some of the reports were "not lockups"; that is, they did not result in isolation. The social worker insisted that any disciplinary report indicates maladjustment which reflects badly on the inmate.

Another distinguishing feature of D board "not provens," or like dispositions, is the manner in which the decisions are communicated to the inmate. The innocence of the inmate is not really proclaimed; to do so would seem to call into question the presumption of truthfulness of the officer's report — a presumption vital to the disciplinary process as administered at Concord. Rather, the inmate is told that he will be given the "benefit of the doubt" due to some uncertainty as to the facts. Exoneration thus becomes an act of grace and not a triumph of the justice of the inmate's defense or a recognition of a genuine absence of sound evidence.

The process is not, however, arbitrary. An inmate will not be convicted if the evidence is wholly unpersuasive or leaves very substantial doubts. And where the evidence appears weak a suspended sentence is usually granted, a disposition that may represent a compromise on the question of guilt itself.[21] A more direct compromise occurs when the charge is "filed." In such a case it will not be disposed of but will be recalled if the inmate is later accused of a similar violation.

If a sanction is to be imposed, including a suspended sentence, a member of the board will usually propose the disposition after the inmate has left the room. If the others seem to agree, the members' suggestion becomes the decision of the board, and the inmate is called back in to be informed. The process usually takes a couple of minutes. Sometimes another member of the board will prefer a higher or lower sentence, and a compromise is common. The social worker rarely takes an active role in this process and usually goes along with the lighter sentences when the other two members are split. Because of the consensus nature of the selection of sanction the membership of the board is very important. If the assistant deputy is familiar with the inmate and speaks up for him, it is unlikely he will get more than a warning or a suspended sentence. The presence of an antagonistic member, on the other hand, may result in a harsher sentence. This is illustrated by a very interesting case.

CASE 6

Inmate *K* was charged with refusing to obey an order. He was found with his shirt outside of his trousers in the dining room. When instructed to tuck it in, he said that he was not going to take any more orders and that as far as he was concerned his continued detention was illegal. The inmate was referring to a dispute about his discharge date that had arisen that morning. He was due to leave on a Monday. This was the preceding Friday and he had just given a pint of blood. Inmates volunteering to give blood are granted by statute a nonforfeitable five day reduction of their minimum sentence. Thus, by giving blood the inmate claims to have pushed his discharge date back five days. He accordingly asked to leave immediately after giving the blood. Apparently he had been informed by his social worker that giving blood that close to discharge would not result in an earlier discharge since the papers from Boston could not be prepared quickly enough. Yet, the inmate had his mother come to the prison on this Friday to take him home. The inmate had barged into a job transfer board session on the morning of the violation to complain about his illegal detention. He was very upset, and it seemed clear that he could not last the weekend without a lockup. The head social worker was quite angry with the inmate and thought about locking him up for coming into the meeting against orders not to do so. The social worker was on the disciplinary board that was now hearing inmate K's dining room violation case. The chairman of the board was also at the job transfer board hearing but took a more understanding attitude towards the inmate's disappointment at not leaving early. Moreover, he thought the best disposition of this case would be the one that would permit the prison to be rid of K at the earliest possible date. The third member was unfamiliar with the day's events and wanted to see if the inmate would be willing to apologize for his poor attitude. The inmate apparently knew what he must do to ride out this new complication and came in appearing quite contrite and confessing error.

Over the strong protest of the social worker the inmate was given a two day suspended isolation sentence. His papers were processed that day and he left the next day. Had the social worker prevailed he would have put K in the hole for three days or a week. Since each day of isolation would have resulted in three lost days of good time credits and since this inmate was serving his full sentence (reduced by good time credits earned), a sentence of isolation would have extended his period of incarceration beyond even the Monday date. When the board informed the inmate of his suspended sentence, it conceded openly that it knew the inmate was "snowing" the board by his show of an improved attitude but nevertheless pointed to that as the crucial determinant of the suspended sentence.

The number of days of isolation is guided by very general ideas about how many days each violation is worth. There can, however, be substantial variations in the severity of sentences for the same offense. For example, when questioning members independently, I was told that the average penalty for fighting is five days unless the fight took place in a crowded place like the dining room in which case 10 days might be given. Another member told me that the average was only two to three days and that five was normal for a dining room altercation. Refusals to work usually result in two to three days isolation although sometimes a warning might be given if the circumstances of the particular case indicate more of a disagreement than a real refusal to work. Destroying state property might range from a warning to the maximum allowable 15 days isolation. Clothing violations ordinarily result only in warnings.

Within the range of sanctions typically associated with each violation, the board selects a sentence based on the circumstances of the case, the attitude of the inmate, and his past disciplinary record. The board's decision, as previously noted, may also be influenced by the desire to treat inmates equally. Furthermore, though generally not a factor, the effect of the disciplinary action on the inmate's parole eligibility may be considered. This is illustrated in the next case.

CASE 7

Inmate A was charged with possession of drugs and being under the influence of alcohol. He was working in the Fernald School for Retarded Children program. He was thus living in the farm dormitory and was due to appear before the parole board in 12 days. Some pills were found in his socks, and he had alcohol on his breath when arrested. Despite this damaging evidence, A insisted that he had been framed by others and was utterly innocent.

The charges were serious, and the board was inclined to give him at least 10 days of isolation. In light of the fact that he had already lost his position on the farm, his opportunity to continue in the Fernald School program, and most likely, parole for at least one more year, the board decided to give him only five days isolation.

The disposition that is decided upon is noted in the small space provided on the disciplinary report, and the report is then signed by the chairman. No explanation of the proceedings or the reasons for the choice of sanctions is recorded on the form. The inmate may be told briefly of the important factors of decision especially when a particular fact or attitude weighed in his favor. If the complaining officer wants an explanation of the disposition, he can ask one of the board members; no formal effort is made to explain the disposition to him.

g. Appeal

No formal appeal of a disciplinary board decision is possible. In very unusual circumstances the board on its own motion may reconsider a case if new facts are discovered. The lack of any right to appeal is thought necessary to preserve the appearance of complete integrity of the D board. Also, it is believed that sanctions must be swiftly dispensed to have the greatest impact on the maintenance of discipline.

Informal appeals, however, can be made in two ways. First, an inmate can exercise his right to send a sealed, uncensored letter to the Commissioner of Corrections protesting this or any other action of the prison staff. Some complaints are occasionally received by the Commissioner's office as a result of an inmate's unhappiness with the actions of the D board. No evidence of a reversal of a D board decision by this process was discovered.

The restoration of lost good time may be considered a second method of reconsideration. Lost good time credits may be restored after a long period of good behavior upon application to the superintendent. The period of good conduct must generally be one year, but an inmate with a serious disciplinary record may warrant consideration after only six months of improved behavior. The inmate either applies in writing himself or some staff member may call the superintendent's attention to his good behavior. The superintendent will then review the file and may ask to talk with the inmate. In appropriate cases the superintendent will recom- . mend restoration of a certain number of lost credits to the Commissioner of Corrections. These recommendations are ordinarily granted as a matter of course.

The restoration of lost good time is a discretionary act of the superintendent. The extent to which the device is used varies widely in the Massachusetts system according to the views of the superintendent in charge of each institution. Before the present superintendent came to Concord, restorations were almost never recommended. The former superintendent believed that a man must pay for his offenses and that restoration denied a fair reward to the inmate who never had any disciplinary problems. The present superintendent, on the other hand, believes restoration to be a proper and important rehabilitative tool which is especially useful for inmates who have difficulties shortly after arrival but who have otherwise behaved themselves. He rejects the argument that this practice is unfair to the perfect inmate by noting that the one-time troublemaker had to serve time in the hole and was probably denied a variety of other prison benefits because of his misconduct.

Referral to the Criminal Courts

Rule violations which are very serious and constitute felonies are reported to the District Attorney for criminal action. All escapes and attempted escapes which are very close to implementation are also reported to the District Attorney. Related rule infractions such as possession of a saw are handled as disciplinary violations. Destruction of state property is usually handled by the D board unless the amount of damage was very substantial. An assault on an officer will be reported to the District Attorney only if the officer requests that court action be taken. For some officers who receive minor assaults frequently, going to court is simply too much of a bother. Inmates found with hypodermic needles must be reported to the courts.

The D board is often used as a screening agency to recommend to the superintendent whether court action should be initiated. If the board so recommends, the inmate will be held pending court action and will not be independently punished by the D board. If the D board feels that it can impose a sufficient sanction, it may ask the officer to lessen his charge from "arson," for example, to "suspicion of starting a fire" or "disturbance in shop." In that way the D board can more easily avoid referral to the court. The next case illustrates the use of the D board for this screening purpose.

CASE 8

Inmate X was charged with suspicion of arson. Within five or six minutes after leaving his cell for dinner, the wing officer noticed a fire in X's cell. The mattress was completely in flames. X was apprehended in the dining room and taken into custody.

The inmate protested his innocence. He stated that he had reason to believe that an inmate who lived in his wing named Joe had started the fire as a frameup. He did not know Joe's last name. The motive was alleged to be punishment for X's support of the administration. For example, the guys would complain how bad the food was, and X said he would tell them that he thought with the money available the prison did a good job of feeding the inmates.

A shakedown of X's cell revealed nothing that could have been used to start the fire; X did not smoke so he carried no matches. X was committed to Concord for arson, and this was an important element in his apprehension on this charge. He was very nervous and quite frightened; he was presently being treated by a doctor for emotional disorders. It was his first disciplinary violation in his six months of incarceration. The inmate Joe — who was identified by the board — was said to be the kind of person who could have started the fire to cause X to get locked up. In light of these factors, the board tended to believe X and thought the evidence insufficient to prove his guilt.

Inmate X was very grateful for the exoneration and was very anxious for Joe to be punished for framing him. The board, however, quickly dismissed any action now against anyone X might name. If the board did seek to punish someone else, X would be likely to receive even more trouble from the other inmates. And the board told X, it could not on his testimony alone charge Joe with the offense. X was urged not to take independent action against anyone and assured that the responsible parties, if any, would be dealt with eventually on other charges.

Collateral Uses of The Disciplinary Hearing

a. Educative function

To varying degrees the disciplinary hearing is used to convey to the inmate the reasons for certain rules and procedures. The extent to which this function was emphasized depended upon who chaired the D board sessions. When the superintendent sat as chairman, a considerable effort was made to convince the inmate that the rule violation in question was inconsistent with the best interests of the prison community. For example, the prison has a rule against inmates working in the laundry doing "special presses" for their friends. An inmate found with laundry not belonging to him was accused of violating this rule. The inmate's defense was that he was only doing a favor for a friend; he was not charging anything for the work and did not see anything wrong with it. The superintendent asked him who did the work for the inmates without friends in the laundry. The inmate's first response was that that was their problem. Then, the superintendent asked him if he thought that was fair. Whether because he actually believed it or because he was trying to impress the D board, the inmate seemed to agree that "special pressings" for friends denied equal treatment to all inmates and hence were unfair. The same approach was taken in many cases. An inmate charged with illegal possession of coffee was told that the coffee was innocent enough but that possession of anything that large was a serious security risk. This educative philosophy was not as apparent when the deputy superintendent was chairing the meeting. It is unclear whether the difference was one of approach or reflected the fact that the superintendent was more conscious of my presence than the deputy superintendent.

Sometimes a lockup will serve more as an example for the other inmates than to correct the misbehavior of the particular inmate. When this is the case, the lockup and the preliminary detention may be regarded as a sufficient sanction, and a warning will be the only formal sanction. An example of this occurred in the prison's effort to crack down on the "special pressing" problem in the laundry. The shop officer ordered two inmates locked up for pressing violations and then notified the assistant deputy superintendent that the inmates had otherwise good work records. This communication was revealed to the other members of the board, and the consensus was that the shop officer only wanted a formal show of support for his crackdown efforts and did not want serious punishment for the two inmates. A warning was the disposition in each case.

b. Investigative function

The D board occasionally acts as an investigatory body. In this capacity, the board will hear a nondisciplinary matter in an effort to question an inmate about a personal problem or to uncover evidence of misconduct by others. The next case illustrates this practice.

CASE 9

Inmate *Y* had requested assignment as a permanent "runner" in the New Line. These positions are usually filled by persons who are unable to work elsewhere in a more productive capacity. Such a request by a healthy inmate usually is a sign of trouble within the general population. Thus, inmate *Y*'s case was heard by the D board rather than by the job transfer board.

Inmate *Y* appeared with a badly beaten right eye. He claimed that he received it falling off the toilet in his cell; in the hearing he continued to maintain that position, but he smiled occasionally when it was asserted that everyone knew that was a lie. He had a good job in the kitchen. He indicated that he wanted to be assigned to the New Line because he preferred to work in smaller groups. He turned down offers of different employment in smaller groups within the general population. The real reason for his request seemed apparent: he wanted to be removed from the general population because he thought it would be safer to be out of reach. He expressed it as: "I just want to do the best time I can and get out."[22]

From the beginning of the hearing, it seemed fairly clear that the transfer would be denied. The purpose of the hearing was to forcefully probe into the reason for the request. Who assaulted the inmate and for what reason? All efforts to find out failed. Several possible answers occurred to the board members and were suggested to the inmate. Was he a big shot who had lost his power inside? Had he made an unnatural advance on a young inmate and been met by retaliation by a friend? Whatever the reason,

inmate *Y* was frightened and wanted the security of the New Line. The board tried to emphasize that anyone he named would not be apprehended immediately; rather, he would be watched and charged when caught violating another rule.

After the inmate's transfer was denied and he left the room, a member of the board speculated that the inmate had "made a mistake" inside, was reprimanded by other inmates, and now was scared. If he followed the "inmate code" more closely in the future, it was thought that probably he would be left alone. Nonetheless it is likely that the staff would watch the inmate a bit more closely. A couple of months later it appeared that the inmate's orientation into the prison community had been completed successfully and he was leading an uneventful life in the kitchen job.

A RATIONALE FOR
DECISION-MAKING

NECESSARY GOALS

The foregoing discussion has been largely descriptive. It is based on four months of observations and interviews at Concord. It cannot be considered definitive; nor can it be said with confidence that it does not contain error of fact or inference. It does, however, convey a sense of the decision-making process in one prison community. Although some evaluative comments may be found in the previous section, this section has been reserved for tentative conclusions as to how decisions in a prison community ought to be made.

If the prison experience is successfully to persuade inmates not to continue criminal careers, the prison community should be one that pursues *inter alia* these goals:

1. To maximize the opportunities for a "cooperative regime" wherein all participants — inmates and staff alike — pursue complementary rather than contradictory goals.
2. To promote interaction between inmates and staff to the end that the utility of conventional norms may be demonstrated.
3. To maximize in every way consistent with the needs of security and administra-

tion respect for human dignity and the principle of self-determination.

4. To develop a rational scheme of rewards and deterrents administered in a manner that is perceived as fair and just.

These goals may not be entirely exclusive of one another; they are intended to achieve the same purpose. The hope is that the correctional institution will convince its charges that crime is unacceptable. A process of "persuasion" rather than one of "rehabilitation" is preferred because it is not clear that a democratic society should claim the right to reshape in an involuntary setting human personalities. Rather, it is felt that the goal should be to demonstrate why conformity with certain fundamental norms is in the best interests of all members of the society. While this view may be naive and hopelessly optimistic, it seems highly desirable in a prison that the utility and moral force of the rule of law be demonstrated. If persons, who by their antisocial acts have indicated a lack of faith in the rule of law, are forced to live in a community in which the rule of law is adhered to and enjoyed there may be reason to hope that they may live under the rule of law upon release. The chances that they will do so must at least be improved; such chances are surely impaired by an involuntary scheme of regulation that is perceived as arbitrary or unjust.

NOTES*

1. "The prison is not an institutional septic tank for societal waste; it is a structural part of the correctional system." Comment, "The Inadequacy of Prisoners' Rights to Provide Sufficient Protection for Those Confined in Penal Institutions", 48 *N.C.L. Rev.* 347, 843 (1970). As Chief Justice Burger has said:

> The system of . . . justice must be viewed as a process embracing every phase. . . . We can no longer limit our responsibility to providing defense services for the judicial process [alone and] yet continue to be miserly with the needs of correctional institution and probation and parole services.

Burger, "The State of the Judiciary" — 1970, 56 *A.B.A.J.* 929, 934 (1970). Only last year was a casebook printed covering the newly emerging field of prisoners' rights. *See, e.g., S. Krantz, The Law of Corrections and Prisoner's Rights, Cases and Materials xiii* (1973).

2. Law schools are, however, beginning to offer instruction on the law of criminal corrections. *See* Rubin, "The Law Schools and the Law of Sentencing and Correctional Treatment", 43 *Texas L. Rev.* 332 (1966). A number of clinical programs have begun also. *See generally* Jacob and Sharma, "Justice After Trial: Prisoner's Need for Legal Services in the Criminal-Correctional Process", 18 *Kan. L. Rev.* 493, 604–621 (1970).

3. *Cf.* Mueller, "Punishment, Corrections and the Law" in *The Tasks of Penology* 77–78 (H. Perlman & T. Allington eds. 1969).

4. For a history of the development of treatment methods and philosophy in American prisons *see*, *American Correctional Association, Manual of Correctional Standards* 3–30 (3rd Ed. 1966) [hereinafter cited as *Manual*]; "E. Sutherland & D. Cressey, *Principles of Criminology*" 503–510 (7th Ed. 1966) [hereinafter cited as *E. Sutherland & D. Cressey*]; Rothman, "The Invention of the Penitentiary," 8 *Crim. L. Bull.* 554 (1972); "State Correctional Institutions for Adults", 13 *Crime & Delinquency* 185, 185–187 (1967).

5. Ruffin v. Commonwealth, 62 Va. (21 Gratt.) 790, 796 (1871).

6. *See Manual supra* note 4, at 7, 17. Rehabiliation, although an articulated goal of the sentencing courts (*see* Williams v. New York, 337 U.S. 241 (1949)), is not necessarily the goal of the prison administrator. He is normally concerned more with the security of the institution. Seliger, "Toward a Realistic Reorganization of the Penitentiaries", 60 *J. Crim. L.C. & P.S.* 47, 48 (1969).

7. "S. Rubin, *Law of Criminal Correction* 111 (1963).

8. This process of individualized program planning is referred to as "classification".

9. *See President's Commission on Law Enforcement and Administration of Justice, Task Force Report: Corrections* 53 (1967) [hereinafter cited as *Corrections Task Force*]; Note, "Prisoners' Gain Time: Incentive, Deterrent, or Ritual Response", 21 *U. Fla. L. Rev.* 103 (1968).

10. "Statutes regulating the maintenance and care of prisoners and the power of their keepers to control them are rare. The legislative standards that do exist are for the most part vague." Goldfarb and Singer, "Redressing Prisoners' Grievances", 39 *Geo. Wash. L. Rev.* 175, 180 (1970).

11. A starting bibliography can be found in 27 *The*

---

*This article has been abridged and its footnotes have been edited and renumbered.

Record 188 (1972). A more comprehensive bibliography is R. *Singer Prisoners' Legal Rights: A Bibliography of Cases and Articles* (2d ed. 1974). Both sources can be supplemented for later articles by using the Bibliography Section of the *Prison L. Rptr.*

12. This is a phrase adopted by Erving Goffman to refer to institutions which capture the time and interest of its members to such an encompassing degree as to be called "total." Such institutions include besides prison and concentration camps, homes for the aged, mental hospitals, army barracks, boarding schools, and convents. *See* Goffman, "On the Characteristics of Total Institutions: The Inmate World and On the Characteristics of Total Institutions: Staff-Inmate Relations" in *The Prison* 15–106 (D. Cressey ed. 1961) [hereinafter cited as Goffman].

13. "The wretched physical conditions pale in importance . . . beside the total arbitrariness of the bureaucracy that rules every aspect of their existence." Wick, "Procedural Due Process in Disciplinary Hearings: The Case for Specific Constitutional Requirements", 18 *So. Dak. L. Rev.*, 309, 310 (1973).

14. A minor exception is the authority given to the deputy superintendent, acting alone, to withdraw the privilege of owning a personal radio for the remainder of the inmate's term of incarceration for allowing a radio to leave one's possession without permission. This policy was adopted and announced by posted notice in order to combat the use of radios as wagering collateral and payments. An inmate may write the deputy to offer an explanation for the apparent violation, but in the several cases that arose under this regulation such defenses were rejected.

15. "The amount and type of disciplinary actions received by a prisoner determines when he will be paroled." Clark, "Prisons: A Perspective From Within," 6 *Suffolk U.L. Rev.* 785, 793 (1972). Since the inmate's file follows him throughout the institutional setting and has an effect on the grant or denial of parole, where the facts show lack of guilt, this should be clearly noted on the record. This would also aid the later adjustment committee's considering sanctions for any future offenses charged. Due process hearings or notice may be required before bad conduct reports are placed in an inmate's file. *Compare* Cluchette v. Procunier,

328 F. Supp. 767 (N.D. Cal. 1971), *with* Braxton v. Carlson, 483 F.2d 933 (3d Cir. 1973). The inmate under the model regulations is allowed access to his file and any reports or records relied upon at his disciplinary hearings.

16. When an officer sees what he considers to be a violation of one of the rules, he can do one of four things: 1. ignore the violation; 2. reprimand the inmate and give him a warning; 3. inflict summary punishment (such as extra work or denial of privileges); or 4. file a disciplinary report. At present, the officer's decision is not reviewable. It is recommended that before a charge can be brought there be an investigation of the incident by supervisory personnel. *See* Brant, "Prison Disciplinary Procedures: Creating Rules," 21 *Clev. St. L. Rev.* 83, 86 (1972). Chief Justice Burger has indicated that there is an urgent need for carefully selected and trained corrections personnel. Since line personnel are not adequately trained or qualified, the need for review of their discretionary acts is especially great. *See* Note, "Prisoners' Rights Under Section 1983", 57 *Geo. L.J. 1270* (1969).

17. The Third Circuit Court of Appeals has recently held that a disciplinary proceeding before the adjustment committee (federal system) is not merely a guilt adjudicating hearing. "It is also part of the rehabilitation and correctional system for determining the institutional program and service to which the prisoner should be referred." Braxton v. Carlson, 483 F.2d 933, 939 (3d Cir. 1973).

18. This prehearing detention would appear valid only in cases where a serious offense is charged.

19. The prisoner's right to be heard by the disciplinary board may well be meaningless unless he has some assistance in marshalling the facts or arguing in mitigation. This is especially so because as the Supreme Court has recognized, "penitentiaries include among their inmates a high percentage of persons who are totally or functionally illiterate, whose educational attainments are slight and whose intelligence is limited." Johnson v. Avery, 393 U.S. 483, 487 (1969).

20. This case seemed to cry out for counsel and examination of witnesses.

21. Very few suspended sentences are granted. The figure may be as low as 16%.

22. The staff thus supported the intra-inmate power structure and helped to continue in effect the "inmate code."

16. THE DECISION TO GRANT OR DENY PAROLE

ROBERT DAWSON

1966 *Washington University Law Quarterly* 243, © 1966. Reprinted by permission.

■ This article represents the findings of the American Bar Association's Survey of Parole Board decisions in three states: Kansas, Michigan, and Wisconsin. Dawson, utilizing an observation-type methodology combined with case examples, concludes that parole boards, more so than other agencies in the criminal justice system, exercise their discretionary power with very little review or oversight from outside scrutiny. This article provides a thorough analysis of just how parole boards arrive at their decision to grant or deny parole to a prison inmate. Further, Dawson calls for the implementation of policies which would provide for more equitable paroling decisions. He suggests that administrative self-controls are as essential to equitable decisions as formal, legal controls. ■

DISCRETION IS EXERCISED at all stages of the criminal justice system. Police sometimes make decisions not to arrest suspects despite adequate evidence for doing so. Prosecutors may not prosecute, or not fully prosecute, those against whom they have evidence sufficient to obtain a conviction. Trial judges sometimes dismiss cases or acquit defendants for reasons unrelated to guilt or innocence. After conviction, trial judges usually exercise great discretion in sentencing. And the decision to grant or deny parole lies almost entirely within the discretion of the parole board.

The parole board's discretion, like the discretion exercised by other criminal justice agencies, is as a practical matter free of legal controls. It is virtually impossible in an individual case to challenge a parole board decision successfully by legal processes. Not only are provisions lacking for effective judicial review, but there are few legal standards to which the decisions must conform. When discretion has been granted, its exercise is often regarded as a matter not of concern to the law and lawyers — the law sets the boundaries of discretion; it does not interfere with decisions within those boundaries.

The fact that a decision-maker has discretion does not excuse a lawyer for abandoning inquiry into a decision-making process. It is important to understand how discretion is exercised, even when there is very little that can presently be done to challenge a given decision; the lawyer must know whether there is a need to create control devices, and if so, which are feasible and will produce the fewest unwanted side effects. Knowledge of a discretionary decision-making process cannot be obtained simply by reading appellate cases. Different research techniques must be employed to discover the factors that influence discretion. The purpose of this article is to report the results of field research into the exercise of discretion by parole boards in Kansas, Michigan, and Wisconsin, and to suggest some of the difficulties likely to face those who undertake the task of effectively controlling parole board discretion.

PAROLE DECISION-MAKING

The process of making parole decisions begins even before incarceration; the timing of release on parole is significantly and purposely affected by decisions made at the charging and adjudication stages of the criminal justice system. For a wide variety of reasons, including limitations upon enforcement resources and considerations of "public welfare," police and prosecutors frequently do not charge a defendant with all the offenses for which they have sufficient evidence of guilt, thereby limiting the use of consecutive sentences where those are permitted by law. Also, they frequently do not charge the most serious offense possible or may not invoke an habitual criminal statute against a defendant with a prior criminal record. The obvious effect of these decisions is to impose limits on the duration of incarceration which would not otherwise exist.

Similarly, the adjudication process has a significant impact upon the parole board's decision. The vast majority of convictions occur upon guilty pleas. A major reason for this is the practice of plea bargaining; the defendant agrees to plead guilty in exchange for leniency in the disposition of his case, for example, probation consideration, a charge reduction, or a shorter sentence.[1] For those defendants who are incarcerated following a bargained plea of guilty, the adjudication process imposes limits on the parole board's ability to defer release.

Charging and adjudication decisions which affect the parole decision are made, in part at least, for that very purpose. For instance, there is considerable evidence that an important reason defendants bargain for guilty pleas is to eliminate the possibility of a long sentence which, although the parole board has the power of earlier release, would create the possibility of a long period of incarceration.

There are significant variations among the laws of the states concerning the extent to which the trial judiciary may participate in determining the length of incarceration.[2] In many states, the trial judge has discretion to select the maximum sentence, within statutory limits, and may thereby limit the duration of incarceration.[3] In other states, the trial judge has authority to select the minimum sentence and can thereby determine the parole eligibility of the offender.[4] In either event, the trial judge's sentencing decision has a significant, direct impact on the parole decision.

Some states have attempted to eliminate trial judge participation in determining the length of incarceration by requiring imposition of a sentence provided by statute. In Kansas[5] and Michigan[6], for example, the trial judge is required to impose the maximum sentence provided by statute for the offense of which the defendant was convicted. The purpose of such provisions is to eliminate the possibility of trial judge imposition of maxima which force release of defendants prematurely. In part, attaining the objectives of such statutes is obstructed by the practice of charge reduction in exchange for guilty pleas; the statutory maximum attached to a less serious offense than that which the evi-

dence supports is imposed instead of the longer statutory maximum attached to the offense originally charged.[7] This practice diminishes the parole board's scope of discretion contrary to legislative intent.

In other situations, mandatory sentences are intended to restrict the discretion both of the sentencing judge and the parole board; this is the case with regard to the mandatory minimum sentence which is quite long. The usual response to such legislation is to reduce the charge (in exchange for a plea of guilty) to one which carries a lower mandatory minimum sentence or which permits the trial judge to exercise discretion in setting the minimum.[8]

In most states, there are statutory parole eligibility requirements which must be met before the parole board is authorized to release an inmate. Normally, parole eligibility is attained when the inmate has served his minimum sentence, his minimum sentence less allowances for good institutional behavior, or a percentage of his maximum sentence, depending upon the jurisdiction. In many states, certain offenders are excluded from the possibility of parole.[9] These legislative restrictions on the authority of the parole board to release inmates from prison are subject to considerable administrative manipulation. If an inmate is ineligible for parole because he is serving a life sentence or because he has not yet served a rather high minimum sentence, it is common for the executive clemency power of commutation of sentence to be used to give him immediate parole eligibility, thereby permitting his release when the parole board deems proper.[10] The obvious effect of these practices is to enlarge the parole board's discretion and to frustrate legislative intent in determining parole eligibility.

The information available to the parole board concerning an inmate whose case it is considering is of obvious importance. The parole board cannot give weight to factors in the case about which it has no information, and while a parole board may (and does) disregard certain information made available to it on grounds of irrelevancy, the availability of information at least creates the opportunity for its use in decision-making. In Kansas at the time of the field survey, the parole board had very little information upon which to base its decision. It has only a brief description of the offense, the sentence, a record of disciplinary violations while in the institution, and a notation of whether any detainers were on file against the inmate. By contrast, in Michigan and Wisconsin, the parole board was provided with a present-ence report, inmate classification reports, progress reports by institutional personnel, reports on inmates participating in therapy, and an institutional summary and recom-mendation, as well as the basic information provided in Kansas. The information made available in the latter states permit the parole board to take into account factors which it could not were it given only the in-formation provided the Kansas parole board.[11]

Once the parole board arrives at a deci-sion, there is very little effective review. In two of the three states studied, there is, in a formal sense, administrative review of the parole board's decision. In practice, this amounts to little more than giving formal ap-proval to the decision made by the parole board and, furthermore, only decisions to grant parole receive even this modicum of review.[12] In none of the three states is there judicial review of parole board decisions.[13]

PAROLE CRITERIA IN PRACTICE

In practice, the parole decision is based upon numerous considerations, only some of which are reflected in the statutes which pro-vide the legal criteria for the decision. It is useful to group these considerations into three categories, although, admittedly, this introduces an element of artificiality into the analysis. In one category are the factors which a parole board considers for the pur-pose of determining the probability of recidi-vism by the inmate if released on parole. A parole board is vitally concerned with the probability of recidivism. That is viewed as the index of the extent to which the inmate has been rehabilitated; it is also some mea-sure of the risk to society which his release would entail.

Recidivism probability is by no means the sole concern of a parole board. A second category of factors consists of those which, in the view of a parole board, justify granting

parole despite serious reservations about whether the inmate will recidivate. Indeed, in some instances, a parole board may be-lieve an inmate is very likely to commit a criminal offense if released but, for other reasons, may feel compelled to grant parole. A third category, the converse of the sec-ond, consists of those factors which, in the view of a parole board, justify a parole de-nial despite its own judgment that if released the inmate would be very unlikely to recidi-vate.

THE PROBABILITY OF RECIDIVISM AS A
CONSIDERATION IN THE PAROLE DECISION

A basic consideration in the decision to grant or deny parole is the probability that the inmate will violate the criminal law if he is released. If for no other reason, parole boards are concerned with the probability of recidivism because of the public criticism which often accrues to them when a person they have released violates his parole, espe-cially by committing a serious offense.[14] But they also regard the parole decision as an in-tegral part of the rehabilitation process and consider the probability of recidivism to be an index of the extent to which the inmate is rehabilitated.

Parole boards do not use a fixed or uni-form standard of recidivism probability to determine whether an inmate should be paroled. A parole board may demand a low probability of recidivism in some cases while it may be satisfied with a very high probabil-ity in others.

It is clear from the field study that in no case does a parole board require anything approaching a certainty of non-recidivism. Considering the nature of the judgment in-volved, that would be an unreasonably high standard. It is also clear that in all cases the parole board requires at least some evidence that the inmate may make his parole; it is difficult to imagine a parole following a state-ment by an inmate that he will immediately commit a new offense, no matter how minor. The standard varies, then, from great doubt as to parole success to great confidence that the inmate will make it through his parole period and beyond without a mishap.

The standard varies depending upon a number of factors. It varies according to the seriousness of the offense which the parole board anticipates the inmate will commit if he violates his parole. If a parole board believes an inmate has assaultive tendencies and that if he violates parole he will do so by committing a physical assault, perhaps homicide, it will demand a great deal of proof that he will not recidivate before it releases him. If an inmate has limited his offenses to forgery, however, and it seems unlikely he will do anything more serious than violate parole by becoming drunk and forging a check, the board may use a considerably lower standard of likelihood of parole success. There are a number of other factors which raise or lower the standards.[15]

While the probability of success required varies from case to case, the factors to which the board looks to determine the probability remain relatively constant. Obviously not all of them are present in every case. A number recur with sufficient frequency to permit isolation and discussion.

1. *Psychological Change*

Illustration No. 1: The inmate, age twenty-three, has originally received a two to five-year sentence for auto theft. He was paroled and was returned to the institution within four months for parole violation. About three months after his return, he and two other inmates escaped from within the walls. He was apprehended quickly and was given a three to six-year sentence for the escape. Two and one-half years after the escape he was given a parole hearing. Despite his escape record, he was recommended for parole by the institution screening committee. The psychologist's report showed that he received frequent counseling and had apparently benefited from it. A parole board member asked him the usual questions concerning any altered viewpoint on his part or any change that had taken place within himself. The inmate was able to explain that he had begun to understand himself better after many talks with the psychologist and felt that his past behavior would not be repeated since he now understood how senseless it had been. The psychologist's report indicated the inmate had actually gained much insight into his motivation. The board unanimously decided to grant parole.

The indication of parole success most frequently searched for at parole hearings in Michigan and Wisconsin is evidence of a change in the inmate's attitudes toward himself and his offense. This is commonly referred to as an inmate's gaining "insight" into the problem which caused his incarceration. This criterion is based on the assumption the offense was the result of a personal problem, and unless some gains are made in solving that problem the likelihood of recidivism is high. Rehabilitation, then, becomes a matter of changing the problem aspects of the inmate's personality. There are some cases in which the parole board apparently feels the offense was truly situational — that is, the result of a peculiar combination of circumstances external to the inmate which are unlikely to recur.[16] These are rare, however, and it is an unusual case in which a parole board becomes convinced of reformation without some basic personality change. Paroles are often granted without evidence of psychological change,[17] but it is clear the parole board considers it the best indication of successful adjustment on parole.[18]

In Kansas, evidence of psychological change is usually not a factor in the parole decision. This is not necessarily because the parole board considers it to be irrelevant. Rather, it seems to be based on the fact that at the time of the field survey the parole board had very little social and psychological data on parole applicants. There were also no programs in the institutions for aiding in changing attitudes, and the time spent in parole hearings was inadequate to permit questioning beyond cursory inquiry into disciplinary infractions and the parole plan.

The factor of psychological change is frequently expressed in terms of when the inmate has reached his peak in psychological development. The problem of parole selection becomes one of retaining the inmate until he has reached his peak and then releasing him; incarceration after this point is regarded as detrimental to adjustment on parole.[19] Often the institutional summary and recommendation, prepared specially for the parole board, will indicate that further incarceration will not help the inmate — that the institution has done as much for him as it can. Conversely, when an inmate is receiving counseling or therapy and it is reported that he has made some gains in insight but more can be done, the parole board is likely to take the position that the inmate has not reached his peak and will deny parole to permit further treatment. Alcoholics and narcotic addicts seem unique in that the parole board apparently takes the position that the longer the incarceration the better the chances of rehabilitation. These inmates will sometimes be denied parole at the initial hearing for this reason despite other favorable factors.

Parole board members recognize that it is often very difficult to apply the criterion of psychological change. A member of the Michigan parole board states: "A parole board's most difficult task is to determine if any worthwhile change has taken place in an individual in order that he might take his place in society." In Michigan, the parole board frequently questions the inmate about his offense in order to determine whether he freely admits his guilt and has feelings of remorse for his conduct. These are regarded as favorable signs that an inmate has taken full responsibility for his offense and has begun the process of rehabilitation. Denial of guilt or lack of remorse does not preclude parole, because criteria other than probable success are considered, but it is an extremely unfavorable factor.

The difficulty which parole board members experience in attempting to determine whether there has been a change in the inmate's attitudes finds expression in a universal fear of being "conned."[20] The parole board shows considerable concern about the inmate who is too glib, who seems to have everything down pat and is so smooth that every detail of his story fits neatly into place. The board members resent inmates who seem to be trying to "con" them or to "take them in." One parole board member in Michigan showed considerable concern in particular over the difficulty which "psychopaths" cause a parole board which looks for signs of psychological change in inmates:

I believe the psychopath is especially adept at simulating rehabilitation and reformation and gives parole boards as much trouble as he does psychiatrists. I believe that they can be characterized only through a careful case history of their actions and that any standard description of them lacks a sharp focus unless it relates to their past behavior extended over many years.

Board members especially suspect simulation in the claims of inmates who report remarkable insight and gains from therapy. For this reason, they frequently question such an inmate on whether he found it difficult at first to talk about his problems in therapy. They are much more favorably disposed toward the inmate who found insight hard to gain at first, rather than one who claims he found it easy to understand himself and to profit quickly from counseling or psychotherapy.

Illustration No. 2: The screening committee of the institution recommended granting parole in this case. The inmate had received intensive psychotherapy, four months in group therapy and ten months individual therapy. The committee felt it should concur with the psychiatrist who recommended parole because of the progress made in therapy. The parole board granted parole.

Difficulty discovering whether an inmate has made progress in understanding himself accounts in large part for the great reliance which parole board members place on the recommendations of the counselors and psychiatrists who treat inmates. The Michigan parole board pays close attention to psychological and psychiatric reports, when available. Because of personnel shortages, many inmates are not diagnosed or treated by psychologists, psychiatrists, or social workers. However, examinations are made on repeated offenders, those with case histories involving assaultive criminal acts, and those who exhibit some apparent psychological disturbance. The parole board very often follows the recommendation of the counselors or psychiatrists treating the inmate. In Wisconsin, both the institutional committees, which make recommendations to the parole board, and the parole board place considerable emphasis upon the recommendations of psychiatrists who have observed or treated particular inmates. If an inmate received therapy and the prognosis is hopeful, it weighs heavily in favor of parole, although this fact alone may not be sufficient reason to persuade the board to grant it. However, if an inmate makes no effort to obtain therapy, or worse, refuses it, he is almost certain to be denied parole unless other very important positive factors are present. A negative recommendation from a psychiatrist treating an inmate almost invariably results in denial of parole.[21]

2. *Participation in Institutional Programs*

Illustration No. 3: The inmate, sentenced for forgery, had been a valuable asset to the institution because he was an experienced electrician. The institutional recommendation was for parole denial, characterizing him as a "chronic offender." The social services supervisor noted that no one has observed any change in him and he had not requested psychotherapy. When he was called into the parole hearing room, the first question was whether he had a job plan if released. The prisoner indicated that he wanted to look for work as a refrigeration mechanic. A parole board member then noted the inmate's drinking problem and its possible effect in the future. The prisoner indicated he felt he could make it. The parole board member than asked the inmate if he had done anything about his alcohol problem while confined. The inmate indicated he could not do anything about it because he was working seven days a week in the institution. The parole board member asked which was more important, working at the institution or seeking psychiatric help concerning the very problem that would bring him back to the institution. He told him if he really wanted psychotherapy he could have received it despite the seven-day work schedule at the institution. The inmate was asked what in his present situation had changed that would make him a good parole risk. To this the prisoner replied that he would have to make it or give up. He claimed that if he works steadily he has no problems, and that as long as he has work on the outside he feels he can adjust on parole. A parole board member then noted to him that working was not the problem because he always had a good work record and was considered a very skilled person. He was told that this type of case was the most difficult to decide, principally because of the alcohol problem involved. After the hearing, the board unanimously denied parole.

In many institutions there are a number of programs and activities designed to assist the inmate in changing his attitudes and eliminating the problems thought to be causative of his criminal conduct. Examples of these are group and individual therapy, alcoholics anonymous, self improvement (Dale Carnegie) courses, academic education and vocational training, and opportunity for religious training and worship. One of the indications of probable parole success used by the board is the extent to which the inmate has availed himself of these programs. This is viewed as indicating that the inmate is making a serious attempt to rehabilitate himself. The inmate who participates in these programs is regarded as a better risk even if no noticeable personality change is effected than is the inmate who is just "serving his time" with no genuine effort at change.

If an inmate appears before the parole board with a problem which might be alleviated by participation in any of these programs, he may be urged to participate if parole is denied. He may in fact be told that in his case, participation is the surest way to be paroled.

One of the difficult problems in applying this criterion is the availability of institutional programs, particularly psychotherapy. This is a problem of particular concern to the Michigan parole board because at the state prison the average caseload per counselor is 325. One parole board member stated:

What good does it do to select a good risk for a parole camp, thinking that fresh air and sunshine will automatically rehabilitate him, and not provide him with anyone to discuss his personal problems with over a period of three or four years? I have asked dozens of inmates if they have ever had an opportunity to discuss personal problems with anyone during a period of many years' imprisonment and most of them have said that they have not. I believe that psychological treatment, counseling, and guidance must begin with the inmate's entrance into an institution and should be a continuing process leading up to parole. I do not believe that custodial care alone ever led to any spontaneous rehabilitation of an inmate.

Concern over lack of adequate personnel for bringing about change in imprisoned offenders is illustrated by the statement of another board member: "It would almost be better not to have any counseling or psychotherapy available than to have a negligible amount and claim we have sufficient to cause any change for the better in an inmate."

The availability of programs is an important factor in the weight given to participation or failure to participate in programs. At the time of the field survey, Kansas had virtually no counseling or similar programs in its adult penal institutions. As a result, the parole board was unable to use this factor in its decisions. In Wisconsin's new medium security institution, however, many programs are available. At that institution, the parole board gives even more attention to participation in programs than it does at other Wisconsion institutions.

There is evidence that in some cases in which parole is denied, the parole board may be concerned about the effects on the other inmates of a parole grant to one who has not availed himself of any of the institutional programs. One parole board member in Wisconsin said that if an inmate appeared for parole and all prognosticating factors were in his favor for adjustment under supervision, and even if he, the parole board member, thought the individual would successfully complete parole, he still would vote to deny parole if the inmate had made no effort at all to change himself by participation in institutional programs. Thus conceived, the parole decision becomes a means of encouraging participation in the institution's programs, much as it may be used to encourage compliance with the institution's rules of discipline.

3. *Institutional Adjustment*

Illustration No. 4: The inmate had received concurrent sentences totaling three to fifteen years for assault with intent to rob, assault and armed robbery, and larceny. He had served four years at the time of the hearing. Parole had been denied at two previous hearings. The inmate had maintained he was innocent. Institutional reports characterized him as a guardhouse lawyer who was always critical of other inmates, had a quick temper, and was difficult to get along with. His adjustment in his work assignment in the laundry was satisfactory, although he was always finding fault with the institution. The institutional committee recommended denial of parole because of the inmate's hostility to authority. At the hearing, the inmate still asserted his innocence. In denying parole, the board listed the following reasons: "resents institutional authority, jail house lawyer, denies offense, has a bad temper, has a generally poor institutional adjustment."

One factor in the parole decision is the way in which the inmate has adjusted to the daily life of the institution. In Michigan and Wisconsin, records of conformity to institutional disciplinary rules, of work progress and adjustment, and of other contacts by institutional personnel bearing on adjustment are contained in the case file. In Kansas, information of the inmate's institutional adjustment is limited to a record of disciplinary infractions. The parole board in each of the states apparently regards the inmate's ability to conform to the institution's rules and to get along with other inmates, custodial personnel, and supervisors as some indication of his probable adjustment under parole supervision. Most inmates appearing for parole have a record of fairly good institutional adjustment. The fact that for many of them parole is denied indicates that good adjustment itself is not sufficient for a parole grant. It is likely that good adjustment is a minimum requirement for parole, one which must be met in order to qualify an inmate for favorable parole consideration but which is itself not sufficient for a favorable decision. In Kansas, where parole information is scanty, the fact that the board has a record of disciplinary infractions probably gives the factor of institutional adjustment greater weight than in the other two states. Also, both members of the Kansas parole board were former wardens, persons who would be expected to give more weight to institutional adjustment.

In all three states, poor adjustment can be a negative factor in the parole decision, sufficient in itself for a parole denial. For example, if an inmate with a record of assaultive behavior continues this pattern within the institution, it is regarded as evidence that there has been no personality change. It is often difficult to determine whether the board is interested in the inmate's disciplinary record as an indication of his probable adjustment on parole or whether it is concerned about the effect which parole of an inmate with a bad institutional record would have on the efforts of the institutional administrator to maintain discipline. In many cases it seems likely that the board is interested in both.

4. *Criminal Record*

Illustration No. 5: The inmate was a fifty-three year old man serving two concurrent terms of three to five years for forging and uttering. He was an eleventh offender. He had served almost two years of the present sentence and was appearing for his first parole hearing. He had made a good institutional adjustment, but the screening committee of the institution recommended a denial of parole because of his criminal record. His record began in 1927 and involved convictions and prison sentences for abduction, rape, larceny, and forgery. The interview did not last longer than two or three minutes, only long enough for the inmate to smoke a cigarette. He was asked if he had a final comment to make and, after he left the hearing room, the board briefly discussed his prospects if released. No parole plan had been developed. The board members unanimously denied parole without further discussion.

Most inmates appearing for parole hearing have had at least one criminal conviction prior to the one for which they were sentenced. The extent and nature of the criminal record is a factor of considerable importance in the parole decision.[22] The inmate's criminal record is regarded as evidence of his potentiality for "going straight" if released on parole. Other factors being equal, it will take more evidence of change in attitude to convince the parole board that an inmate with a long record has reformed than one without.

Statutes in some states exclude the possibility of parole or greatly postpone the parole eligibility of inmates with prior convictions. A Kansas statute provided that inmates who have served two prior terms in a penitentiary are ineligible for parole.[23] Even in a jurisdiction with liberal parole eligibility laws, an extensive prior criminal record may result in a routine denial of parole at the first hearing. In the illustration case, the inmate received his first parole hearing under Wisconsin law[24] after two years. Although there would normally be a strong expectation that a forger would be released at the end of two years in Wisconsin, parole was routinely denied because of the long criminal record. It could theoretically be asserted that routine parole denials because of prior record would be less likely to occur in a jurisdiction, like Michigan, where parole eligibility depends upon a judicially set minimum sentence,[25] because the trial judge could be expected to increase the minimum as a result of the prior criminal conduct. The Michigan parole board has frequently complained, however, that inmates sentenced from Detroit with long records are often given minimum sentences which are so short that they compel routine denial at the first hearing. This can be explained largely by the necessity for keeping minimum sentences low in Detroit in order not to interfere with guilty plea bargaining.[26]

Although routine denials at the initial hearing because of prior record are common in Michigan, the parole board has consciously refrained from using a rule of thumb excluding parole consideration for serious recidivists. One member of the board said that he does not believe in any rule of thumb such as four-time losers cannot be rehabilitated, but believes that the process of maturation comes late with many persons and that rehabilitation can take place within the personality of a multiple offender as well as a first offender.

In many cases it seems clear the board is more concerned with whether an inmate has had prior penitentiary experience than with the criminal record itself. Indeed, an inmate with only a juvenile record, an adult arrest record, or adult conviction resulting only in probation will be regarded by the institution and the parole board as a "first" offender. Parole may be granted rather early despite prior failure under community supervision on the theory that the inmate's first adult institutional experience may have had a shock value.

The parole board also considers offenses the inmate has admitted committing but for which he has not been convicted. In both Michigan and Wisconsin, an offender who has confessed to a number of offenses is normally charged only with the one or two most serious ones. The uncharged offenses are described in the presentence report for consideration by the trial judge in sentencing. The presentence report describing the uncharged offenses is normally included in the parole board case file. Doubtless, the uncharged offenses influence the board in its decision. Members of the Michigan parole board stated they consider the presentence report to be particularly valuable in determining the extent and nature of the uncharged offenses.

A member of the Wisconsin parole board said uncharged offenses are not, without more, an important factor in the board's estimation of probable parole success. As an example, he cited a case of a young man who for the first time in his life went on a drinking spree and committed ten burglaries. The mere fact that he committed ten burglaries probably would not influence the parole board in its decision to grant parole. The parole board member added, however, he did not intend to say that if the numerous offenses committed by an inmate, whether charged or not, indicated a pattern of serious behavior and a seriously disturbed personality, they would not be taken into consideration. He concluded that what the offenses represent in terms of the individual's entire personality and the risk to the community is considered, rather than the isolated fact that he committed a certain number of offenses.

5. *Prior Experience Under Community Supervision*

Illustration No. 6: The inmate was serving a one to four-year sentence for larceny. He was sentenced in December 1953, paroled in July 1955, and violated his parole in November 1955. The violation consisted of drinking and absconding. This was his first parole hearing since his return as a violator nine months ago. Prior to the sentence for this offense he had been on probation for a different offense and had violated probation. The Board unanimously denied parole. One member, in dictating his comments on the case, said the inmate had been back in the institution only nine months and while his institutional adjustment was good, he was a previous probation and parole violator, had an alcohol problem, and was not interested in treatment.

The inmate's experience under community supervision is an important consideration in the parole decision. Many of the inmates appearing for parole hearings have had probation, which they may or may not have violated, and some of them are serving a sentence imposed because they violated

probation.[27] Many inmates with long criminal records have had experience on parole as well as probation; this is regarded as an especially important indication of what behavior can be expected of them if they are paroled.[28]

The extent the parole board should rely on the inmate's parole experience is a problem which inevitably arises when, as in the illustration case, an inmate who has been returned to the institution as a parole violator appears before the board in a hearing for re-parole. More evidence of a change in outlook is required to convince the board to parole him than when he originally was given parole. Parole boards in the states studied do not have a flat rule with regard to re-paroles. Many inmates are given second paroles and some even third paroles, although the board may even warn them that this is their "last chance," and that a violation of this parole will result in service of the maximum sentence.[29]

Illustration No. 7: The inmate was sentenced to two and one-half to five years for larceny by conversion. He had already served twenty months. He had a long criminal record and had previously been in three other prisons in various states on charges of breaking and entering. All of his prior sentences were "flat" sentences and he had never spent time on parole. The inmate demonstrated some signs of beginning to understand his problem. His case was continued for ten months, an indication that he probably would be paroled at his next hearing.

The absence of experience on parole may be a favorable factor. In the illustration case, one of the parole board members said they were in effect promising a parole grant because although the inmate had a long prior record, he had never had a parole from any institution and it was not actually known what he could do under supervision. The board is understandably unwilling to assume that recidivism without parole is a clear indication of a high probability of recidivism with parole.

6. *Parole Plan*

Illustration No. 8: The inmate, a youth, had no family to which he could return upon release. He indicated a desire to work as a machinist and live at the

YMCA in a particular small city. The pre-parole report pointed out that it was probably impossible for a seventeen year old boy to secure employment as a machinist and, in any event, such positions in that particular small city were practically non-existent. The parole agent conducting the pre-parole investigation reviewed the inmate's long juvenile record and concluded that placement in a YMCA was unrealistic because he needed considerably more supervision. The agent felt the youth was not a proper subject for a group home because he had leadership qualities which might lead other boys into trouble. He was too old for a foster home and probably would not adjust in that setting. Therefore, the agent felt the only alternative available was to place the inmate on a farm until he reached an age when he could support himself fully without control and discipline. The board paroled the inmate to a farm placement.

The inmate's parole plan — his employment and residence arrangements — is considered in some cases an important factor in determining the probability of parole success. It is considered a favorable sign if an inmate has made a serious attempt to develop a suitable parole plan because it indicates he is thinking about his future. Even when a parole plan has been developed and its feasibility verified by the pre-parole investigation, it is still necessary to determine whether it will help or hinder the inmate's adjustment on parole.[30]

When an inmate's parole plan seems inadequate, the parole board may deny parole or defer it for a short time. If the original plan seems inadequate but an alternative has been developed by the field agent conducting the pre-parole investigation, or is otherwise available, the parole board may immediately grant parole on the condition that the inmate accept the new plan. Unlike other factors relating to probable parole success, then, the parole plan can be manipulated in order to increase the probability of success. In the illustration case, the job plan was not feasible and the residence plan was considered inadequate. A new job and residence plan was developed and parole was granted on the basis of it.

In Wisconsin, the Special Review Board, the release authority for persons incarcerated under the Sex Crimes Law,[31] makes extensive use of special parole plans for certain types of offenders. The Board's experience has been that the best solution in incest cases is to parole the inmate to a place other than that where the relative with whom he was having incestuous relations lives. Similarly, the Board has developed "protective placements" in rural areas of the state for higher risk indecent liberties cases.

The unavailability of employment for parolees and its general inadequacy causes problems. Statutes in some states require the inmate to have a job before he can be released on parole. Parole boards and field agents find it difficult to comply with these statutes and often must be satisfied with only a vague promise of a temporary, unsubstantial job, or even with no job offer but only an expectation that some job can be found shortly after release. If the parole board feels unemployment may seriously jeopardize adjustment on parole, it may deny parole until the employment picture brightens. With many unskilled workers, this necessitates a denial of parole in the winter in the expectation that the possibility of securing unskilled employment will be greater in the summer and the inmate can be paroled then. Normally, the parole board must be satisfied if the inmate has only a possibility of an unsubstantial job. In cases in which prior involvement with the law has repeatedly occurred during periods of unemployment, however, the board may refuse to parole the inmate unless he has a firm offer of substantial employment.

Normally, the inmate's residence plan is investigated to verify that he will be accepted in the home or institution and to determine what the physical conditions are and who the inmate's associates will be. The parole board usually attempts to persuade the inmate to return to his family, if he has one and they are willing to take him back, especially if he is young.

The attitude of the community in which the inmate wishes to reside and work is sometimes considered an important factor in adjustment on parole. This is especially likely if the inmate plans to go to a small community, where the attitudes of a number of citizens may make a substantial difference. If the inmate plans to work and live in a large city, a negative attitude by some of its citizens may make less difference.

7. Circumstances of the Offense

Illustration No. 9: The inmate was convicted of armed robbery and was sentenced to two to fifteen years, of which he had served eighteen months at the time of the hearing. He had no previous convictions and only a few arrests for misdemeanors. The inmate's account of the offense was that he held up a bus and was arrested almost immediately. His file showed he had been destitute at the time of the offense, was unemployed, and had been sleeping in parks. The file also showed a good work record when he was employed. He had a letter to show the parole board verifying the fact that if there were an opening he could get his old job back. He was granted parole subject to home and employment placement.

The basic indication of probable recidivism used by the Michigan and Wisconsin parole boards is evidence of personality change during the period of institutionalization. There are cases, however, in which the parole board may regard the offense as situational in nature and not necessarily the result of a personality defect. If the parole board has some assurance that the situational factors have changed during the period of incarceration, it may be willing to grant parole despite lack of evidence of personality change. In the illustration case, the offense seemed the result of the inmate's prolonged unemployment, and the parole board became convinced that the probability of success on parole would be high if the inmate were employed.

The number of cases in which the boards seem to regard the situational factors as predominating is small. Certainly, in comparison with the number of cases in which inmates explain their criminal conduct in situational terms — bad associates, drinking, unemployment, family disputes — the number of cases is small. It is difficult to determine whether the situational factors in the offense go exclusively to the probability of parole success or also to a judgment of the moral blame which the inmate should bear for his conduct. In the illustration case, one member of the board concluded that al-

though there was no excuse for the offense, the inmate's circumstances did appear to be desperate at the time he committed it, implying that the offense was "understandable."

THE DECISION TO GRANT PAROLE FOR REASONS OTHER THAN THE PROBABILITY OF RECIDIVISM

In practice, inmates are paroled who would not be released if the probability of recidivism were the sole criterion for the decision. Often, inmates are paroled despite the board's judgment that they are likely to commit new criminal offenses. That a parole board sometimes feels compelled to parole inmates who are not rehabilitated may in part reflect deficiencies in institutional treatment programs. It is clear, however, that even great advances in that area would not entirely eliminate the necessity for making decisions of this kind.

1. Seriousness of the Anticipated Violation

Illustration No. 10: The inmate, a fifty year old man, had served two years on concurrent sentences of one to five and one to seven years for forgery. No parole plan had been developed. He was a seventh felony offender. His record for forgery extended back to 1933. He had served two previous prison terms. The institution made the following parole recommendation: "Seventh offender. Chronic offender. Social adjustment in institution was good. Psychiatrist seemed to think superficial progress was being made, however, never accepted alcoholism as a problem. Deny." A parole board member began discussing with the inmate the necessity for accepting alcoholism as a problem and told him he knew he would be back as a parole violator if he did not stop drinking. He suggested the inmate join Alcoholics Anonymous after release. The board voted to grant parole.

Parole board interest in predicting behavior on parole does not end when the probability of the inmate's violating the law becomes apparent. The board is also deeply concerned with the type of violation likely to occur if the inmate does in fact violate. The board is willing to parole on less evidence of probable success when it is apparent that a violation, if it occurs, is not likely to be serious. In the illustration case, one of the parole board members said he was voting for parole because the inmate was the type of individual who just wrote small checks when drunk and who did not constitute a serious threat to the community. Another board member said that he was voting to grant parole but added that "all we're granting with tongue in cheek."

The potential benefit from further institutional treatment is also a factor in these decisions. Thus, although one inmate was clearly alcoholic and had a long record of arrests for public intoxication, he was paroled at his initial hearing. The parole board concluded he was a harmless person. It could see little point in keeping him in the institution any longer because he had shown little indication of having enough strength to quit using alcohol. The board concluded, therefore, not only had the institution been unable to do much for the inmate, but it was extremely unlikely he would ever be able to make significant gains in solving his problem.

Finally, the board is concerned in these cases about the effect of parole on the inmate's family. If the inmate is retained in the institution there is little opportunity for him to make significant contributions to the support of his dependents. If he is paroled, however, he at least has the opportunity to support his family. In Wisconsin, nonsupport offenders normally are paroled as soon as they are eligible. The parole board states there are three reasons for this policy: they are unlikely to commit a serious violation of the criminal law, the institutional program is of little aid in their rehabilitation beyond the first several months, and parole may provide financial support for the family for a time as well as the benefits which may accrue from having a father in the family again.

2. *Mandatory Release Date Near*

Illustration No. 11: The inmate was a nineteen year old girl serving a sentence of six months to one year for larceny. Her prior record consisted of one conviction for drunkenness, for which she successfully completed a one-year probation period. At the time of the hearing she had served eight months on the sentence. Her conditional release date would be reached in another three months. If parole were

denied, she would be released then and, after one month under supervision, would receive an absolute discharge. The board decided to parole her.

Parole boards sometimes find themselves in the position of choosing between a need to retain the inmate in prison and a need for supervision and control over him after he is released. This occurs when at the time of the parole hearing the inmate has only a short period to serve until he must be released from the institution. These are all cases in which the maximum sentence, whether set by statute or by the trial judge, is, in the view of the parole board, too short under the circumstances. The parole board frequently paroles an inmate despite its estimate of a high probability of recidivism, if, in its view, parole supervision is needed more than continued institutionalization.

In Kansas and Michigan, the inmate must be released unconditionally when he has served his maximum sentence, less allowances for good time. No period of parole supervision follows release. When the inmate has only a short period to serve until his maximum, less good time, the parole board frequently feels it is forced to parole him to provide supervision and control over him when he is released. In Michigan, the inmate must be discharged from parole supervision when he has served his maximum sentence, less good time earned in the institution and on parole, and in Kansas, when he has served his maximum, less good time earned while incarcerated.

In Wisconsin, the inmate must be released from the institution when he has served his maximum sentence, less good time, but the release is conditional and a mandatory period of parole supervision follows during which the releasee is subject to the same condition and possibilities of revocation which apply to parolees released by act of the parole board. He must be discharged from parole when he has served his maximum sentence without allowance for good time. When, as in the illustration case, the maximum sentence is short, the period of mandatory parole supervision following release at the maximum, less good time, is, of necessity, quite short. In the illustration case, the period of supervision would have been one month had the inmate been kept until her mandatory release date. Nevertheless, the parole board felt that further incarceration would be useful in her case. Thus, it was forced to choose between what it regarded as an inadequate period of institutionalization and an inadequate period of post-incarceration supervision. It chose to lengthen the period of supervision at the expense of the institutionalization.

The position might be taken that this is one factor to consider in determining whether the maximum sentence should be fixed by the trial judge or set by statute. Thus, it could be argued that paroles based on the approach of the mandatory release date would be less frequent when the maximum is set by statute than when set by the trial judge. One would expect to find, therefore, that this is more of a problem in Wisconsin than in Kansas and Michigan.[32] This does not seem to be the case. There may be any number of reasons for this, including, perhaps, the fact that the Wisconsin parole board may be more liberal in granting paroles than the boards in Michigan and Kansas. Another reason may be that in Wisconsin the mandatory release is followed by a mandatory period of supervision. Unlike the boards in the other two states, the parole board in Wisconsin must simply determine whether the period of supervision permitted by the good time awarded the prisoner is adequate.[33] It is only when the maximum sentence is quite short that there is any need for a parole to increase the length of the period of supervision. In Wisconsin, one finds such paroles when the maximum is short, while in Kansas and Michigan, one finds such paroles when the inmate has been denied parole in the past or has been paroled and returned for a violation.[34]

3. *Length of Time Served*

Illustration No. 12: The inmate had received a sentence of three to twenty years for armed robbery, auto theft, and forgery. He was paroled after three years but shortly thereafter violated his parole and received a new sentence for operating a con game. He served three years since his last parole. His criminal career began twenty years previously and involved numerous convictions. The psychiatric report was that the inmate was "instinctively vicious. Any rehabilitative

program will be futile." The institutional recommendation was that the inmate "has adjusted in excellent manner in institution. Has served lengthy sentence. Should be tried. Grant." The parole board decided to grant parole.

Every decision to grant parole reflects the opinion of the parole board that the inmate has served enough time, but there are some cases in which the length of time served is itself the most significant factor in the case. This typically occurs when an inmate has received a relatively long sentence, but fails to respond to the rehabilitative programs at the institution. In addition, he may have been tried on parole once or twice and had his parole revoked. The parole board may then be faced with the choice of denying parole when it is evident that further institutionalization will not increase the probability of success on parole or of granting parole to an inmate who presents some risk of violation.

In the illustration case, one of the parole board members commented that "just maybe" the inmate will make parole after so long an institutionalization. He felt that in such cases institutionalization reaches a point when it serves no purpose in terms of rehabilitation. The only question remaining is that of protection of the community, he continued. In this case, the board members all felt they would have to try the inmate on parole sooner or later, but none expressed any confidence in his capacity for success.

A factor mentioned in many cases of this type is maturation. When a relatively young man receives a long sentence and serves a fairly long term before parole, the board may comment that despite the absence of any apparent effect of the institution's program, he may have matured enough to enable him to live a lawful life in the community.

4. *Parole to a Detainer*

Illustration No. 13: A twenty-seven year old man serving a one to five-year sentence for larceny appeared before the parole board for a hearing. He had a long criminal and juvenile record. While on parole in Ohio, he came to Wisconsin and committed the offense for which he was serving time. An institutional psychologist said the inmate had admitted using narcotics and drugs; he stated that the prognosis was poor. The institutional committee recommended parole to a detainer, partly because only about seven months remained until conditional release would be required; he had served approximately three years of a one to five-year sentence, and it was thought he might as well start on his Ohio sentence. The final decision of the board was to grant parole to the Ohio detainer. The chairman commented that he did not think Ohio would come after the inmate, in which event he would be detained at the prison until his conditional release date. None of the board members felt the inmate could possibly adjust on parole. The board rationale in this case was dictated by the chairman: "Claims he owes Ohio five years. He has been locked up for the past sixteen years except for twenty-nine months. Gullible, ambitionless, and no insight. Has used heroin. Practically hopeless."

The parole decision may be influenced by the fact that a detainer has been filed against the inmate. The prisoner against whom a detainer is filed may be charged with a crime for which he has not yet been tried, may be a probation or parole violator from another state, may be wanted for completion of a prison term which was interrupted by an escape, or may have been ordered deported by a court or administrative agency.

The effect of a detainer on the parole decision varies from state to state. In some states, a detainer automatically precludes the inmate from the possibility of parole.[35] Sometimes this position is based on the view that parole implies community supervision — that a "parole to a detainer" is not really a parole and, hence, not within the authority of the parole board. In the three states, the parole boards do parole to detainers, although this is specifically authorized by statute in only one of them.[36] However, the circumstances under which they parole to a detainer vary.

The problem of whether an inmate should be paroled to a detainer normally arises only when prior attempts to secure removal of the detainer have failed. Sometimes the trial judge may be successful in obtaining removal of a detainer at the sentencing stage. If a defendant whom the judge has sentenced to prison is wanted in other counties of the

state, he may order that the defendant be taken to those counties and tried for the offenses before being transported to the correctional institution. If a defendant is wanted in another state or by federal authorities, the judge may arrange to increase the sentence in exchange for an agreement to drop the detainer, or he may grant the defendant probation or a suspended sentence and turn him over to the requesting authority.

In some correctional institutions, officials contact authorities which have lodged detainers against inmates in an attempt to discover their intentions. Effort is made to persuade the requesting authority to drop the detainer or at least to specify the circumstances, such as the number of years the inmate must serve, under which they would drop it.[37]

There are some circumstances under which an inmate of a correctional institution may demand disposition of a detainer against him as a matter of right. If the detainer represents an untried charge, the inmate may be able to require that he be taken from the institution and tried, or that the state be barred from ever trying him on that charge, on the ground that he is enforcing his right to a speedy trial. In some states, statutes give an inmate this right.[38] Even in a state which contains full provision for mandatory removal of detainers, the problem of parole to a detainer remains with respect to detainers for revocation of probation or parole and deportation detainers. Unless institutional authorities are successful in negotiating their removal, the problem comes before the parole board.

In Kansas, the parole board grants parole to inmates who have detainers filed against them as soon as they are eligible. The board apparently does not distinguish between in-state, out-of-state, and deportation detainers, nor between detainers based on charges yet to be proved and detainers for revocation of probation or parole. During one day's hearings, seven inmates were paroled to detainers. In many of these cases, it was apparent that the inmate would not have been paroled had there not been a detainer lodged against him. In each instance, the board explained to the inmate that it could do nothing but parole him to the detainer. Apparently, no effort was made during the inmate's confinement to determine whether the requesting authority is willing to drop its detainer. When an inmate has been paroled to a detainer and the requesting authority fails to take custody of him at the institution, the detainer is dropped and the inmate is scheduled for the next parole hearing to be held at his institution to determine whether he should be paroled to community supervision.

The Wisconsin parole board's policy on paroles to detainers was detailed in a booklet published shortly after the field survey was conducted, but reflected practices in effect at the time of the survey:

Persons eligible for parole under Wisconsin Statute but against whom detainers have been filed by Federal, Immigration, Out-of-State or local authorities may be granted parole to the detainer. Normally, parole is not granted to a detainer unless the usual criteria for parole selection can be met.

Institutions will be responsible for correspondence on parole planning with authorities who file detainers except when the detainer has been filed by a paroling authority. In such cases the Parole Board will be responsible for the necessary correspondence. (Institutions should refer cases of this type to the Parole Board.)

Detainers from other states placed against persons serving sentences in Wisconsin Correctional Institutions normally fall within three groups:

1. Those cases in which the individual was under field supervision at the time he was received.
2. Those in which the individual had been previously convicted in another state and it is expected that he will, upon release from a Wisconsin Institution, go to an institution in the other state to serve his unexpired term. As a matter of practice, parole is usually not granted to this type of detainer until such time as the applicant has less time remaining to serve in Wisconsin than he will have to serve in the other state.
3. Those in which the individual has been charged with an offense in another state but has not yet been tried. In this situation, it is expected that the individual will be taken to court in the other state to face prosecution when paroled in Wisconsin.[39]

In Michigan, paroles to detainers are specifically authorized. The statute provides: "Paroles-in-custody to answer warrants filed by local, out-of-state agencies or immigration officials are permissible, provided an accredited agent of the agency filing the warrant shall call for the prisoner so paroled in custody."[40] The effect of the detainer on the parole decision differs depending upon the type of detainer involved.

Detainers filed by agencies within the state of Michigan are usually for the purpose of having the inmate answer an untried felony charge. If an inmate who has such a detainer filed against him is not regarded as parolable at the time of his initial hearing, a "custody parole" is almost always given to allow disposition of the untried charges. If the local requesting authority upon notice of the parole does not take custody of the inmate at the institution, the detainer is considered dropped. If the requesting authority takes custody, the inmate is not permitted to make bond while waiting trial or disposition, and, regardless of the outcome of the proceedings, he is returned to the institution after their completion. If a new prison term is imposed, he will become eligible for parole again when he serves the new minimum sentence, less good time. If no new prison sentence is imposed, he will be reconsidered for parole in the usual manner.

In acting on a detainer filed by another state to bring an inmate to trial in that state, the parole board decides whether the inmate should be paroled to the community. When an inmate is released on such a detainer it is with the intent that if he is found not guilty, or if the charges are dropped, he will be placed on parole supervision in the other state. Commenting on this type of parole to a detainer, one parole board member stated, "We must handle such cases with the expectation that the inmate may be released entirely from custody, and cannot afford to take the long risk if the person is deemed not a proper subject for return to society." The board apparently works on the assumption in this type of case that the inmate will be set free in the other state, although he may be convicted and sentenced to prison. Therefore, the board apparently requires that the inmate be parolable under the usual criteria.

If the detainer issued by another state is for the return of the inmate as a probation or parole violator or an escaped prisoner, the board has more indication of what treatment is to be accorded the prisoner by the requesting jurisdiction. Because the risk of the inmate's being freed is considerably less than when the detainer is based on untried charges, the parole board is likely to be considerably more liberal in its attitude toward parole. The board learns the length of the sentence remaining for the prisoner to serve and the character of the parole supervision in the state. If, for example, the parole board considers the inmate a menace to society and learns that the period of time remaining to be served in the requesting state is limited, it would decide against honoring the detainer. If the parole board believes the inmate is ready for community supervision, it may suggest to the requesting state that the inmate be released to that state for dual parole supervision.

The effect on the parole decision of a detainer filed for deportation of an inmate varies depending on the country to which the inmate is to be deported. In considering deportation to Canada or Mexico, the board, aware of the ease with which the parolee can return to Michigan, tends to be somewhat cautious in granting parole. Nevertheless, even in these cases, the board is sometimes willing to grant parole when otherwise it would not. One parole board member noted:

In some quarters of this state, and particularly among some members of the judiciary, there is present a philosophy that we should not clutter up our institutions with persons who are deportable, and that we should, as a matter of fact, pursue a very liberal policy in such cases. I do not think that the board subscribes to this philosophy, nor does it operate under it to the extent that some would desire.

A greater degree of liberality is evident in considering paroles to detainers for deportation to countries overseas.

5. *Reward for Informant Services*

Illustration No. 14: The inmate has been convicted of assault with intent to rob, for which he was placed on probation. After one year on probation, he violated and received a prison sentence of one to ten years. This was his initial parole hearing. The sentencing judge and the prosecuting attorney both recommended a parole denial. He had a prior record of assault. His I.Q. was recorded

as sixty-three. Shortly before his hearing, the inmate had learned of an escape plot involving four inmates who were hiding in a tunnel. He tipped off a guard and the inmates were apprehended. The board decided to grant parole.

In current administration, the services of informants are sought and rewarded by enforcement officials. Typically, the informant has engaged in criminal behavior himself. The most persuasive inducement and reward for the information is lenient treatment of the informant. The leniency may take the form of failure to arrest for minor offenses, refusing to charge an informant despite sufficient evidence, convicting him of a less serious offense, or probation or a lighter sentence.

Occasionally, the parole decision may be used as a reward for informant services, especially for information about the activities of inmates in the correctional institution. In the illustration case, the inmate would not have been paroled on the basis of his rehabilitation. His informant services were not discussed during the parole hearing, but the board was told of them before the hearing and discussed them after the inmate left the hearing room.

In many states, statutes authorize the granting of special good time to inmates who perform extra work or other meritorious duties, including giving information to prison officials.[41] It is not certain how often these provisions are used to reward inmate informant services and, if they are used, whether they are effective in eliminating the need to use the parole decision for the same purpose.[42]

The chairman of the Michigan parole board indicated in a speech the difficulty which the informant causes the board in reaching a decision:

Parole was designed to serve society as a means of assisting the individual to make the transition from prison confinement to existence in the free community. There are times, however, when offenders render great assistance to law enforcement or perform some valorous or meritorious act. Testifying against dangerous criminal offenders and thereby placing their own lives in jeopardy, saving the life of an officer or helping him in a serious situation, and giving information preventing a serious escape threat of dangerous persons are acts which seem to warrant special consideration. As valuable as these acts may be, they must be interpreted as to the intent of the individual in performing them. It is said that "virtue is its own reward," but sometimes people expect something more tangible — say, a parole! The motivation of the individual and the circumstances in which his valor was evidenced are as important here as they are in the crime for which he was sentenced. They may be sincere expressions of a better set of social values, or they may be selfish efforts to gain personal advantage even if it means taking a personal risk. Such acts can be a spectacular evidence of deep significance or only an exhibition of self-aggrandizement.[43]

In some situations there may be a need, which parole can meet, for the removal of the informing inmate from the institution for his own safety. It is not clear whether this is an important consideration in the decision to grant parole to the informant and, if so, whether a transfer of the informant to another institution would be a satisfactory alternative.

THE DECISION TO DENY PAROLE FOR REASONS OTHER THAN THE PROBABILITY OF RECIDIVISM

Parole is often denied to inmates for reasons other than perceived probability of recidivism. Often this decision is made despite the board's own estimate that the inmate would very likely complete his parole period successfully if he were released. That this should occur is surprising in view of the chronic crowded conditions of most prisons. Ironically, however, in some situations prison overpopulation may be a factor contributing to a decision to deny parole despite a high probability of parole success. It might be argued, for example, that when a parole board denies parole to a good risk because it is enforcing prison discipline, a major reason it feels compelled to do so lies in the strain on prison discipline created by over-crowding.

It has been contended that parole boards tend to be too "conservative" in their release practices. In part this contention goes to the point that parole boards may require too high a probability of parole success before granting parole, but it also may go to

policy considerations upon which parole denials are based in cases in which the board's own requirements of probable parole success have clearly been met. This may be the situation, for example, with regard to denials because the inmate has assaultive tendencies or because a parole grant would subject the correctional system to severe public criticism.

1. *Cases Involving Assaultive Behavior*

Illustration No. 15: The inmate, thirty-one years of age, was convicted of carrying a concealed weapon and sentenced to one to five years. When he was arrested on the present offense, he was believed to be trying to draw a gun on the arresting officer. His prior record consisted of convictions for "shooting another" and for felonious assault. He had been denied parole at a previous hearing because of several misconduct reports from the institution, one of which consisted of possession of a knife. Since his last hearing, however, he had received no misconduct reports. When the questioning of one of the board members revealed he was thinking of a parole grant, the other member interrupted him with: "I want a discussion on this." The first member replied that the record showed the inmate had greatly improved his attitude since the last hearing. Nevertheless, the inmate was told his case would have to be discussed with other members of the parole board and he would hear their decision in about a month.

Parole boards tend to be more conservative in their release practices when the inmate has demonstrated he is capable of assaultive behavior. Sometimes this consideration is regarded as sufficiently important to justify a denial of parole to an inmate who would otherwise be regarded as having a sufficiently high probability of parole success to justify release. The rationale is, of course, that the parole board has an obligation to protect the public from possible assaultive behavior which overrides its obligation to release inmates at the optimum point in their rehabilitative progress.

The Michigan parole board has a practice of refusing to grant parole to an inmate with a demonstrated capacity for assaultive behavior until the case has been discussed by the full five-man membership of the board in the executive session. In the illustration case, one of the two parole board hearing members said after the inmate left the room that he did not believe parole was appropriate because of the inmate's history of assaultive conduct. He said he believed a further psychiatric evaluation would be necessary since on at least three occasions the inmate had proved himself capable of serious assaultive behavior.

Shortly after the field survey was conducted, the Wisconsin parole board adopted the policy of requiring a discussion in executive session before an inmate with a history of assault who may be paroled. In these cases, the two members of the board conducting the parole hearing tell the inmate a discussion with a third member is necessary before a decision can be made. The director of the Social Service Department of one of the institutions noted that both institutional authorities and the parole board are more cautious in cases involving assault, particularly in cases of murder, because although the probability of recidivism may be low, the probable seriousness of the new offense, if one is committed, is great.

Normally, the board determines whether the inmate is capable of assaultive behavior on the basis of his prior record and the offense for which he is serving time. The board may also have the benefit of a psychiatric evaluation. In such cases, the latter is given great weight. An evaluation which concludes that the inmate is still capable of assaultive behavior or is still too dangerous for release will almost automatically result in a denial of parole.[44]

2. *Supporting Institutional Discipline*

Illustration No. 16: The inmate, twenty-six years of age, was convicted of larceny in a building and received a sentence of one and one-half to four years. This was his first parole hearing. A parole board member questioned the inmate about his institutional record, which showed he had three institutional reports, two for being "lazy" and refusing to work and one for having dice in his possession. He had several misdemeanor arrests and at one time had been arrested on a narcotics investigation charge. An immediate parole was not granted but the

case was continued for office review in six months. It was explained to the inmate that his institutional record had been poor and that if he corrected this and tried to obtain some help from his counselor, he would be given consideration again in six months.

Maintaining discipline among inmates is a major concern of all prison administrators. Although there are wide variations among penal institutions as to the degree to which the details of daily living are regulated by the administration, even in relatively permissive institutions there are disciplinary rules and sanctions for their infraction. Infractions of prison discipline are often interpreted by the parole board as signs of what the offender is likely to do when he is released on parole. They suggest an inability of the offender to adjust to his position and to respect authority. Quite a different consideration is primary, however, when the board denies parole because of the effect its decision may have on prison discipline. The major interest shifts from a concern with the future adjustment of the offender to a concern with order and control in the penal institution. Parole becomes an incentive for good behavior and a sanction against undisciplined conduct by inmates.

It is frequently not easy to distinguish between actions of the board which are designed to have an impact on the discipline of the institution and those which relate to the offender's future adjustment. It is likely that even the parole board members are unable to articulate clearly their reasons for reacting as they do to inmates with disciplinary problems. In Kansas, a parole board member may sometimes say, "How can you expect to be paroled when you can't even behave in the institution?" which might be interpreted by the inmate to indicate the board feels he lacks sufficient control. On the other hand, the board member will sometimes say, "I can't parole anyone who has become involved in so serious a breach of prison discipline," which might more readily be interpreted as supportive of prison discipline. Treating misbehavior during confinement as an unfavorable sign for future parole success leads in most cases to the same decision which would be made if the order of the institution were the sole consideration.

Parole is only one of many sanctions which are used to maintain discipline in penal institutions. Violations of disciplinary rules may result in denial of certain privileges or in solitary confinement. Repeated disciplinary violations may result in a transfer of the inmate to a less desirable institution. In most states, good time laws permit reduction of the maximum or minimum sentences, or both, as a reward for infraction-free conduct, and permit revocation of reductions already given for disciplinary violations. In some states, parole eligibility may be specifically contingent on the existence of no recent disciplinary infractions.

That parole is used to support institutional discipline may reflect the failure of these other devices to provide the necessary controls. This may be particularly true of the good time laws. In some institutions, it seems clear that good time laws have degenerated into automatic reductions of sentence, possibly as a result of the heavy release pressures of prison overpopulation, and thus have little, if any, effect on the conduct of inmates. A member of the Michigan parole board indicated that in practice the good time system has broken down and that it is an exception for an inmate to appear before the parole board who has not earned all possible regular and special good time. The board member indicated that in order to be denied good time, an inmate would have to "spit in the warden's eye."

It is difficult to determine whether it is possible, assuming for the moment it is desirable, to strengthen other control devices enough to enable the parole decision to remain free of the necessity for its use as a disciplinary device. It is probably true that, assuming administration of the good time laws has resulted in their uniform application without regard to conduct, the parole decision is currently a necessary device for control within the institution. Certainly the Model Penal Code regards it as a proper use of parole because it authorizes a denial of parole when the inmate's "release would have a substantially adverse effect on institutional discipline."[45] It is impossible to know whether this reflects a judgment that parole must inevitably be used as a control device, or whether, given current conditions, it must be so used. It would be possible to devise a system whereby the institution did preliminary screening of parole applicants and had the power to postpone parole hearings several months on the basis of institutional misconduct. This would have the effect of retaining the parole decision as a sanction for nonconformance to the institution's code, while at the same time relieving the parole board from the necessity of taking prison discipline into account when it makes parole decisions.

3. *Minimum Amount of Time*

Illustration No. 17: The inmate, age twenty-two, had been convicted of unlawfully driving away an auto, for which he received two years' probation. After he had served twenty-one months on probation, it was revoked for failure to report, failure to pay costs and restitution, and involvement in an auto accident. The judge imposed a prison term of six months to five years, stating to the inmate that he would probably be back home in about four and one-half months. He spent two months at the main prison and was then transferred to the prison camp where he had served almost a month by the time of his parole hearing. The camp recommended a short continuance of the case on the ground little was known about the inmate. Most of the hearing was consumed by the parole board attempting to explain to the inmate that he had been in the institution "too short a time for the offense" and, further, that the institution knew little about him. The board explained it could not conscientiously recommend parole for him in light of its lack of knowledge of his case. The case was continued for discussion in executive session.

A problem which some parole boards must frequently face occurs when an inmate appears for his initial parole hearing after he has served only a short length of time, normally under six months. Whatever the reasons, the parole board is likely to be quite reluctant to give serious consideration to the case until the inmate has served more time. The normal disposition when such a case appears is to schedule a rehearing, or sometimes only a conference in executive session, in several months, at which time the decision to grant or deny parole will be given usual consideration.

Because of its sentencing structure, the problem is particularly noticeable in Michigan. There, the maximum sentence for most offenses is fixed by statute but the judge has discretion to set any minimum sentence he wishes.[46] Regular and special good time are deducted from the judicially set minimum to determine parole eligibility,[47] and the inmate normally receives his first parole hearing one or two months before he becomes eligible for parole. As a result, when the judge sets a minimum sentence of six months, the inmate is eligible for parole after he has served about four months and appears for his first parole hearing after he has served only three months. The typical disposition of such cases is a continuance for six months or a year, at which time he will be given usual parole consideration.

It is possible, of course, to have a judicial minimum system which does not as readily lead to the difficulties experienced in Michigan. Under the judicial minimum system proposed in the Model Penal Code, the judge may not set the minimum sentence at less than one year.[48] With the necessary allowances for deducting good time and scheduling the hearing a month in advance of parole eligibility, this would normally result in an inmate's not receiving his first parole hearing before he has served nine months.

A potential problem of the same type was handled by parole board policy in Kansas and Wisconsin. There, inmates of the reformatories and women's prisons are by statute eligible for parole as soon as they arrive at the institution. In each state, the inmate, although stautorily eligible for parole immediately, does not normally receive his first parole hearing until he has served nine months of his sentence. This doubtless reflects a judgment that about that much time is necessary before it makes sense to consider the question of parole.

While there seems to be a consensus that a minimum time, probably between nine months and one year, is necessary before serious consideration should be given to parole, there is lack of agreement as to why this is true. One reason given is that the institution is incapable of having any rehabilitative effect on the inmate in less time. The assumption is that all persons sentenced to prison are in need of rehabilitation, which takes time, or at least that it takes time to determine whether they are in need of rehabilitation.[49] A related reason sometimes given is that the parole system and institution are incapable of formulating sound post-release programs for inmates in less time. Further, parole boards sometimes contend that adequate information on the inmate cannot be obtained in less time and, therefore, a short continuance is necessary in order to obtain information. At other times, however, parole boards have indicated a certain minimum time is necessary in order to justify the risk entailed by every decision to grant parole. The assumption in such cases is that the inmate has served such a short length of time that the parole board can afford to be more conservative in its release decision. Also implicit is the fear that if an inmate were granted parole after serving only four or six months and violated parole in a spectacular fashion, the parole board would be subject to more than the usual amount of criticism.

4. *To Benefit the Inmate*

Illustration No. 18: The inmate, a young man who appeared to be in his late teens, had come from what many would describe as a "good home." He had two brothers, both of whom were ordained ministers, and his parents were respected members of the community. The inmate's father constantly demanded more of the inmate than the latter thought he had the ability to accomplish and continually compared him unfavorably with his older brothers. This comparison was also made by the inmate's school teachers because the inmate, although of high average intelligence, did rather poorly in school. Nevertheless, he had completed all but part of his senior year in high school by the time he had been sentenced to the reformatory. In its pre-parole summary, the classification committee of the institution recommended that the inmate be permitted to complete his high school education, on the ground that it would aid him in the achievements of which he was capable. Some members of the parole board believed that if the inmate finished high school, he might go to college. The parole board decided to defer the case for five months to permit the inmate to complete his high school education prior to his release.

Cases sometimes arise in which it may appear to the parole board that a denial of parole would bring a benefit to the inmate which would be unobtainable if parole were granted. It is arguable, of course, that whenever the board denies parole because it believes the inmate has not reached the optimum time for release in terms of rehabilitation, this is, in reality, a benefit to the inmate. But there are other cases in which the benefit obtainable only through a parole denial may be at least as real, but may have no direct connection with the inmate's rehabilitation. Perhaps the clearest examples are those in which the inmate is suffering from a physical illness which is correctable in the prison but which release to the community would aggravate, or those in which the inmate would benefit from devices, such as dental plates or a hearing aid, which could be provided at no cost to him if he remains an inmate but which may not be as readily obtainable on the outside.[50] The illustration case is one in which the benefit accruing to the inmate by remaining in the institution is related both to his rehabilitation and to his more general welfare. The parole board may sometimes be faced with the dilemma of having an inmate who in terms of its rehabilitation standard might best be released, but who in terms of the interest of the institution in the inmate's total welfare ought to be retained to receive a special benefit which the institution can provide.

5. *To Avoid Criticism of the Parole System*

Illustration No. 19: The inmate had been convicted of embezzling $25,000 from a veterans' service group. He had absolutely no prior criminal record. Before the offense he had been a prominent member of the community and was well liked. This was his initial parole hearing. When the parole board learned that as a result of the offense the attitude of the community was very much against the inmate, it voted to deny parole.

There is a feeling shared among many parole board members that the success of the parole system depends in part on whether it achieves public approval and confidence. In some states the parole board publishes literature on the parole system for the public, and members make speeches or give demonstrations of parole hearings to civic and social groups. The parole board may also invite community leaders to be present at parole hearings and observe how the board functions.

While a desire to be free of public criticism and to gain the confidence of the public is a characteristic probably common to all criminal justice agencies, the parole board seems particularly sensitive. Whatever the reasons for this concern, it is sometimes reflected in the parole decision. Parole boards are often reluctant to release assaultive offenders despite their own estimate of the high probability of parole success. One reason for this is the board's concern for the safety of the community — that while the probability of recidivism may be low, the seriousness of the violation, if it occurs, is likely to be quite great. But another reason for the board's reluctance to release assaultive offenders is its concern about adverse public reaction if the offender violates parole in a spectacular manner.[51]

The concern about public criticism is even more clearly an important factor in the trust violation cases. The parole board normally views public or private officials who have embezzled funds as good parole risks in terms of the likelihood of parole success. One parole member even said that he thought these persons should not be sent to prison since, because of the unusual publicity surrounding their apprehension and conviction, they are very unlikely to repeat the same or a similar offense. Nevertheless, the question whether they should be paroled raises the difficult problem of determining what weight the parole board should give to community attitudes. If the attitude of the community toward the inmate is good, he is likely to be paroled as soon as he is eligible. When the community attitude is negative parole is likely to be denied. One reason may be that a negative community attitude is likely to seriously hamper the inmate's efforts to adjust. Another reason, and probably the more important one, is that parole of such an inmate would expose the board and the parole system to public criticism. One parole board member expressed his attitude toward the trust violation cases in terms of a dilemma, stating that to some extent a parole board must defer to certain community attitudes but that no parole board member can go beyond a certain point without violating his own conscience.

The board's concern with public criticism of the parole system also affects the parole decision in cases in which the inmate or a member of his family has attempted to put unusual pressure on the parole board for his release. This normally occurs in cases in which the inmate has received a long sentence, often a life sentence. The inmate may write letters to influential persons in state government or to anyone else whom he thinks might be able to influence the board. Sometimes, the inmate or his family may hire attorneys whom they think have unusual influence with the board. The attitude of the parole board in such cases toward the release of the inmate is likely to be extremely negative. In one case, a member of the board said that if a lifer who wrote great numbers of letters trying to get someone to influence the board would cease writing for six months, he would be released, but so long as he persisted in his present behavior the board member was determined that he "do it all."[52] If the board were to grant parole to such an inmate on the merits of the case, it would expose itself to the accusation that the parole grant was the result of special influence. The board prefers to keep the inmate in prison rather than incur that risk.

CONTROLLING PAROLE BOARD DISCRETION

One of the important problems in corrections is finding ways to accommodate the need for discretion and flexibility in making decisions with society's need to assure itself that fair and sensible decisions are indeed being made — to control discretion without destroying it.

If one regards discretionary decision-making and controlled decision-making as completely incompatible, this must seem an impossible task; either the person making the decision has discretion or he applies rules, and there is no middle ground. However, there are many subtle differences among kinds of decisions measured by the extent to which the decision-maker decides according to his own norms or is subject to legal controls and checks.[53] It is important to re-examine our thinking to determine to what extent discretion and legal control are compatible and whether they can work together.

Control of discretion is often thought of exclusively in terms of *legal* control. Some persons may not trust controls which are neither legislative nor judicial; to them they may seem illusory or, at best, less than adequate. Yet, when one examines the parole decision it becomes clear it is subject to controls despite the fact that legal controls are almost totally lacking. If it is a mistake to regard legal controls and discretion as completely incompatible, it is perhaps an even greater mistake to regard the legal system as the only means of controlling discretion.

It is important (1) to re-examine our thinking about legal control of discretion and (2) to explore means of control other than traditional legislative and judicial ones.[54]

LEGISLATIVE AND JUDICIAL CONTROLS

Concern with individualization is an important reason legislatures have failed to provide meaningful standards for correctional decision-making and courts have refused to review actions of the decision-makers.[55] Indeed, Professor Kadish has remarked that the emphasis upon individualized decision-making in corrections "has resulted in vesting in judges and parole and probation agencies the greatest degree of uncontrolled power over the liberty of human beings that one can find in the legal system."[56]

It is apparent from a comparison of statutory parole criteria with decisions made in practice that there is very little relationship between them and that statutory criteria do not, in fact, provide meaningful guides for the parole board. Some criteria, such as those requiring consideration of the welfare of society and of the inmate, are too general to have any real effect on the decision. Other criteria are specific, but a parole board is likely not to consider itself bound to conform to them when the individual case seems to require a contrary result. This is clearly true, for example, with respect to the decision to parole the minor property offender and the nonsupport violator despite parole board expectation of recidivism, and the decision to parole an inmate who has been unable to obtain employment in a state which imposes that as a prerequisite to parole.

One reason parole boards may be willing to ignore statutory criteria is that the legislature has frequently indicated, in effect, that it is entirely proper to do so. Typically, parole statutes are careful to state that the matter of parole is entirely within the "discretion"[57] of the parole board or that whether the statutory standards are met is a matter for its "opinion."[58] Some statutes specifically state that the parole board's decision is not subject to judicial review;[59] even in the absence of such a provision, courts uniformly hold that they will not review the decision to determine its conformity with statutory criteria.[60]

Furthermore, statutory parole criteria do not speak to many significant issues, most importantly, the circumstances under which a parole board may deny release despite its opinion that the inmate is unlikely to recidivate.[61]

The inadequacy of current statutory criteria was recognized by the drafters of the Model Penal Code,[62] and an effort was made to provide criteria which would be meaningful guides to the parole board:

> Whenever the Board of Parole considers the first release of a prisoner who is eligible for release on parole, it shall be the policy of the Board to order his release, unless the Board is of the opinion that his release should be deferred because:
> (a) there is substantial risk that he will not conform to the conditions of parole; or
> (b) his release at that time would depreciate the seriousness of his crime or promote disrespect for law; or
> (c) his release would have a substantially adverse affect on institutional discipline; or
> (d) his continued correctional treatment, medical care or vocational or other training in the institution will substantially enhance his capacity to lead a law-abiding life when released at a later date. . . .[63]

Although this formulation is a great improvement over present statutes, the manner in which it is intended to function is troublesome. The Code specifically precludes judicial review to enforce compliance with the statutory criteria.[64] The draftsmen nevertheless felt that a careful statutory formulation of release criteria would be helpful on the theory that if the statutory criteria are realistic, parole boards will be guided by them without judicial enforcement.[65] Although much depends upon the attitudes of parole board members, experience under present statutes strongly indicates that the most likely parole board reaction to this provision would be to ignore it.

There is considerable difficulty in providing effective judicial review of the parole decision, even if legislatures or courts[66] desired to provide it. A verbatim record of the parole hearing would probably have to be kept, and the court would have to be given access to the parole board case file, which contains information regarded by many as confidential. But even more importantly, while the inmate can be depended upon to challenge parole denials, there are problems in obtaining review of parole grants. The inmate is certainly unlikely to challenge a grant of parole, and it is doubtful whether under present procedures any public official can be expected to have sufficient interest in the parole grant to challenge it. It is, nevertheless, difficult to arrive at the position that parole denials should be subject to judicial review without also taking the position that grants should be subject to similar review.

Even if these problems could be overcome, there are perils in providing legal supervision of the parole decision. One of the major purposes of having official discretion is to permit individualized decision-making. Nowhere in the criminal justice system is the propriety, and even necessity, of individualized decision-making more clearly recognized than in the parole decision. The risk is that legal supervision would destroy the ability of the parole board to consider each case fully upon its own facts.

The individualized nature of each parole decision is best seen in the board's judgment about the rehabilitation of an inmate considered for parole. This is, admittedly, a difficult judgment to make under the best of circumstances. Even with predictive devices and elaborate parole success studies, determination of the probability of recidivism is virtually a matter of intuition based on experience but unaided by rules or even firm guidelines. It would obviously be inappropriate for a court to substitute its judgment for the parole board's on this question.

Yet observation of practice clearly indicates that many parole decisions — probably even a majority of them — do not rest entirely upon the board's estimate of the probability of recidivism. Many also rest upon factors which can best be termed "policy considerations" — fairly easily applicable value judgments developed by the parole board from long experience. Indeed, in many cases, an inmate may be released on parole because of a policy consideration despite an estimated high probability of recidivism, or may be denied parole despite an obviously low probability of recidivism. A value judgment which a parole board is likely to make is that offenses against the person are far more serious than offenses against property. This judgment is reflected in the practice of readily releasing minor property offenders despite an estimated very high probability of recidivism, and the reluctance to release assaultive offenders despite an estimated low probability of recidivism. In other cases, a parole board may grant parole to an inmate solely because he has performed valuable services to the institution or may deny parole to enforce institutional discipline or to avoid public criticism of the parole system.

To the extent parole decisions are based on these policy considerations they are not fully individualized decisions. It is possible to isolate many of these factors and to make judgments about their propriety which would result in legal approval or disapproval. But it would be a mistake for a legislature or court to make a judgment about the propriety of a particular policy consideration without detailed understanding of the reasons the parole board has for it and of the context in which it appears. Considerable knowledge of the nature of the parole decision-making process is essential. Assuming the necessary knowledge, however, a generalized decision can be made about whether particular policy considerations ought to influence the parole decision, and this judgment can be legally enforced without doing damage to the goal of individualized parole decisions and without destroying parole board discretion.

It would be illusory, however, to believe that the formal legal system is capable of controlling all the subtle variables which make the difference between sound and unsound discretionary decision-making. Of necessity, much needs to be left to the administrators and to the development of administrative self-control.

ADMINISTRATIVE SELF-CONTROLS

Although the parole decision is not subject in any significant degree to formal legal controls, it would be incorrect to assume that, therefore, it is subject to no control. In fact, in some states it is subject to fairly significant control imposed by the administrators of the parole system without legal compulsion. But there are important differences among the states in the degree to which the parole decision is subject to administrative self-controls.

Six parole board practices found in one or more of the three states studied exert significant control over the parole decision: board members subject themselves to persuasion by all interested parties; formulate and explain reasons for particular decisions; voluntarily disqualify themselves for bias; impose administrative review on themselves; test the bases for decisions by encouraging empirical research; and publish the criteria to be used.

One of the most important occasions for self-control is the parole hearing. A hearing is required by statute in Michigan,[67] but not in Kansas[68] or Wisconsin. Nevertheless, parole hearings are held regularly in each of these states. They differ significantly, however. In Michigan and Wisconsin, parole hearings last for ten to twenty minutes; they are conducted in a leisurely fashion and the inmate is given opportunity to make virtually any statement he wishes. In fact, one of the major objectives in the parole hearing in those states is to have the inmate talk about himself and his offense as much as possible. In Kansas, on the other hand, parole hearings last for two or three minutes each. The parole board may conduct as many as 135 hearings a day;[69] there is time only to ask the inmate a few brief questions and to dismiss him. He is not permitted to make statements except in response to questions posed by board members.

In Kansas, the parole board permitted attorneys and members of the inmate's family to be present at the parole hearing and to make brief statements.[70] In Michigan and Wisconsin,[71] friends, relatives, and attorneys are not permitted to attend parole hearings. They may present their views to a member of the parole board prior to the hearing. A memorandum of the conversation is prepared by the member contacted for the parole board's case file.

In Michigan and Wisconsin, the parole boards are careful to explain to the inmate the reason for the decision reached. They are especially careful to explain parole denials and to suggest what, if anything, the inmate can do to improve his chances for parole later. Furthermore, they record a brief statement of their reasons for the decision for the inmate's case file. Although these statements are quite brief, the necessity for making them requires some reflection on the grounds for the decision.

On several occasions in Wisconsin, various parole board members disqualified themselves from participating in the decision. One parole board member stated he did not participate in cases involving sex offenses against children or the use of weapons because he "saw red" in those cases.

In Michigan, two members of the parole board conduct hearings, but a third member reviews the case file before the hearing and votes for or against parole. In Wisconsin, under present procedures, two members of the parole board conduct the parole hearing and make the decision to grant or deny parole. However, if the two hearing members vote to parole an inmate serving a life sentence or one incarcerated for assaultive conduct, a third member reviews the case and must concur with the hearing panel before parole can be granted. In Kansas and in other cases in Wisconsin, there is no real administrative review of the decision reached by the parole board members who conduct the parole hearing.

In Wisconsin, the parole board has encouraged research into its practices and procedures, and especially the criteria it uses. On one occasion, it encouraged research into the empirical bases of assumption it made in paroling nonsupport offenders. The board which is authorized to release offenders committed under the Wisconsin sex crimes law[72] encouraged research into the efficacy of its use of special protective placements on farms.

The Michigan Department of Corrections published a pamphlet which describes the entire parole system and contains a brief statement of parole criteria used by the parole board.[73] The Wisconsin Department of Public Welfare published such a pamphlet in 1959[74] and revised it in 1963.[75]

Although it is possible to control discretion without destroying it, a continuing effort is required. It is not enough simply to provide legal mechanisms for setting decision standards and reviewing decisions made. The persons who exercise discretion must be encouraged to engage in a constant process of self-examination and critical review and improvement of their practices and procedures. Only when this occurs can society be assured that official discretion is being exercised fairly and sensibly.

NOTES*

1. See Newman, *Conviction*, 76–130, (1966); Newman, "Pleading Guilty for Considerations: A Study of Bargain Justice," 46 *J. Crim. L., C. & P.S., 780, (1956);* Note, "Guilty Plea Bargaining: Compromises by Prosecutors to Secure Guilty Pleas," *112 U Pa. L. Rev.*, 865, (1964).
2. See "Statutory Structures for Sentencing Felons to Prison," 60, *Colum. L. Rev.*, 1134 (1960).
3. For example, the trial judge in Wisconsin has discretion to select the maximum sentence within the limits imposed by the legislature. *Wis. Stat. Ann. § 959.05* (Supp. 1966). The trial judge does not select a minimum sentence. Minima are provided by statute, and the inmate attains parole eligibility when he has served his statutory minimum sentence, one-half of his judicial maximum sentence, one-half of his judicial maximum sentence, or two years, whichever is shortest. *Wis. Stat. Ann. § 57.06(1)* (Supp. 1965). First degree murder is punishable by life imprisonment, but the trial judge must impose the life sentence. *Wis. Stat. Ann. § 959.05* (Supp. 1966). Parole eligibility is attained when the inmate has served twenty years,

*Footnotes have been abridged, edited, and renumbered.

less allowance for good behavior within the institution (which may reduce the minimum to as low as 11 years and 3 months). *Wis Stat. Ann.* § 57.06(1) (Supp. 1965).

4. In Michigan, for example, the trial judge has discretion to select the minimum sentence. *Mich. Stat. Ann.* § 28.1081 (Supp. 1965). Parole eligibility is attained when the inmate has served his judicial minimum sentence, less allowances for good behavior. *Mich. Stat Ann.* § 28.2304 (Supp. 1965).

5. *Kan. Laws 1903*, Ch. 375 § 1, the provision in effect at the time of the ABF field survey, required the trial judge to impose both the maximum and minimum sentences provided by statute. In 1957, the trial judge was authorized to select the minimum sentence but was still required to impose the maximum provided by law. *Kan. Stat. Ann.* § 62-2239 (1964). The provision permitting the trial judge to select the minimum sentence has been declared void because of vagueness. State v. O'Connor, 186 Kan. 718, 353 P.2d 214 (1960).

6. For most offenses, the Michigan trial judge is required to impose the maximum sentence provided by statute and has discretion to select the minimum sentence, but for several offenses punishable by life imprisonment the trial judge is authorized to select both the maximum and minimum sentences. *Mich. Stat. Ann.* § 28.1031 (Supp. 1965).

7. For a detailed discussion of this response to mandatory sentencing provisions see Ohlin & Remington, "Sentencing Structure: Its Effect Upon Systems for the Administration of Criminal Justice," 23 *Law & Contemp. Prob.* 495 (1958).

8. In Michigan, the offense of sale of narcotics is punishable by a mandatory minimum sentence of 20 years. *Mich. Stat. Ann* § 18.1122 (1957). The routine response is to reduce the charge to possession of narcotics, which permits the trial judge to select the minimum sentence. *Mich. State. Ann* § 18.1123 (1957).

9. For a brief but useful description of existing parole eligibility requirements see *Model Penal Code* § 305.10, comment (Tent. Draft No. 5, 1956).

10. In Kansas, commutation of sentence occurred in 225 cases in an 18-month period; during approximately the same period about 750 inmates were paroled from the state penitentiary. *Kansas Legislative Council, Report and Recommendations: The Penal and Correctional Institutions of the State* pt. II, Special, at 19 (1956).

11. In Michigan and Wisconsin, one of the prime considerations in the decision to grant or deny parole is any change in the inmate's attitude toward himself, his offense, and persons in authority. In Kansas, since information of this kind is lacking, the parole board cannot base its decisions on that consideration. See notes 16–21.

12. In Kansas, the parole decision is made at the conclusion of the parole hearing. Parole board decisions made at the penitentiary were in theory recommendations to the governor because by statute his assent was necessary to make a parole grant valid. *Kan. Laws 1903*, ch. 375, § 9. The governor's consent is not necessary for paroles from the reformatory and women's prison. *Kan. Stat. Ann.* §§ 76-2315, -2505 (1949). In practice, however, the governor's consent was given automatically and there was no actual gubernatorial review of the parole board's decision. The 1957 revision of the Kansas parole laws eliminated the requirement of consent of the governor. *Kan. Stat. Ann.* §§ 62-2232, -2245 (1964).

In Michigan, legal authority to grant parole is placed in the five members of the parole board, to be exercised by a majority of the five. *Mich. Stat Ann* §§ 28.2305 (1954). Only two members of the parole board conduct parole hearings. Prior to the hearing, a third member has examined the case file and has voted to grant parole, deny parole, or defer to the judgment of the two hearing members. If the hearing members' votes combined with those who have reviewed the file constitute a majority vote of the board either for or against parole, that is the decision of the parole board and there is not further review. If a majority vote is not obtained after the hearing, the case is referred to an executive session of the entire parole board; it is discussed, and a vote is taken. There is no administrative review of a parole board decision.

In Wisconsin, legal authority to parole rests with the Director of the State Department of Public Welfare. *Wis. Stat. Ann.* §§ 57.06, .07 (1958). The parole board is an advisory group to the Director. Three members of the parole board conduct hearings. If the hearing members decide to grant parole, they forward that recommendation to the Director for his approval. If only two of the three hearing members vote to grant parole, the decision is reviewed by the Director of the Division of Corrections within the State Department of Public Welfare. A unanimous vote of the hearing members almost always receives approval from the Director of the State Department of Public Welfare. When there is a split vote, the Director of Corrections usually votes with the two affirmative votes and parole is ultimately granted. Parole board decisions to deny parole are not reviewed.

Administrative review of the parole decision performs almost none of the functions which are normally associated with administrative review. The reviewing authority is likely to consider only the effect of the grant on the public relations of the parole system. For example, in recent years only one Wisconsin parole board decision to grant parole has been "vetoed" by the Director and that was on the ground that a parole would result in great criticism of the parole system because of the extensive publicity surrounding the original offense and the relatively short time the inmate had been in prison.

13. *Mich. Stat. Ann.* § 28.2304 (Supp. 1965); see, e.g., Garvey v. Brown, 99 Kan. 122, 160 Pac. 1027 (1916); Tyler v. State Dep't of Pub. Welfare, 19 Wis. 2d 166, 119 N.W. 2d 460 (1963)

14. A parole board is likely to think of the probability of recidivism in terms of the probability of parole success. A parolee who completes his parole period without revocation of his parole is a success; one who has his parole revoked — in most cases for conviction of or commission of a new offense — is a failure.

15. For a discussion of many of these factors see p. 370, "The Decision to Grant Parole for Reasons Other Than the Probability of Recidivism"; and p. 376, "The Decision to Deny Parole for Reasons Other Than the Probability of Recidivism."

16. See p. 370.

17. See p. 370, "The Decision to Grant Parole for Reasons Other Than the Probability of Recidivism."

18. The emphasis placed by parole boards on psychological change creates problems when dealing with mentally defective inmates because of the extreme difficulty of effecting change with present prison resources.

19. Often when the parole board releases an inmate who has served a long sentence, it will refer to psychological change in the inmate in terms of maturation. Some parole board members have remarked that for certain types of offenders the only hope of rehabilitation lies in the slow processes of maturation.

20. This fear prevailed even among members of the Kansas parole board, which puts little emphasis upon psychological change in making its decisions. In one case, the inmate seemed to the parole board to be too glib, so it quickly dismissed him and denied parole on the ground he was a "con man."

21. In one Wisconsin case, the screening committee recommendation was as follows: "Paranoid psychosis. Thinks wife maneuvered him into murdering her. Psychiatrist reports too dangerous for release. Deny." The parole board quickly denied parole on the basis of the psychiatric recommendation.

22. In a study of parole criteria used by the Wisconsin parole board, the inmate's prior criminal and juvenile record was the factor mentioned by the board most frequently as a strong reason for denial of parole. "Hendrickson & Schultz, A Study of the Criteria Influencing the Decision to Grant or Deny Parole to Adult Offenders in Wisconsin Correctional Institutions," p. 36–37, 1964 (unpublished thesis in University of Wisconsin School of Social Work).

23. *Kan. Laws 1903*, ch. 375, § 9, repealed by *Kan. Laws 1957*, ch. 331 § 37.

24. *Wis. Stat. Ann.* § 57.06 (Supp. 1965). See note 3.

25. See note 4.

26. The pressures to reward a guilty plea with leniency in sentencing appear to be greatest in the urban areas, apparently because that is where the problems of court congestion are most severe. It would be expected, therefore, that one would find shorter sentences from the urban areas of a state than from the rural. This expectation seems substantiated in all three states, although no systematic exploration of this thesis was made. For a brief discussion of guilty plea bargaining in the three states see notes 1–8.

27. There is an indication that inmates committed to the Wisconsin State Reformatory for probation violation are routinely denied parole at their initial hearing, held after nine months in the institution. It is clear the nature of the probation violation is as important as the fact of violation. In one case at the Reformatory, an inmate who was appearing for his initial hearing on a probation violation commitment was denied parole. He had been placed on probation on a conviction for armed robbery. He violated probation by carrying a gun and the probation was revoked. He admitted to the parole board that he had intended to use the gun in a hold-up to get money to abscond from the state.

28. Again, it is clear that the nature of the violation is as important as the fact of violation, particularly whether the violation and the original offense form a pattern which seems to indicate a personality trait and whether there is any evidence of a change in the problem aspects of the inmate's personality. However, the supervisor of the Social Service Department at the Wisconsin State Prison stated that he believed that normally parole violated by a new offense is much more of a negative factor than is a technical violation.

29. Some of the re-paroles probably occur because the mandatory release date is approaching and the board prefers to give the inmate some community supervision even though he has shown a tendency not to profit from it in the past.

30. The pre-parole report in Kansas simply verifies home and job arrangements, if any. No attempt is made to evaluate community sentiment or the suitability of the placement plan. Parole board members in Kansas complained frequently about the scanty information they received from the field.

31. *Wis. Stat. Ann* § 959.15 (1958).

32. In Wisconsin, the maximum sentence is selected by the trial judge, while in Kansas and Michigan it is usually fixed by statute.

33. In Wisconsin, juvenile boys transferred from the training school to the reformatory are subject to the release jurisdiction of the adult parole board. Because they are still juveniles, however, the conditional release law does not apply to them. When they reach the age of twenty-one they must be released unconditionally. It is a common practice for the parole board to grant paroles to juveniles who are approaching age twenty-one simply to give them a period of supervision in the community, which would be denied them under release by operation of law.

34. The problem was particularly acute in Michigan due to an administrative directive which prohibited the parole board from forfeiting good time earned in the institution when an inmate violated parole. This resulted in a number of returned violators having only a short time remaining until their mandatory, unconditional release date. In some of these situations, the parole board felt it was forced to grant parole in order to provide the inmate with some community supervision.

35. *Tappan, Crime, Justice and Correction* 724 (1960): "In some states any prisoner who is wanted under a detainer for further court action or imprisonment is automatically rejected [for parole] unless or until the writ is lifted."

36. *Mich. State Ann.* § 28.2303(c) (1954).

37. *Tappan*, at note 59, at p. 724 n. 32.

38. E.g., *Mich. Stat. Ann.* §§ 4.147, 28.969 (Supp. 1965); *Wis. Stat. Ann.* 955.22 (Supp. 1966).

39. *Wis. Dep't of Public Welfare, Parole Board Procedures and Practices* 11 (Feb., 1959).

40. *Mich. Stat. Ann.* § 28.2303(c) (1954).

41. The Kansas statute provided: "The board of administration is hereby empowered to adopt a rule whereby prisoners . . . may be granted additional good time for . . . giving valuable information to prison officials. . . ." *Kan. Laws 1935*, ch. 292, § 1.

42. For example, it is probably true in Michigan that the great majority of prison inmates are routinely awarded the maximum possible good time and special good time.

43. Address by R. H. Nelson, Chairman, Michigan Parole Board, at a meeting of Michigan prosecutors, July, 1957.

44. For example, an institutional recommendation such as the following is virtually certain to result in a parole denial: "Paranoid psychosis. Thinks wife maneuvered him into murdering her. Psychiatrist reports too dangerous for release. Deny."

45. *Model Penal Code* § 305.9(1)(c) (Proposed Official Draft 1962).

46. *Mich. Stat. Ann.* §§ 28.1080, .1081 (1954).

47. *Mich. Stat. Ann.* § 28.2304 (1954).

48. *Model Penal Code* § 6.06 (Tent. Draft No. 2, 1954).

49. In one case, the parole board denied parole to an inmate who had served only three months, commenting: "He has only been in the institution for three months and I believe this is too short a time to expect a change in him if it is possible for any change to occur in such an individual."

50. The *Model Penal Code* authorizes denial of parole to obtain a benefit for the inmate which is related to his rehabilitation. *Model Penal Code* § 305.9(1) (Proposed Official Draft 1962) provides in part:

> Whenever the Board of Parole considers the first release of a prisoner who is eligible for release on parole, it shall be the policy of the Board to order his release, unless the Board is of the opinion that his release should be deferred because:

> . . . .

> (d) his continued correctional treatment, medical care or vocational or other training in the institution will substantially enhance his capacity to lead a law-abiding life when released at a later date.

51. One member of a parole board indicated that although parole prediction studies have shown that murders, sex offenders, and men who have committed assaults are among the best parole risks, the fact remains that if one is paroled and repeats the same type of crime, the unfavorable publicity is many times that when a sixth forgery offender is paroled and again forges checks.

52. One parole board uses a special investigator attached to the corrections department to investigate suspected attempts to secure parole through unethical pressure.

53. Professor Davis asserts that it is possible to place all official action on a scale extending from the most clearly uncontrolled discretionary decisions through numerous subtle gradations to those decisions most governed by legal rule. See *Davis, Administrative Law*, 81–82, (1965).

54. Although all of what will be said concerns the parole decision, much of it is applicable to other correctional decisions and, indeed, to other discretionary decisions in the criminal justice system.

55. There are other reasons: unwillingness to face the tough problems of formulating adequate standards; little or no information about the decisions that are actually made in practice; lessened concern about the potentiality of injustice to the individual because of his status as a convicted criminal; desire to defer to the expertise of correctional personnel; and with respect to judicial review, fear that the courts will be flooded by requests for review from petition-minded inmates.

56. Kadish, "Legal Norm and Discretion in the Police and Sentencing Processes," 75, *Harv. L. Rev.* 904, 916, (1962).

57. See, e.g., *Conn. Gen. Stat. Rev.* § 54-125 (1958).

58. See, e.g., *N.J. Stat. Ann.* 30:4-123.14 (1964).

59. See, e.g., *Mich. Stat. Ann.* § 28.2304 (Supp. 1965), which provides: "The time of his release on parole shall be discretionary with the parole board. The action of the parole board in releasing prisoners shall not be reviewable if in compliance with law."

Model Penal Code § 305.19 (Proposed Official Draft 1962) provides: "No court shall have jurisdiction to review or set aside, except for the denial of a hearing when a right to be heard is conferred by law: . . . (2) the orders or decisions of the Board of Parole regarding . . . the release or deferment of release on parole of a prisoner whose maximum prison term has not expired. . . ."

60. See note 13.

61. See notes 44–52.

62. *Model Penal Code* § 305.14, comment (Tent. Draft No. 5, 1956):

Under present parole practice, the release of eligible prisoners is purely discretionary and no formal criteria have been established in the statutes, aside from general principles relating to public safety. Nor has there been any standardized administrative policy in the matter: parole decisions rest on the intuition of the paroling authority, largely unguided by the laws that establish this broad grant of power or even by specific board standards. . . .

63. *Model Penal Code* § 305.9 (Proposed Official Draft 1962).

64. See note 59.

65. *Model Penal Code* § 305.13, comment (Tent. Draft No. 5, 1956):

Although the timing of release is governed by the "opinion" of the Board upon these points, and so not subject to judicial review, we consider that the consistency, equality and soundness of release decisions will be enhanced by thus focusing attention of the Board on these specific grounds for the postponement of release. . . .

66. Courts have demonstrated great reluctance to review parole decisions; this is curious since many of them have apparently been able to overcome a similar reluctance to review the exercise of discretion by trial judges in sentencing.

67. *Mich. Stat. Ann.* § 28.2305 (1954). Despite the fact that many states do not by statute require parole hearings, they are regularly conducted in virtually all of the states. See *Model Penal Code* § 305.10, comment (Tent. Draft No. 5, 1956).

68. After the field survey, the Kansas statutes were amended to require a parole hearing. *Kan. Stat Ann.* § 62-2245 (1964).

69. The Kansas parole board attempted to hear all the cases at a particular institution in one day, while in Michigan and Wisconsin, the board often spent a week or more per month hearing cases at each of the institutions.

70. It was rare for an attorney to appear at a parole hearing. Because there was no provision for appointing counsel for the indigent, one member of the Kansas parole board stated that he felt it was unfair to permit retained attorneys to appear at the hearing.

The 1957 revision of the Kansas parole laws provided:

The board shall not be required to hear oral statements or arguments by any person not connected with the correctional system. All persons not connected with the correctional system presenting information or arguments to the board shall submit their statements in writing, and shall submit therwith an affidavit stating whether any fee has been paid or is to be paid for their services in the case, and by whom such fee is paid or to be paid, and stating that the amount of any fee which has been paid or which is to be paid for their services in the case was not or is not to be determined on the basis of the granting or denial of parole. Such affidavit shall be a public record. *Kan. Stat. Ann.* § 62-2248 (1964).

71. The Wisconsin policy prohibiting the appearance of attorneys at parole hearings is stated in *Wis. Dep't of Public Welfare, Parole Board Procedures and Practices* 10 (Feb., 1959): "Attorneys, members of inmates' families, or others are not permitted to make appearances either for or against parole at parole hearings. Such persons may, if they wish, make their views known to the Parole Board by letter or can arrange to see the Board at its offices in Madison." In a revision of that pamphlet, the parole board states: "Persons representing prospective parole applicants may appear before the Parole Board by appointment in the Madison Office of the Board. Special arrangements can be made to see Board members at places other than the Madison Office. However, the Board does not make appointments to see persons representing parole applicants at the institution of confinement during the month of the applicant's hearing." *Wis. Dep't of Public Welfare, Parole Board Procedures and Practices* 16 (June, 1963).

The *Model Penal Code* once contained a provision authorizing the appearance of retained counsel at the parole hearing. Later, that provision was eliminated. See *Model Penal Code* § 305.7, status of section (Proposed Official Draft 1962).

72. *Wis. Stat. Ann.* § 959.15 (Supp. 1966).

73. *Mich. Dep't of Corrections, Parole in Michigan* 4–5 (undated).

74. *Wis. Dep't of Public Welfare, Parole Board Procedures and Practices*, (Feb., 1959).

75. *Wis. Dep't of Public Welfare, Parole Board Procedures and Practices*, (June, 1963). In Tyler v. State Dep't of Pub. Welfare, 19 Wis. 2d 166,

119 N.W.2d 460 (1963), the Wisconsin Supreme Court quoted extensively from the pamphlet. It stated that an administrative order of the Director of the State Department of Public Welfare requires the parole board to follow the statements made therein.

17. IN SEARCH OF EQUITY: THE OREGON PAROLE MATRIX

ELIZABETH L. TAYLOR

Federal Probation © March 1979. Reprinted by permission.

■ In an attempt to decrease the discretionary powers of parole boards that Dawson discussed in the preceding article, the Oregon Parole Board developed a matrix system. This new system of parole decision-making attempts to eliminate unfettered discretionary powers to determine when rehabilitation has been accomplished, with resultant inconsistency of decisions and disparity being replaced by a system of "just deserts." This new matrix system is built around specific and narrowly-drawn guidelines. Parole dates are determined primarily upon the seriousness of the offender's crime and the history of their criminal behavior. The recently instituted matrix system, asserts Taylor, increases equity, reduces anxiety for inmates, and strengthens the entire system of criminal justice. ■

DURING THE PAST several years, criminal justice agencies in general and parole boards in particular have increasingly become the subject of criticism. Popular scapegoats, parole boards have been disparaged by the public media, district attorneys, judges, politicians, citizens, and prisoners. The Oregon Board of Parole is no exception.

In Oregon, criticism concentrated around what was perceived as arbitrary, capricious, and disparate decision-making by the parole board. The lack of published standards to guide decision-making, combined with the lack of written reasons for decisions, contributed to this perception. Additionally, the durational uncertainty of prison terms caused much unrest for both prisoners and prison administration alike. Prisoners often did not know until well into their terms how long they would actually have to serve. Prison administrators could not effectively manage bed space and transitional programs without the knowledge of whether prisoners were near release or not. These problems became increasingly critical as the institution population continued to grow.

These criticisms led to a movement for more durational certainty in prison terms with a variety of bills to attain this objective surfacing during the 1977 session of the Oregon Legislature. The final result, after months of consideration, was the passage of House Bill 2013. This bill, itself supported by the Board of Parole, was an aggressive response to the criticisms of Oregon's parole system. The purpose of this article is to analyze the movement for greater determinacy in Oregon and its impact upon parole practice. This experience may provide useful insights for other states facing similar concerns.

HISTORICAL SKETCH OF THE OREGON PAROLE BOARD

The Oregon parole system dates back to 1905 when paroling authority was first given to the governor. As one might expect, Oregon governors had little time to thoroughly consider individual cases and paroles were seldom granted. In 1915, Oregon's first parole office was appointed. Nevertheless, few changes occurred in the ensuing years. Not many paroles were granted and the supervision of parolees was practically nil.

In 1937 Governor Martin appointed a special commission on the Improvement of Oregon's Parole, Probation and Sentencing System. This commission was composed of three associate justices of the Oregon Supreme Court, two circuit judges, one district attorney, the chairman of the State Probation Commission, one member of the Board of Governors of the Oregon State Bar, and the chairman of the House and Senate Judiciary Committees of the 1937 State Legislature. Wayne Morse, then serving as administrative director of the United States Attorney General's Survey of Release Procedures and formerly dean of the

University of Oregon Law School, chaired the commission. In December of 1938, the commission submitted its findings and recommendations to the governor. Two bills, drafted by the commission, were subsequently passed by the state legislature creating Oregon's first parole board, with three part-time members. Although the Board became full time in 1969 and its membership was expanded to five in 1975, its basic operations and procedures remained the same until 1977.

Traditionally, Oregon parole boards believed that the primary purpose of incarceration was rehabilitation, but that the rehabilitative process could not be completed while in prison. The Board's basic function, therefore, was to determine who was "ready" for release into the community on parole without unreasonable risk to the public at large. To accomplish this, officials believed that broad, unchecked discretion was necessary. This philosophy governed the Board's decisionmaking until 1975.

POLITICAL ENVIRONMENT

About 1975, vocal dissatisfaction on the part of Oregon's citizenry toward what it perceived as an overly lenient and unresponsive criminal justice system became apparent. Violence seemed to appear everywhere, especially on the front page of the daily newspapers. Disagreements between various components of the criminal justice system frequently were aired through the mass media. Elected officials, in particular, chose newspapers as their battleground.

At the same time, prison administrators found their populations growing substantially[1] and, as a result, began to experience serious management problems. Not only had the size of the population at criminal risk increased,[2] but expanded police efforts and more vocal public demands for stringent prosecution and punishment contributed to a rising rate of prison commitments. Furthermore, the median length of stay in state institutions had increased significantly.[3]

Consequently, the Board of Parole found itself in a dilemma. Overcrowding created prisoner unrest and an increase in incidents of misconduct. But the Board's practice at that time of routinely deferring release for prisoners reported by the prisons to have violated institutional rules resulted in still more overcrowding.

Additionally, prison officials were frustrated by the unpredictability of release decisions. Lack of firm release dates created a barrier to rational planning for programming and for population management. Prisoners, moreover, found uncertain release dates and the absence of articulated reasons for parole decisions to be anxiety-inducing and seemingly irrational.

Oregon judges were also expressing concern and discomfort with the parole process. Functionally, the parole board was, in many respects, the sentencing agency for all felons committed to prison, because it had control (within the judicially imposed maximum sentence, less good time) over the duration of the prisoner's term and of the period of parole supervision. Many of the judges were frustrated by the lack of explicit criteria in parole decision-making, and there seemed no way for them to participate or intervene in the process. As a result, the judiciary began exerting pressure on the legislature to amend the statutes to permit greater judicial intervention. Some supported mandatory minimum sentences with the total elimination of parole. Most, however, favored retaining the parole board with some additional judicial control and participation in the setting of prison terms.

Moreover, the parole board's visibility made it a target for general frustration with the criminal justice system. Since prosecutors, courts, and legislators had no control over the release of inmates, anything that went wrong was obviously the fault of the parole board, which had been either too harsh or too lenient. Civil libertarians saw the Board's practices as arbitrary, capricious, biased, and too punitive, while law enforcement personnel felt the Board lacked accountability to the public and was too lenient. The media was always quick to cover a sensational story regarding a parolee who had committed a new crime or the plight of an inmate whom the Board had not released. As the attacks on its use of discretion mounted, the Board became more cautious and often deferred release because the inmate was "not ready." Criticism, however, continued to increase.

The public was incensed by incidents resulting from the release of two inmates. Both were convicted murderers: one had been released by the institution administration on a social pass; the other had been paroled by the Board. Shortly after release, both men murdered again. Stiffer penalties were demanded; petitions to reinstate the death penalty were circulated; and proposals for mandatory sentences began to surface.

A number of groups, including the Governor's Task Force on Corrections (appointed by Governor Bob Straub to design a 15-year master plan for corrections in Oregon), a research team from the *Oregon Law Review* (an American Bar Association funded project), and the Interim Joint Judiciary Committee of the Oregon legislature initiated studies of the correctional system. Interestingly, the findings of these groups differed significantly from those embraced by the public. These groups concluded that building a large, new prison would be an expensive, short-lived and unacceptable solution. Instead, they looked to community corrections programs and to reform of policies and practices of the institutions and the parole board. Basically, they suggested that inmates commited for less serious crimes be incarcerated for shorter, more certain terms. Recommendations aimed at the parole board included proposed requirements that the basis for parole decision-making be explicit; that the board develop guidelines articulating the weight given to specific factors considered and that these guidelines be made available to prisoners and to the public; and that the uncertainty of terms be reduced.

During this period, the Board itself was undergoing structural and philosophical changes. Between 1974 and 1975 two members left the Board and, consequently, with the statutory increase from a three to five-member board, four members were appointed. The change in membership stimulated an atmosphere for innovation. New members felt uncomfortable having unguided discretion and far-reaching responsibility without rules and guidelines for decisionmaking. Consequently, the Board

began to examine its decisionmaking process. Members scrutinized the actions of previous Oregon boards, studied the policies and practices of other paroling jurisdictions, and reviewed recent texts by academicians involved in the study of criminal justice. From this, the Board developed and began to use a "guideline" model for decisionmaking. This model was the prototype of the rules and guidelines adopted by the Board under the State Administrative Procedures Act in January 1977.

HOUSE BILL 2013

During the 1977 legislative session, the Oregon legislature was deluged by proposals for mandatory sentences. The public was continuing to demand stiffer penalties with less emphasis on rehabilitative programming. At the same time, Oregon judges were exerting substantial pressure on the legislature to strengthen their role in the prison term decision.

Rather than eliminate the parole release authority, as some had suggested, the legislature chose to adopt a model supported by the parole board itself. Through its development and adoption of explicit rules based on a "just deserts" principle, the Oregon Board had already structured its own discretion. The House Judiciary Committee, upon consideration of testimony and proposals by, among others, Peter Hoffman of the U.S. Parole Commission, Andrew von Hirsch of Rutgers University, and Ira Blalock, chairperson of the Oregon Board of Parole, endorsed House Bill 2013. The bill was passed by the 1977 legislature and was enacted into law.[4]

As enacted, HB 2013 required the Oregon Board of Parole to operate under what is primarily a "just deserts" model. In doing this, the bill required the parole board to structure and limit its discretionary powers through promulgation of published rules. Increased due process was also mandated.

Specifically, the new law required the parole board to establish a matrix of ranges for terms of imprisonment to be served for felony offenses prior to release on parole based on offense and offender characteristics.[5] These ranges must be designed to achieve the primary objective of punishment commensurate with the perceived seriousness of the prisoner's criminal conduct. That is, ranges are to give primary weight to the seriousness of the present offense[6] and the criminal history of the prisoner. To the extent not inconsistent with this primary goal, the deterrence of criminal conduct and the protection of the public from further crimes by the prisoner were additional objectives.

Thus, the Oregon legislation calls for a "modified just deserts" rationale, which provides that the Board consider not only the seriousness of the offense but also the secondary objectives of deterrence and incapacitation. This allows the Board some leeway to consider the risk of recidivism. Nonetheless, "just deserts" is the limiting principle — prediction, incapacitation, and deterrence may only be considered to the extent that punishment imposed is justly deserved given the seriousness of the criminal conduct. The Board was also required to adopt rules regulating variations from the ranges to be applied when aggravating or mitigating circumstances exist.

In addition, the Board was required to conduct its hearings to determine the duration of imprisonment within the first 6 months of the prisoner's incarceration. Thus, each prisoner, as well as the administration, would know near the beginning of his or her imprisonment the probable duration of confinement prior to release on parole or, in rare cases, release upon expiration of sentence.

Almost all prisoners in Oregon now are released via parole. Under exceptional circumstances, however, the parole board may deny parole, in which case the prisoner is released by expiration of sentence.[7]

Once a parole release date has been set, release can be postponed beyond the scheduled date only if: (1) the Board, after a hearing, determines that the prisoner has engaged in serious misconduct during his confinement (rules must define serious misconduct and specify allowable periods of postponement), (2) psychiatric or psychological diagnosis of present severe emotional disturbance has been made, or (3) the prisoner's parole plan is inadequate under the Board rules specifying the elements of an adequate parole plan. The Board may postpone release for up to 90 days for an unacceptable parole plan. Findings and written reasons must be provided when release is deferred.

Through HB 2013, the Oregon legislature has specifically structured the parole board's discretion in determining the duration of imprisonment and the granting of parole release through its requirement for explicit guidelines. In addition to reducing the disparities through the use of explicit criteria, the legislation also increases due process protections afforded prisoners by providing for written notice of hearings, access to information relied upon, and the requirement of written reasons for parole decisions.

The legislation has also enhanced cooperation among the various components of the criminal justice system. Criteria for parole decisionmaking is now available to law enforcement agencies, corrections agencies, and the judiciary. Of great significance is the Advisory Commission on Prison Terms and Parole Standards established by the legislation. This Commission is composed of the five parole board members, five circuit court judges appointed by the Chief Justice of the Oregon Supreme Court, and the legal counsel to the governor, who serves as an ex-officio member voting only to break ties. The Administrator of the Corrections Division acts as an advisor to the Commission. All judicial commission members serve staggered 4-year terms. The purpose of the Advisory Commission is to propose to the Board rules to be adopted in the establishment of the ranges for prison terms, as well as the rules regulating variations from the ranges when aggravating or mitigating circumstances exist.[8] Although advisory in nature, the Commission wields great strength due to the communication and cooperation it creates between the judiciary and the parole board. The Commission combines the sentencing expertise and sensitivity to the public of the judiciary with the experience of the parole board in the development and application of explicit guidelines all individual cases under the jurisdiction of state institutions. The involvement of the Administrator of Corrections has made the Commission aware of problems and needs of the institutions and correctional programs and how they may be affected. The judiciary's involvement in the policy and rule making of the parole board has increased confidence in those guidelines systemwide.

In addition to their involvement in the Advisory Commission, the judiciary has been given further opportunities for input into the parole release decision by HB 2013. The judiciary, at the time of sentencing, is provided a presentence report that includes the same information which will be used by the parole board in establishing a release date. The judge's sentence and reasons for its imposition then become the framework within which the prison term will be defined. The legislation also allows the judge to impose a minimum term of up to one-half of the executed sentence which must be served prior to parole release. The parole board, however, may override such a sentence upon affirmative vote of at least four members of the Board. In addition, when a judge imposes two or more consecutive sentences, the Board must sum the ranges established for the offense when determining the prison terms for those prisoners, subject to rules governing aggravation or mitigation.

ADMINISTRATIVE RULES AND GUIDELINES

By January 1977 the parole board had already, on its own initiative, filed its rules under the State Administrative Procedures Act. During the year after the legislation became effective, the Advisory Commission on Prison Terms and Parole Standards met three times to review the Board's existing rules and guidelines and to propose revisions to the Board. The Board accepted the recommended changes and filed them for public comment with the Secretary of State in March 1978. During the next two months, public hearings were held to take testimony from interested persons in a variety of locations around the state, including within the prisons.

The Board's administrative rules cover 110 pages, including six exhibits. The heart of those rules is the "matrix" (Exhibit 1), which indicates the ranges of time to be served in light of the seriousness of the

Exhibit 1. Total Time to be Served*

	Criminal History/Risk Assessment Score			
	11–9 Excellent	8–6 Good	5–3 Fair	2–0 Poor
	Offense Severity Rating (All ranges in Categories 1–6 shown in months)			
Category 1	≦6	≦6	6–12 (4–8)[1]	12–22 (8–18)
Category 2	≦6	6–10 (4–8)	10–18 (8–14)	18–28 (14–24)
Category 3	6–10 (4–8)	10–16 (8–12)	16–24 (12–20)	24–36 (20–32)
Category 4	10–16 (8–12)	16–22 (12–18)	22–30 (16–24)	30–48 (24–42)
Category 5	18–24 (12–20)	24–30 (20–26)	30–48 (26–40)	48–72 (40–62)
Category 6	36–48	48–60	60–86	86–144
Category 7				
Subcategory 2	8–10 yrs.	10–13 yrs.	13–16 yrs.	16–20 yrs[2]
Subcategory 1	10–14 yrs.	14–19 yrs.	19–24 yrs.	24–Life

1. Months in parentheses represent ranges for youthful offenders (21 or younger at time of conviction).
2. See Exhibit 2 for subcategory explanation.
*From Oregon Administrative Rules, 254-30-032.

crime and the prisoner's criminal history and perceived risk of repetition. All felonies are categorized within seven severity ratings (Exhibit 2). The harm done or risked by the commission of the offense was considered in determining the "severity rating" of each crime. Twenty-one crimes have been further "subcategorized" based upon the specific circumstances surrounding the particular episode.

The prisoner's prior criminal history is assessed through the use of a "criminal history/risk assessment" scale (Exhibit 3). The instrument weighs prior convictions; prior incarcerations; age at the time of first incarceration; prior escapes and failures on probation and parole; alcohol or heroin abuse problems; and a 5-year conviction-free period in the community.

The rules governing parole board decisionmaking and actions require the Board to specifically record how it has assessed the guidelines in each prisoner's case and the specific reasons for any departure therefrom. If a prisoner is dissatisfied with a decision of the Board, internal administrative review by the chairperson and state judicial review can be sought.[9]

The structuring of the parole board's discretion through explicit rules and guidelines has prompted the Corrections Division to do likewise. The Division has developed rules for determining custody status of prisoners and classifications for types of supervision of parole and probation cases using the parole board guidelines as a base. In addition, the parole board and Corrections Division have developed joint rules governing sanctions for serious misconduct by prisoners and defining specific procedures. There is a general movement within the entire corrections system in Oregon to structure board discretion by explicit rules and guidelines, stimulated by the Board's efforts in this area. The development of these rules has increased cooperation and coordination between the various parts of the system. In addition, several Oregon judges have begun to utilize a sentencing matrix based primarily on the Board's matrix to assist in the determination of appropriate sentence length.

POLICY IN PRACTICE

Given the present state of corrections, HB 2013 seems to be the best available option if justice and fairness are to be sought. The decision to make such a major policy change concerning rehabilitation was not an easy one. The Board sympathizes with the views of Willard Gaylin and Dave Pathman in their introduction to *Doing Justice*:

It is not easy to abandon the rehabilitative model, for it was a scheme born to optimism and faith, and humanism. It viewed the evils in man as essentially correctable, and only partially the responsibility of the individual . . . The simple fact is that the experiment has not worked out. Despite every effort and every attempt, correctional treatment programs have failed. The supporters of rehabilitation will say, and perhaps rightly so, that it was never really given a complete chance, that it was only accepted in theory, while in practice the system insisted on maintaining punitive practices. On the other hand, the question remains whether one can reasonably continue to expect anything different given the extended trial that rehabilitation has had.[10]

But for all of its altruistic intentions, the rehabilitative model has in many ways been a very punitive one. Indeterminacy and unfettered discretion were frequent byproducts of that system. Injustices can be easily cloaked beneath the helpful hand of rehabilitation. As McMurphy fatally discovered in Ken Kesey's *One Flew Over the Cuckoo's Nest*, where a prisoner traded a determinate jail sentence for an indeterminate mental hospital sentence, it is possible literally to be "treated" (rehabilitated) to death.[11]

By adopting the "just deserts" model, Oregon has announced that the commission of certain acts is wrong and demands punishment. Furthermore, the state has admitted that prisons actually punish. More importantly, though, the state has limited the degree of punishment depending upon the seriousness of particular crimes and has emphasized fairness. At the very least, an attempt is being made to prevent further injustices and inequities in the system.

Nevertheless, the new legislation and administrative rules of the parole board, although innovative, are not welcomed by all.

Exhibit 2. Offense Severity Scale*

Offense	Rating

Murder
  Subcategory 1 (stranger to stranger, extreme cruelty, prior conviction for murder or manslaughter, significant planning/preparation) — 7
  Subcategory 2 (all other cases) — 7

Treason — 7

Manslaughter I — 6

Kidnapping I — 6

Rape I
  Subcategory 1 (stranger to stranger, aggravated custodial interference, breaking/entering, weapon, serious physical/emotional harm, female victim under 12 years old) — 6
  Subcategory 2 (all other cases) — 5

Sodomy I
  Subcategory 1 (same as Subcategory 1 — Rape 1) — 6
  Subcategory 2 (same as Subcategory 2 — Rape 1) — 5

Robbery I
  Subcategory 1 (discharge of firearm/actual use of weapon; explicit threats by word or gesture, of death or serious bodily harm; serious injury) — 6
  Subcategory 2 (all cases except those described in Subcategory 1) — 5

Assault I
  Subcategory 1 (all cases except those described in Subcategory 2) — 6
  Subcategory 2 (cases in which victim(s) provoked the crime to substantial degree, or evidence that misconduct of victim contributed substantially to criminal episode) — 5

Arson I
  Subcategory 1 (knowing premises were occupied at time of act, actual serious injury) — 6
  Subcategory 2 (all other cases) — 5

Escape I — 5

Burglary I
  Subcategory 1 (involves actually or regularly occupied building where used or threatened to use dangerous weapon and caused or threatened physical injury) — 5
  Subcategory 2 (involves a non-dwelling/value of goods taken is over $5,000 or involves a residence or temporary residence except cases described in Subcategory 3) — 4
  Subcategory 3 (all other cases involving a nondwelling or a residence or temporary residence where defendant is not armed, no extensive property damage and value of goods taken was below $1,000) — 3

Assault II — 4

Kidnapping II — 4

Rape II (non-forcible intercourse involving incapacitated female or female under 14)
  Subcategory 1 (all cases except those fitting Subcategory 2) — 4
  Subcategory 2 (not both under 16 and incapacitated; no coercion or undue influence; and no position of trust (e.g., counselor, doctor) — 3

Sodomy II — 4

Compelling Prostitution — 4

Robbery II — 4

Criminal Activity in Drugs (involving minors)
  Subcategory 1 (furnishing heroin or other opiates; or sale for profit of any drug) — 4
  Subcategory 2 (furnishing any drug other than heroin, opiates or less than one ounce of marihuana) — 3
  Subcategory 3 (furnishing less than one ounce of marihuana) — 2

Criminal Activity in Drugs (other)
  Subcategory 1 (manufacture, cultivation or sale for profit, or possession with intent to sell for profit of any heroin or opiate derivative) — 3
  Subcategory 2 ([same as above] of any other drug) — 2
  Subcategory 3 (manufacture for own use or possession for own use) — 1

Note: Possession of less than one ounce of marihuana is not a crime

Coercion; Theft by Extortion
  Subcategory 1 (threat of serious bodily harm or death) — 4
  Subcategory 2 (all others) — 3

Manslaughter II — 3

Bribe Giving — 3

Bribe Receiving — 3

Sexual Abuse I — 3

Riot — 3

Burglary II
  Subcategory 1 (over $5,000 loss) — 3
  Subcategory 2 ($1,000 to $5,000 loss) — 2
  Subcategory 3 (less than $1,000 loss) — 1

Theft I, Theft of Services; Theft by Deception; Forgery 1
  Subcategory 1 (theft or receiving of over $5,000) — 3
  Subcategory 2 (theft or receiving of $1,000 to $5,000; of a firearm or explosive; of a livestock animal; or theft during a riot or catastrophe) — 2
  Subcategory 3 (theft under $1,000 except those included in Subcategory 2) — 1

Perjury — 2

Escape II
    Subcategory 1 (all cases of escape except   2
    those fitting Subcategory 2)
    Subcategory 2 (escape from minimum cus-   1
    tody for no more than 30 days)
Failure to Appear I   2
Bribing a Witness   2
Witness Receiving Bribe   2
Criminally Negligent Homicide   2
Criminal Mistreatment   2
Custodial Interference   2
Rape III   2
Sodomy III   2
Abandon Child   2
Theft by Receiving   2
Unauthorized Use of a Motor Vehicle
    Subcategory 1 (injury to others or loss, de-   2
    struction or severe damage to vehicle or
    property)
    Subcategory 2 (other)   1
Arson II   2
Robbery III   2
Assault III   2
Sports Bribery   2
Sports Bribery Receiving   2
Ex-Convict in Possession   2

Sale Related (firearms)   2
Carrying a Weapon with Intent to Use   2
Promoting Prostitution   2
Obtaining Drugs Unlawfully   2
Poaching
    Subcategory 1 (poaching of game valued   2
    over $3,000 or commercial operation)
    Subcategory 2 (other)   1
Supplying Contraband   1
Hindering Prosecution   1
Bigamy   1
Incest   1
Criminal Nonsupport   1
Theft: Lost, Mislaid   1
Criminal Mischief 1   1
Forged Instrument   1
Forgery Device   1
Fraudulent Use of a Credit Card   1
Fraudulent Communication Device   1
Promoting Gambling   1
Possession of Gambling Records 1   1
Tampering with Drug Records   1
Welfare Fraud   1
Felony Traffic   1
Interception of Communication   1

*From Oregon Administrative Rules, 254-30-030

Exhibit 3.   Criminal History/Risk Assessment Score*

Item	Score

(A) No prior felony or misdemeanor convictions as an adult or juvenile=3
One prior conviction=2
Two or three prior convictions=1
Four or more prior convictions=0   ____

(B) No prior incarcerations (i.e., executed sentences of 90 days or more) as an adult or juvenile=2
One or two prior incarcerations=1
Three or more prior incarcerations=0   ____

(C) Age at first commitment of 90 days or more
    26 or older=2
    19 thru 25=1
    18 or younger=0   ____

(D) Never escaped, failed parole or probation=2
One incident of the above=1
Any two or more incidents of the above=0

(E) Has no admitted or documented heroin or opiate derivative abuse problem, or has no admitted or documented alcohol problem=1
One or more of the above=0   ____

(F) Verified period of 5 years conviction free in the community prior to present offense=1
Otherwise=0   ____

Total History/Risk Assessment Score: ____

(1) Do not count convictions over 20 years old, convictions that have been pardoned, or juvenile or adult "status offenses" (runaway, truancy, incorrigibility, drunk in public).

(2) If no prior commitment, use age at present conviction.

(3) Count probation failure only if it resulted from new crime, count any parole failure.

*From Oregon Administrative Rules 30-031

A significant number of inmates and prison reform groups are extremely disturbed by the use of the word "punishment" and the minimization of rehabilitative considerations under the new system of "just deserts." Some say it is in violation of the Oregon State Constitution, which calls for "reformation," not "vindictive justice." In particular, inmates serving long prison terms feel all hope of release has been taken away. Under the present rules, inmates feel there is no way they can earn early release even if treatment programs are successfully completed. Prison reform and prisoner advocate groups feel it is cruel to remove all hope and incentive for rehabilitation and treatment. Prison officials have expressed concern that they will be unable to coerce prisoners into behaving appropriately absent traditional rewards and that this may cause management problems in the future. The parole board has recently attempted to respond to these concerns by establishing rules provided for periodic reviews to consider certain exceptional circumstances which may warrant modification of the originally established parole date.

By publishing explicit rules, the parole board has made it possible for its critics to be specific. Criticism can now be focused and therefore constructive. The rules have tremendously improved the internal operations of the Board. They offer a reference point for settling disagreements among Board members. This has significantly increased equity in decisions. Additionally, the plea bargaining process is made more fair due to the knowledge on the part of the defendant of the probable duration of his or her prospective incarceration.

Standards for parole decisionmaking have improved the Board's relationship with the Corrections Division and its institutions. Program and custody planning can now take place early in an inmate's term. Prison officials can more effectively manage bed space and program utilization, being assured that they know when release will occur. Rules governing their own decision-making process can now be developed and implemented. Inmate anxiety caused by uncertainty has been reduced. Inmates now know early in their terms when they will be released if no serious misconduct occurs.

Establishment of the Advisory Commission on Prison Terms and Parole Standards has proven a highly successful endeavor. It taps the input and output expertise of the Oregon criminal justice system, while preserving the independence of both the judiciary and the parole board. It strengthens the system by its very existence through communication, coordination, compromise and understanding.

The durational prison term decision in Oregon is delegated to a small specialized body: the parole board. This specialization allows for ongoing consultation and sharing of views, as well as a view of the full spectrum of cases committed to prison. This, combined with use of the guidelines matrix, reduces unwarranted disparity in prison terms, as well as uncertainty on the part of both the prisoner and the system. Nevertheless, the ability to respond to significant changes in circumstances is retained.

Oregon, by embracing the "just deserts" model, has admitted that for a variety of reasons — lack of resources, lack of sufficient knowledge, and so on — the "coercive rehabilitation model" in prisons has failed.[12] And, although HB 2013 by no means presumes to provide the total solution, its supporters believe the new system is a step in the right direction. Through further research and study, the Oregon Board of Parole hopes to gain new insights in the development of a truly just and humanistic model for parole decisionmaking in Oregon.

NOTES*

1. In 1973, the average daily population in Oregon prisons was 1781. In 1975 this figure was 2254. Personal communication with Neil Chambers, Executive Assistant to Administrator of Corrections Division, November 6, 1978.
2. I.e., population between the ages of 15 and 29.

*Footnotes have been abridged, edited, and renumbered.

See Governor's Task Force on Corrections, *Oregon Corrections Master Plan*, (December, 1976), p. 9.

3. In 1973, the median time served prior to release was 16.8 months. By 1975, it had increased to 25.2 months.

4. Oregon Revised Statutes, Chapter 144, as amended 1977.

5. The ranges, of course, may not exceed the maximum sentence prescribed by Oregon statute.

6. The harm done or risked by the commission of the offense, as well as the culpability of the offender, defines its seriousness.

7. These exceptional circumstances are limited to: (a) a prisoner sentenced for a particularly violent or otherwise dangerous offense; (b) whose present offense was preceded by two or more Class A or B felonies (the most serious felonies under Oregon law); or (c) whose record includes a psychiatric or psychological diagnosis of severe emotional disturbance. The Board is required to develop specific rules governing such cases.

8. The Commission is advisory and cannot set standards due to the separation-of-powers provision of the Oregon Constitution.

9. Although the extent of judicial review by the State Court of Appeals has not yet been determined, a case is presently pending which is expected to resolve this question. *Harris v. Board of Parole*, Oregon Court of Appeals No. 11130. Other judicial recourse (for example, habeas corpus or mandamus) is also available.

10. *Doing Justice*, A. von Hirsch, New York: Hill and Wang, 1976, pp. xxxvii–xxxviii.

11. Ironically, the Oregon Board of Parole now occupies one of the buildings, formerly part of Oregon State Hospital, in which the movie version of "Cuckoo's Nest" was filmed.

12. This does not mean that rehabilitative programs in prison are to be diminished. It does mean that program participation will be made more voluntary by being substantially detached from the parole release process.

TABLE OF CASES

INDEX

DATE DUE

FE 19 '91			
AP 06 '93			
APR 3 '96			
MAY 13 '96			
OCT 20 '97			
OCT 2 4 2000			
11/7/03			
12/19			

DEMCO 38-297